LAW AND AUTHORITY UNDER THE GUISE OF THE GOOD

The received view on the nature of legal authority contains the idea that a sound account of legitimate authority will explain how a legal authority has a right to command and the addressee a duty to obey. The received view fails to explain, however, how legal authority truly operates upon human beings as rational creatures with specific psychological make-ups. This book takes a bottom-up approach, beginning at the microscopic level of agency and practical reason and leading to the justificatory framework of authority. The book argues that an understanding of the nature of legal normativity involves an understanding of the nature and structure of practical reason in the context of the law, and advances the idea that legal authority and normativity are intertwined. This point can be summarised thus: if we are able to understand both how the agent exercises his or her practical reason under legal directives and commands and how the agent engages his or her practical reason by following legal rules grounded on reasons for actions as good-making characteristics, then we can fully grasp the nature of legal authority and legal normativity. Using the philosophies of action enshrined in the works of Elisabeth Anscombe, Aristotle and Thomas Aquinas, the study explains practical reason as diachronic future-directed intention in action and argues that this conception illuminates the structure of practical reason of the legal rules' addressees. The account is comprehensive and enables us to distinguish authoritative and normative legal rules in just and good legal systems from 'apparent' authoritative and normative legal rules of evil legal systems. At the heart of the book is the methodological view of a 'practical turn' to elucidate the nature of legal normativity and authority.

Volume 6 in the series Law and Practical Reason

Law and Practical Reason

The intention of this series is that it should encompass monographs and collections of essays that address the fundamental issues in legal philosophy. The foci are conceptual and normative in character, not empirical. Studies addressing the idea of law as a species of practical reason are especially welcome. Recognising that there is no occasion sharply to distinguish analytic and systematic work in the field from historico-critical research, the editors also welcome studies in the history of legal philosophy. Contributions to the series, inevitably crossing disciplinary lines, will be of interest to students and professionals in moral, political, and legal philosophy.

General Editor

Prof George Pavlakos (Antwerp and Glasgow)

Advisory Board

Prof Robert Alexy (Kiel)
Prof Samantha Besson (Fribourg, CH)
Prof Emilios Christodoulidis (Glasgow)
Prof Sean Coyle (Birmingham)
Prof Mattias Kumm (New York and Berlin)
Prof Stanley Paulson (St Louis and Kiel)
Prof Joseph Raz (Columbia Law School)
Prof Arthur Ripstein (Toronto)
Prof Scott Shapiro (Yale Law School)
Prof Victor Tadros (Warwick)

Editorial Assistant

Triantafyllos Gouvas (Antwerp)

Recent titles in the series

Volume 3: New Essays on the Normativity of Law
Edited by Stefano Bertea and George Pavlakos

Volume 4: Hannah Arendt and the Law
Edited by Marco Goldoni and Christopher McCorkindale

Volume 5: The Logic of Autonomy: Law, Morality and Autonomous Reasoning
Jan-R Sieckmann

Law and Authority under the Guise of the Good

Veronica Rodriguez-Blanco

·HART·
PUBLISHING

OXFORD AND PORTLAND, OREGON
2016

Published in the United Kingdom by Hart Publishing Ltd
16C Worcester Place, Oxford, OX1 2JW
Telephone: +44 (0)1865 517530
Fax: +44 (0)1865 510710
E-mail: mail@hartpub.co.uk
Website: http://www.hartpub.co.uk

Published in North America (US and Canada) by
Hart Publishing
c/o International Specialized Book Services
920 NE 58th Avenue, Suite 300
Portland, OR 97213-3786
USA
Tel: +1 503 287 3093 or toll-free: (1) 800 944 6190
Fax: +1 503 280 8832
E-mail: orders@isbs.com
Website: http://www.isbs.com

First published in hardback 2014
Paperback edition, 2016

Veronica Rodriguez-Blanco has asserted her right under the Copyright, Designs and Patents Act
1988, to be identified as the author of this work.

Hart Publishing is an imprint of Bloomsbury Publishing plc.

British Library Cataloguing in Publication Data
Data Available

ISBN: HB: 978-1-84946-449-9
PB: 978-1-50990-844-8

Typeset by Hope Services Ltd, Abingdon
Printed and bound in Great Britain by
Lightning Source UK Ltd

Acknowledgments

This book started when my daughter, who is now 13, was only two years old. During these years, she has learned, among many other things, to walk, talk, whistle, ride bikes and horses, write, read and play the cello and the piano. It has been a privilege to be the spectator of all these amazing events. This experience has motivated me to try to understand the interconnections and intricacies between our rational capacities and other potentialities and the way we actualise them as active selves in the context of the law. I wanted to make intelligible the distinctions between 'producing' and 'acting', between contemplation and action, between outward-looking and inward-looking. This book concentrates on these notions and aims to show that these distinctions and concepts shed light on the core idea that law is 'actuality' of our practical reasoning powers. The book defends a robust conception of practical reason and argues that practical reason illuminates two key features of law, authority and normativity.

I could not have embarked on this long journey without the love, strength and stamina of my husband Thomas and the constant support and exemplary dedication of my mother. Words of gratitude also for the encouragement and love of my father and my aunt Lila Casado-Rodriguez.

I am very grateful to the Alexander Von Humboldt Foundation for the funding I have received from 2004–2005 and 2010. The Faculty of Law at Kiel provided me with excellent facilities to finish a first draft of the book and the Faculty of Law at Heidelberg hosted me for the first period of my research in Germany. I am grateful to Professor Alexy and Professor Brugger for their hospitality. Sadly, Professor Brugger did not live to read the completed book. His warm encouragement helped me to keep going, especially at the difficult beginnings of the project.

I could not have finished this book without the support of the Saint Ignatius Centre at Antwerp University and the European University Institute through a Senior Fellowship and a Fernand Braudel Senior Research Fellowship, respectively. I am very grateful to George Pavlakos for his friendship and faith in the ideas of the book and to Dennis Patterson for his absolute trust in this project. The European University Institute provided me with the unique environment to finish my writings and the sunsets of Florence and Tuscany transformed my long hours of work into joy and fulfilment.

I have presented chapters of this book at the Universities of Chicago, Exeter, Florence, Girona, Edinburgh, Frankfurt, Kiel, Loja, Nanterre, McMaster,

Mexico, Oxford, Stockholm and am grateful for the comments I have received from the audiences. I also have accumulated debts with friends and colleagues and would like to thank Stefano Bertea, Francesco Biondo, Brian Bix, Matyas Bodig, Martin Borowski, Pierre Brunet, Enrique Cáceres, Geoffrey Callaghan, Emilios Christodoulidis, Jules Coleman, Sean Coyle, Pietro Denaro, Andrea Dolcetti, Luis Duarte Almeida, William Edmundson, Ken Ehrenberg, Kevin Falvey, Jordi Ferrer, Imer Flores, Michael Giudice, Rene González de la Vega, Andrew Halpin, Matthew Hanser, Anthony Hatzisvorou, Susanne Herrmann-Sinai, John Hyman, Mark Johnstone, Peter Langford, Ben Laurence, Brian Leiter, Erasmus Mayr, Claudio Michelon, Nicolás Muffato, Maria Isabel Narváez Mora, Cristóbal Orrego, Danny Priel, Bert Roermund, Constantin Sandis, Aldo Schiavello, Michael Sevel, Stefan Sciaraffa, Scott Shapiro, Harris Tsarras, Candace Vogler and Natalia Waights Hickman. I would also like to thank Anthea Connolly for her careful proof-reading of the entire manuscript and Luke Price for his research assistance.

I have relied on material that was published in 'Social and Justified Normativity: Unlocking the Mystery of the Relationship' (2012) 25 *Ratio Juris* 409 to write Chapter 5. Chapter 6 was previously published as 'Does Kelsen's Notion of Legal Normativity Rest on a Mistake?' (2012) 31 *Law and Philosophy* 725 and Chapter 7 was published as 'Claims of Legal Authority: the Limits of the Philosophy of Language' in Michael Freeman and Fiona Smith (eds), *Law and Language, Current Legal Issues* vol 16 (Oxford, Oxford University Press, 2013). Finally, I relied on material published in 'If You Cannot Help Being Committed to It, Then It Exists: A Defence of Robust Realism in Law' (2012) *Oxford Journal of Legal Studies* 823 to write Chapter 9 and Chapter 8 has been written on the basis of material that was published in 'Legal Authority and the Paradox of Intention in Action' in *Reasons and Intentions in Law and Practical Agency* (Cambridge, Cambridge University Press, forthcoming 2015). I am grateful to the publishers for granting permission to use these materials.

Contents

Acknowledgments   v

Introduction   1

1   Legal Authority and Normativity: Rediscovering a Hidden
Relationship   11
   1.1 First thread of the web: grasping the question   11
   1.2 Implausibility of performing a complex action: *because an
       authority has said so*   14
   1.3 Autonomy versus heteronomy: a quick glance at the accounts
       of autonomy in Wolff and Kant   16
   1.4 A first approach towards a harmonising project   21

2   Law as an Actuality   25
   2.1 Three questions   25
   2.2 Lessons to learn from two conceptions of intentional action:
       action in terms of the two-component view *versus* action
       according to the 'guise of the good' model   25
   2.3 Legal rules, reasons and the asymmetrical view   28
   2.4 'Following legal rules' as a naive explanation of intentional
       action   30
   2.5 The promulgation puzzle   34
   2.6 Legal normativity again   36
   2.7 The problem of guidance   38

3   The Guise of the Good Model   41
   3.1 The guise of the good model   41
   3.2 The why-question methodology   41
   3.3 Transparency condition and practical knowledge   47
   3.4 A defence of the guise of the good model   52

4   Understanding the Nature and Structure of Practical Reason:
Excavating the Classical Tradition   59
   4.1 Priority of the first-person perspective or deliberative point of
       view as manifesting the form or structure of practical reasoning   59
   4.2 Understanding *Energeia*: an interpretation of the why-question
       methodology   61

4.2.1 Key features of intentional action   61
4.2.2 Aristotle's distinction between actuality and potentiality   65
4.3 Law and *Energeia*: how citizens comply with legal rules?   69

5 A Defence of the Parasitic Thesis: A Re-examination of Hart's
Internal Point of View   75
5.1 Hart's model of intentional action and the parasitic thesis   75
5.2 Hart's non-cognitivist account of intentional action and the
internal point of view   78
5.2.1 Some textual analysis   78
5.2.2 Hart's non-cognitivism   80
5.3 Why did I park my vehicle in the park?: a defence of the parasitic
conception   86
5.3.1 The practical standpoint: the distinction between the
deliberative and the theoretical viewpoints   86
5.3.2 Problems with the 'acceptance thesis'   88
5.3.3 Social version of the acceptance thesis   90
5.3.4 Detached point of view of the 'acceptance thesis*'   92
5.4 Objections to the argument that the detached viewpoint of the
'acceptance thesis*' is merely theoretical and is therefore
parasitic on the 'acceptance thesis*'   94
5.4.1 'Detached point of view' is neither deliberative nor
theoretical, but rather a 'third point of view'   94
5.4.2 We do not, and cannot, commit ourselves to all the
different normative systems that coexist in our practical
experience   97
5.5 Conclusions of this chapter   98

6 A Defence of the Parasitic Thesis II: Does Kelsen's Notion of Legal
Normativity Rest on a Mistake?   101
6.1 Kelsen's jurisprudential antinomy   101
6.2 Kelsen's notion of the 'subjective meaning' of an intentional
action   104
6.2.1 Some textual analysis   106
6.3 A defence of the parasitic thesis   110
6.4 Two possible objections to the parasitic thesis of Kelsen's notion
of subjective intention   116
6.4.1 The parasitic thesis is sound, but Kelsen's inversion thesis
does not need to be parasitic on Aristotle-Anscombe's
explanation of intentional action   116

6.4.2 Kelsen can prescind from the 'subjective' meaning 118
6.5 Conclusions of this chapter 118

7 Authorities' Claims as Expressions of Intentions 123
7.1 Character of authorities' claims 125
7.2 Expressions of intentions about how actions will be performed 131
7.3 Authorities' claims as expressions of intentions 135

8 Authority and Normativity: A Defence of the 'Ethical-Political'
Account of Legal Authority 139
8.1 Raz's exclusionary reasons and the guise of the good model 139
8.2 Reasons for actions in Raz's legal and moral philosophies 143
8.2.1 Some key distinctions for understanding exclusionary
reasons 143
8.3 A criticism of second-order reasons 144
8.4 The guise of the good model as competing with the exclusionary
reasons model 146
8.4.1 Phenomenological Argument 146
8.4.2 Teleological Argument 148
8.4.3 Analogical Argument 149
8.5 Exclusionary reasons and the paradox of intention in action 152
8.6 Presumption of legitimate authority thesis 160
8.6.1 Equivalence thesis: the presumption of the goodness of
authority as equivalent to the presumption of legitimate
authority 162
8.6.2 The Rule of Law 166
8.6.3 Authorities' claims of moral authority and correctness 168

9 The Epistemology of Modestly Objective Values and Robust Value
Realism 171
9.1 A theoretical response to a deliberative question 171
9.2 Conceptual and practical capacities 174
9.3 Two formulas for identifying the objective grounding reasons
for actions as good-making characteristics of legal rules 179
9.4 Are there *really* robust objective values? a defence of normative
and value realism 181
9.4.1 The story of a philosophical problem: putting Enoch's
robust realism in context 182
9.4.2 Harman's challenge 185
9.4.3 The deliberative indispensability argument: can it stand? 187

10 Possible Objections and Concluding Note   199

    10.1   *First objection*   199
    10.2   *Second objection*   200
    10.3   *Third objection*   201
    10.4   *Fourth objection*   206
    10.5   *Fifth objection*   207
    10.6   *Sixth objection*   210
    10.7   *Concluding note:* law as actuality   213

Bibliography   217
Index   227

Introduction

Contemporary views on the nature of knowledge reaffirm and insist on the priority of theoretical knowledge over practical knowledge. This view is not new, however. It has roots that stretch back through time and an ancient pedigree in Platonist philosophers, for whom it did not make sense to comply with God's intentions without trying to understand them.[1] Platonist philosophers considered that before acting and performing in accordance to the good, it was necessary to understand what the good is. In the same vein, Aristotle – the champion of practical knowledge – believed that a contemplative life is the highest flourishing point for human beings.

One reason for the proclaimed supremacy of theoretical over practical knowledge is that practical knowledge and practical reason are elusive and a full and deep understanding of them raises difficult questions. For example, to understand practical knowledge do we need to reduce them to theoretical knowledge? If practical knowledge is not about true propositions but about 'doing', how do we perceive the 'doing' within time? The complexity of change and time add to the inscrutable character of practical reason and practical knowledge. And what about its metaphysical status? The ontological status of practical knowledge escalates its puzzling nature and even some philosophers, such as Kant, prefer to expel practical reason from the realm of the experiential. Thus, Kant advanced the idea that practical reason *must* belong to the 'non-knowable by experience' and therefore he located it beyond our empirical possibilities.

Modern scientific achievements seem to confirm the primacy of theoretical perspectives over practical perspectives. Technological developments, for instance, have been possible because of our sustained and continuous engagement with science and mathematics. Contrast this with the disasters of two world wars; armed conflict in numerous regions of the world; famine in certain parts of the world in contrast to the abundance of food in other parts; the growth in fear of, and violence towards, a constantly redefined other; and the destruction of our natural environment and resources. It is difficult to believe that the answers to our practical problems reside in something that is about 'practical knowledge' and reasons in acting. It is even harder to believe that there is a 'robust conception of practical reason' that can compete with a

---

[1] A Dihle, *A Theory of the Will in the Classical Antiquity* (Berkeley, CA, University of California Press, 1982).

'robust conception of theoretical reason'. If it is 'knowledge', the practical reason sceptic argues, it is a type of knowledge that is subservient to theoretical knowledge. Practical knowledge is the Cinderella of all types of knowledge, including technical knowledge. If the measure of truth and knowledge is success, then practical knowledge is bankrupt.

However, might it be that our current understanding of practical knowledge cannot help us to alleviate the deepest problems and dilemmas of human action because this understanding is wrong or insufficiently deep? Might it be that we have an understanding of practical reason that is extremely theoretical because, for example, deep understandings of practical reason have been replaced by 'decision-making' theories, game theory and other more 'scientific' or theoretical understandings of practical knowledge. Not surprisingly, the field of economics has thrived. Its success above other disciplines that study human beings, societies and institutions resides in its theoretical understanding of human action and in discarding any robust conception of practical knowledge.

The final triumph of theoretical reasoning comes from within moral and normative philosophy where contemporary philosophical reflections on 'reasons for action' tend to bifurcate reasons for action into motivational and normative reasons for action,[2] leaving the puzzle of how practical reason truly operates intact. They extrapolate the understanding of reasons from the sovereignty of theoretical reflection. Consequently, normative reasons are conceived as being proximate to *right* theoretical reasons, by contrast to motivational reasons, which are conceived as merely psychological states of the agent. Normative reasons theorists have been seen to have the upper hand in this debate because, among many other factors, the Humean account of reasons for actions as merely psychological or desire-based, even in its most sophisticated and refined version, seems implausible and leaves unexplained key features of human agency. In this debate between normative and motivational reason for actions, the nature and understanding of what robust practical reason is, is both simplified and reduced. In the normativist account, a reflection on reasons for action in isolation from the agent is privileged. In other words, reasons for actions are understood in isolation from the agent whose whole parts, according to the classical tradition, act in unity and produce *something* in the world. In the normativist account the question of how agents produce states of affairs and things in the world, which is the bread and water of practical reason and practical knowledge, becomes utterly unintelligible.

---

[2] Candace Vogler calls this 'bifurcationalist psychology'. See C Vogler, *Reasonably Vicious* (Cambridge, MA, Harvard University Press, 2002). In some ways, contemporary philosophy has been trapped by Hume's formulation of the problem, emphasising a division between beliefs and desires.

Human institutions such as law, probably because of a lack of sufficient reflection on robust practical reason among legal philosophers, have also been the subject of reflection from a predominantly theoretical or conceptual perspective. The most important work in twentieth century legal philosophy is called *The Concept of Law*. As the title suggests, it engages with the core features of the concept 'law' and theorises 'law'. Even the main critical accounts of this work, for example Dworkin's theory of legal interpretation,[3] give a theoretical account of law as interpretation. Interpretivist theory provides only a weak portrayal of the full power or faculty of human agency and practical reason.

In this book I will argue that there is a field of study to which we should return to complete our understanding of, and find answers to questions on, the nature of human institutions such as law. In contemporary philosophy this field is called 'moral psychology' and 'philosophy of action', but in the classical tradition it is connected to how things become, and consequently it is linked to action, movement and changes produced by agency. I invite the reader to re-visit a place that has been mainly occupied by Aristotle, Aquinas and Anscombe. I will argue that deep engagement with practical reason and practical knowledge provides the framework to understand two key features of law, ie normativity and authority.

The core argument of the book is that law is a specific 'actuality'[4] of our practical reasoning powers. Practical reason is conceived as a *form* that is displayed in our intentional action, which also has a *form* that involves a *diachronic structure*. To show that law is an 'actuality' of our practical reasoning powers, the book begins by dispelling the mistaken view that practical reason is theoretical reason *plus* something extra, ie volition, will or desire. The study advocates the view that intentional action is the midwife of practical reason. The study then tackles various misunderstandings surrounding intentional action and criticises the view that reduces intentional actions to mental states. The tendency has been either to reduce or to not take sufficiently seriously the idea that intentional action is a *form* which entails a *diachronic structure*. The illusion has been that we can grasp the diachronic structure of intentional action, and therefore of practical reason, if we regard it as constituted by separate components, or as constituted by 'slices' of actions which are caused by mental states. The result is muddled and confused theories that hopelessly attempt to connect mental states and results of actions in a directed and intelligible unity, after having severely chopped and disconnected their parts.

I have said that Aristotle, Aquinas and Anscombe provide the framework for a robust conception of practical reason and for explaining two key features of law: authority and normativity. Nonetheless, the first chapter of the book

---

[3] Dworkin hardly ever uses the term 'practical reason'.

[4] I use the term 'actuality' as coined by LA Kosman in his article 'Aristotle's Definition of Motion' (1969) *Phronesis* 40. See Chapter 4 for a full discussion of the notion of 'actuality'.

begins with a modern and familiar framework which is the antagonism between anarchist and Kantian notions of autonomy. In the first chapter the supposed conflict between authority and autonomy is analysed and it is shown that there is a possible Kantian interpretation of autonomy which makes compatible autonomy and the idea of the authority of the state. The chapter finishes with a promissory note on harmonising the conceptions of practical reason in the classical tradition and Kantian practical reason. This project is, of course, beyond the scope of this book.[5] The contemporary reader is more familiar with the Kantian notion of practical reason than with the idea of practical reason as advocated by Aristotle, Aquinas or Anscombe and therefore this first chapter provides the reader with familiar territory from where reflection on practical reason can begin. Since this is a book on legal authority and normativity, it begins with the anarchist challenge on authority, and because the anarchist challenge is connected to the Kantian notion of autonomy, I have searched for a tentative Kantian answer. The underlying intuition is that the Kantian answer is not far from the answer provided by Aristotle, Aquinas and Anscombe. One of the aims of this chapter is to provide the reader with reasoning that will allow her to go from what is familiar, ie practical reason in Kant, to something less familiar, ie practical reason according to the classical tradition. The first chapter establishes the tasks, ie examining the antagonism between authority and autonomy and possible ways of reinterpreting both authority and autonomy that ameliorate the antagonism between them. The notion of legal normativity, ie how the law is reason-giving, plays a key role in reinterpreting authority and autonomy. Thereafter the book focuses on legal normativity until we return to the question of legal authority in Chapter 8.

In Chapter 2 I explain how law can be reason-giving. The chapter aims to give an account of what legal normativity is in terms of *how* it works and operates in the agent. It is shown how intentional actions of legal rule-following or rule-compliance[6] are explained by the description of the agent who takes the deliberative point of view. It is argued that the agent performs the action *because* of the grounding reasons of legal rules that are understood in the best light by the deliberator or agent himself. In other words, the deliberator follows the legal rule because he can describe his own actions in terms of reasons as good-making characteristics. Traditional wisdom states that intentional actions can be rationalised and that intentions are mental states (such as acceptance, desires, beliefs, and so on). Therefore, following this line of argu-

---

[5] For an attempt to do this see C Korsgaard, 'Aristotle and Kant on the Source of Value' in *Creating the Kingdom of Ends* (Cambridge, Cambridge University Press, 1996) 225 and S Engstrom, *The Form of Practical Knowledge* (Cambridge, MA, Harvard University Press, 2009).

[6] I will use the terms 'rule following' and 'rule compliance' interchangeably for reasons that will become apparent in Chapter 8.

mentation, an intentional action aimed at following legal rules can be explained in terms of 'acceptance' of the rule or other related mental states. I argue that this conception presupposes what I call the 'two-component model' of intentional action. The two-component model sits well with a description of rule-following actions from the third-person perspective. The model assumes that there is symmetry between an explanation of 'following a legal rule' from the third-person point of view and an explanation from the first-person point of view.[7] This assumption of symmetry, however, is mistaken and in Chapters 5 and 6 I defend the parasitic thesis. It is argued in these chapters that an explanation of rule-following from the deliberative point of view in terms of the grounding reasons as good-making characteristics ('guise of the good' model of legal rules) is *primary* to the explanation given by the two-component model in terms of mental states. Chapter 5 shows that Hart's notion of 'acceptance' of the rule of recognition presupposed the two-component model; consequently, it is argued, Hart's notion of 'acceptance' is parasitic upon the 'guise of the good' model of legal rules. Chapter 6 argues that Kelsen's notion of legal normativity relied on a narrow notion of intentional action which is close to the two-component model. A parasitic relationship also seems necessary to make intelligible and much more *complete* the notion of legal normativity.

Chapters 3 and 4 scrutinise the robust conception of practical reason, ie the 'guise of the good' model. In these chapters I directly engage with, and unpack, the key features of this model whilst in Chapter 2 the 'guise of the good' model is applied to the phenomenon of legal rule-following or rule-compliance. Chapter 3 elucidates the relationship between reasons for actions, good-making characteristics and intentional action and defends the guise of the good model against some its critics. Chapter 4 engages with understanding *how* the form or structure of intentional action is able to reveal the form and structure of practical reason. I argue that we need to go deeper into Aristotelian metaphysics to scrutinise what practical reason is and *how* practical reason and intentional action are intertwined. The Aristotelian metaphysical view is that we are creatures of a certain nature and that we possess powers and capacities, amongst which the power of practical reasoning is the

---

[7] Examples of the symmetric view of intentional action can be found in S Perry, 'Political Authority and Political Obligation' in L Green and B Leiter (eds), *Oxford Studies in Philosophy of Law* (Oxford, Oxford University Press, 2012) vol II. Perry points out: 'What should we say about the situation where the lawmaker goes through the motions, as it were, of legislating but does not have the appropriate intention? It seems to me that the right thing to say is analogous to the private law solution to such problems, which is that we attribute intentions based on objective manifestations of behavior. So the lawmaker has in fact made law, despite not possessing the appropriate intention' (34). However, Perry argues that the paradigmatic case is when the 'intention is present'. Perry's test to determine whether 'intention is present' is Enoch's defence of a Gricean theory of intention. For a rejection of Enoch's and Grice's explanation of reason-giving and intention see section 10.3.

most important. Capacities or powers can only be grasped when we are active. But then what does it mean to say that these capacities are 'active' or *actual*? The core argument is that the Aristotelian distinction between actuality and potentiality provides the general framework for understanding the idea of capacity change that underlies the view of practical reason as a capacity or power that changes and manifests itself in different ways.[8] We require, therefore, an understanding of the actuality/potentiality distinction to grasp *how* practical reason as a capacity is able to work, operate, manifest itself and provide the form of our intentional actions. In section 4.2 I explain the actuality/ potentiality distinction and how it illuminates the notion of practical reasoning (capacity) and capacity change. In section 4.3 I analyse the implications of this view for the central inquiry of the book which is an explanation of the legal-rule compliance phenomenon.

Chapter 7 aims to establish the idea that the claims of legal authorities of legitimate authority and moral correctness should be understood as expressions of intentions about *how* legal actions will be performed. It is shown how the claims of legal authorities construed as expressions of intentions shape the law and our attitudes towards legal rules.

The picture of legal rules that starts to emerge is a complex one where expressions of intentions, intentional actions, successful and failed performances, and hypothetical and objective good-making characteristics are all intertwined.

Chapter 8 joins the idea of authorities' claims as expressions of intentions with compliance with the eight desiderata of the Rule of Law to show that together they create a presumption of the goodness of legal authority and, consequently, a presumption of legitimacy. The view that the notion of legal normativity defended in this book and legal authority are incompatible is subsequently discussed. Raz, for example, offers an explanation of the reason-giving character of law that is compatible with legal authority. He adumbrates the view that legal rules provide exclusionary reasons which can explain the service that law gives us and the practical difference in our lives that characterises the authoritative nature of law. The 'guise of the good' model seems unsatisfactory because it cannot explain the 'practical difference' that law makes to our actions and in our lives. However, I adumbrate arguments to show that legal rules as conceived by the 'guise of the good' model can compete with the idea of legal rules as exclusionary reasons. An independent criticism of Raz's notion of authority is also offered. The notion of exclusionary

---

[8] This interpretation is advanced by M Frede, 'Aristotle's Notion of Potentiality in *Metaphysics Q*' in T Scaltsas, D Charles and M Gill (eds), *Unity, Identity and Explanation in Aristotle's Metaphysics* (Oxford, Clarendon Press, 1994) and Makin's commentaries on Aristotle in *Aristotle, Metaphysics Book Q*, Clarendon Aristotle Series (Oxford, Clarendon Press, 2006) 133. Cf WD Ross, *Aristotle's Physics: A Revised Text with Introduction and Commentary* (Oxford, Oxford University Press, 1995).

reasons is caught on the two horns of the following paradox ('the paradox of intentionality'): if we follow legal rules intentionally, then legal rules are not exclusionary reasons. If we do not follow legal rules intentionally, then legal rules do not have a reason-giving character. Therefore, either legal rules are not exclusionary reasons or legal rules do not have a reason-giving character. I put forward arguments to show that only the first option can be attractive, namely we follow legal rules intentionally and therefore legal rules are not exclusionary reasons for actions. Finally, it is argued that legal rules can serve us in a 'ethical-political way' since they offer us grounding reasons as (believed) good-making characteristics. Authorities express their intentions to perform their actions in a moral and legitimate way. Consequently, in the exercise of our practical knowledge and practical capacities, we intentionally follow legal rules or authoritative directives, either recognising the goodness of the authority and creating a presumption of legitimate authority, or avowing the reasons as good-making characteristics of the legal rule or authoritative directive. An objector might argue that this is an unsatisfactory solution to the problem of the compatibility between legal normativity and legal authority as construed by the 'guise of the good' model because the authority of the law is *independent* of our intentions as citizens to give authority to the law, and this view is well grasped and explained by the idea of exclusionary reasons. I advance the following response to this objection. The explanation of legal rules as exclusionary reasons is *parasitic* on the explanation of legal rules under the 'guise of the good' model. From the third-person perspective the explanation of legal rules as exclusionary reasons seems appealing. Thus, as spectators of the authority of legal rules, we think of law as something *independent* of our intentions and we have good reasons to think this. We are, after all, in the position of mere spectators and our knowledge is, therefore, limited; ie we do not, after all, intend to act. From the point of view of the agent (the deliberative viewpoint), however, the explanation is not sound since only legal rules under the guise of the good model can make 'legal rule-following' or 'legal rule-compliance' intelligible, if rule-following or rule-compliance is a sub-species of intentional action. Consequently, legal rules as grounded in good-making characteristics lie at the heart of the phenomenon of 'following authoritative legal rules'.

A second independent argument is adumbrated in response to the latter objection. It seems that the notion of 'service' provided by law involves an ambiguity. On its strong reading this means that the agent cannot assess the merits or reasons for acting according to legal rules and authoritative directives; on a weaker reading it suggests that legal rules and authoritative directives show us the grounding reasons of the legal rules, reasons that we should avow when we follow legal rules. Thus, law invites us to engage with law's reasons. In this way it makes a practical difference to our lives because it shows us reasons as good-making characteristics that we would probably not have considered without the law. Law aims to have an authoritative effect on us in a 'ethical-political' way; ie it gives us good-making characteristics that we can avow, and that can constitute *our* reasons for actions. I defend the 'ethical-political' view of legitimate legal authority and argue that the agent, in the paradigmatic case, needs to engage in deliberation when following legal rules.

In Chapter 9 I defend an epistemology of objective values and advocate a modest conception of objective goods (values). Thus, I suggest that when we deliberate we engage our conceptual and practical capacities and this enables us to grasp the good-making characteristics of legal rules. The grounding reasons of rules as 'good' are learned and perceived in their instantiation of particulars; they should not be interpreted as principles or maxims. We show that when we engage with the good-making characteristics of legal rules, there is continuity between our personal commitments and what is valuable as embedded in our cultural and social fabric.

The idea of particulars that instantiate good-making characteristics plays a mediating role between objective values and our subjective value judgments. The way to understand and grasp values is through our value judgments and conceptions of the good. Our value judgments are directed towards objective values which are instantiated in particulars. Thus, it is argued that the grounding reasons of legal rules as objective goods are identified through two formulas: one for acts ('Identifying Formula for Grounding Reasons in case of Acts', IA) and the other for prohibited acts such as 'do not steal' or 'do not commit murder' ('Identifying Formula for Grounding Reasons in case of Prohibited Acts', IPA), which are the following:

> *(IA): 'A grounding reason as a good-making characteristic of a legal rule is objective if the addressee of the legal rule or authoritative directive cannot reasonably refuse to intend to act under a certain hypothetical description of the grounding reason'.*

> *(IPA): 'A grounding reason as a good-making characteristic of a legal rule is objective if the addressee of the legal rule or authoritative directive cannot reasonably intend to act under a certain hypothetical description of the grounding reason'.*

The chapter finishes with a partial reflection on the metaphysics of value. A full account of a metaphysical position of values is beyond the limits of the book, however I offer a partial defence of normative and value realism. The book adumbrates a modified version of the 'deliberative indispensability of irreducibly normative truths' argument advanced by Enoch[9] and gestures towards the possibility of normative and value realism.

The final chapter of the book analyses some possible objections to the proposed view of legal authority and normativity as conceived under the guise of the good model.

---

[9] D Enoch, *Taking Morality Seriously* (Oxford, Oxford University Press, 2011).

The received view on the nature of legal authority contains the idea that a sound account of legitimate authority explains how a legal authority has the right to command and the addressee a duty to obey.[10] The received view fails to explain, however, how legal authority truly operates upon human beings as rational creatures with specific psychological make-ups. The book takes a bottom-up approach, beginning at the microscopic level of agency and practical reason and leading to the justificatory framework of authority. The book argues that an understanding of the nature of legal normativity involves an understanding of the *nature* and *structure* of robust practical reason in the context of law, and advances the idea that legal authority and normativity are intertwined. This point can be summarised thus: If we are able to understand both how the agent exercises his or her practical reason under legal directives and commands and how the agent engages his or her practical reason by following legal rules grounded on reasons for actions as good-making characteristics, then we can fully grasp the nature of legal authority and legal normativity. The account is comprehensive and enables us to distinguish authoritative and normative legal rules in just and good legal systems from 'apparent' authoritative and normative legal rules in ill-intentioned (of evil) legal systems.

At the heart of this book is the methodological view of a 'practical turn' to elucidate the nature of legal normativity and authority. I hope that this 'practical turn' will be used as a methodology to illuminate other questions on the nature of law and other human institutions.

[10] Note that recent work on legal authority establishes a division of labour between the task of explaining the submission problem, ie the problem of how authorities' directives and legal rules enter into the practical reasoning of the agents, and the justificatory task (see especially Perry (n 7)). The book aims to show that these two tasks cannot be separated, because the justification of legal authority is *primarily* from the first-person perspective or the deliberative viewpoint. Thus, there is continuity between the submission and the justificatory problems of legal authority.

1

Legal Authority and Normativity: Rediscovering a Hidden Relationship

LAW TRANSFORMS OUR lives in the most important way: it changes how we act and because of this it gives rise to fundamental questions. One such question concerns legal authority and individual autonomy and asks: if we are autonomous agents how do legislators, judges and officials have legitimate authority to change our actions and indirectly change how we conduct our lives? We conceive ourselves as active agents who determine *how* and *when* to act, and we conceive ourselves as the planners of our own lives and the creators of change. Law asks us, however, to perform actions that range from the trivial to the complex. Law requires us, for example, to: stop at traffic lights; park our vehicles in specially allocated areas; exercise our professional judgement in a responsible and non-negligent manner; pay our taxes; recycle our rubbish, and so on. Law asks us to perform innumerable tasks, almost all of which we perform intentionally and in full awareness. But how is it possible for me to do, in full awareness, as the law asks and, at the same time, be in control of my own destiny? How is my free will affected by the law?

But how is this possible when I am *simply* trying to *conform* with what the law says? This means, I am trying to follow what the law says without giving much thought or without engaging my will or intention.

Legal and political philosophers have tended to examine legal authority and autonomy and have consequently put forward the following questions: (a) Can there ever be legitimate authority? (b) What are the conditions of legitimate authority? and (c) Does the possibility of *legitimate* authority diminish or assuage the antagonism between authority and autonomy?

I find that posing the problem and the questions in this way is unsatisfactory because it presupposes *what* we need to explain, ie the *nature* of authority and whether there is a 'genuine' antagonism between autonomy and legal authority. Within this framework authority is *given,* and the starting point of the theorist is the following statement: *If there is* a legitimate authority then conditions x, y, and z need to be fulfilled, but it is not shown *how there is or whether there could* be something such as legitimate authority. The received view begins by recognising the phenomenological fact that legal officials and authorities issue commands and directives. It is usually said that if authorities have the right to command and addressees the duty to obey, then the officials have legitimate authority.

Theorists usually argue in favour of a particular political theory, for example, liberalism or perfectionism, and engage with a set of key values, for instance, expert knowledge or democratic values that provide the grounds for 'rights' and 'duties' and that enable us to grasp the conditions of legitimate authority. The traditional strategy, therefore, begins top-down from a plausible view on political theory that leads to the framework that *justifies* authority. There is no doubt that the traditional strategy has provided us with a rich understanding that has advanced our grasp of the *normative conditions* that make *possible* legitimate legal authority. However, the traditional strategy fails to provide a microscopic view of the phenomenon of legal authority and falls short of explaining *how* legal authority truly operates on individual human beings.

By contrast, the strategy of this book is to focus on the agent, ie the addressee of the legal command or directive who performs the action requested by the legal official. This strategy is bottom-up, from the level of agency and practical reason to the justificatory framework of authority. It also begins with the *naive* phenomenological observation that X commands Y to perform the action p (an action p-ing to Y). Thus it is intelligible to us that Y performs the action p as requested by X. The key question that this book aims to investigate is how a legal command or directive, *just because* it is a legal command or directive, *effectively* changes the agent's course of action. A set of sub-questions arise: Does the command intervene in the practical reasoning of the agent or addressee? If this is the case, how does this intervention *operate*? Moreover, what are the limits of our phenomenological observations, in other words can I truly observe that you are performing an action because you are complying with a legal directive or command? What happens in the agent that enables her to comply with the legal command or directive? When we perform an action because we are complying with the legal command or directive, are we still active, self-governed autonomous agents? In what sense are we still autonomous agents? The task of this book is to explain *what* legal authority is and the premise of the study is that this question can only be answered through understanding *how* legal authority operates upon the agent: if we recognise that legal commands or directives intervene upon, affect and change the agent's practical reasoning, then we need to understand and explain *how this happens*.

Answering the question above raises other, difficult, questions, however. For instance we quickly come to see that the question of legal authority is closely tied up with the issue of the normativity of law. Raz,[1] for example, has asserted that to understand what normativity is, we need to understand what reasons for actions are.[2] But reasons for action are not 'free-standing' reasons in the world where agents play no role, they do not stand independently of the agents and their practical reasoning. The philosophical literature on reasons for action is vast and for the last thirty years philosophical studies have focused on the notion of reasons for actions, but few philosophers have concentrated on the *nature and structure of practical reason*.[3] Paraphrasing Raz, understanding the nature of legal normativity involves understanding the nature and struc-ture of practical reason in the context of the law.[4] We have, now, two very closely related issues. The point can be summarised as this: if we are able to understand how practical reason under legal commands, directives and rules operates, and how practical reason operates by following reasons for actions, then we can fully grasp the nature of legal authority and legal normativity. There will be paradigmatic cases[5] of legitimate legal authority, but we also aim to explain cases of legal authority where there is only 'apparent' legit-imacy (see Chapter 9).

The book focuses on unpacking the nature and structure of practical reason so that it may shed light on the phenomenon of legal authority and normativ-ity. I defend the classical view of practical reason and focus on the philoso-phies of actions of Aristotle, Aquinas and Anscombe. However, because the complexities and intricacies of the notion of practical reason, which within this tradition is closely connected to intentional action, will be unfamiliar to some readers, I begin with a more familiar view of practical reason, ie that defended by Kant. The discussion begins with the way in which one specific contemporary view poses the conflict between authority and autonomy.

In this chapter I examine the 'anarchist' view as formulated by Wolff' who aims to show that there can never be legitimate authority since this inevitably undermines our autonomy. We are then faced with two irreconcilable options: if we recognise that the state can have authority over us, then we need to give up the idea that we are autonomous agents, but we cannot give up this idea because it will involve the absurd view that we are not responsible. We, there-fore, give up the idea that is least threatening to our self-understanding, ie that

---

[1] J Raz, *Engaging Reason* (Oxford, Oxford University Press, 1999) 67.

[2] I will use 'reasons in action' and 'reasons for action' interchangeably. At the end of the book the reason for this interchange of terminology will become clear.

[3] For some exceptions, see D Velleman, *Practical Reflection* (Princeton, Princeton University Press, 1989) and *The Possibility of Practical Reason* (Oxford, Oxford University Press, 2000); C Korsgaard, *Sources of Normativity* (Cambridge, Cambridge University Press, 1996) and *Self-Constitution: Agency, Identity and Integrity* (Oxford, Oxford University Press, 2009).

[4] Raz (n 1) 67.

[5] The notion of paradigm follows the idea of core-resemblance that is defended in my article 'Is Finnis Wrong?' (2007) 13 *Legal Theory* 257.

the state has authority over us. In section 1.2 I show that the view of authoritative commands as advanced by Wolff is implausible, but the details of this argument depend on the account of intentional action and practical reason that I defend in Chapters 2, 3 and 4. In section 1.3 I demonstrate that Wolff's conception of autonomy is ambiguous and in section 1.4 I advance a more promising way of understanding the 'apparent' antagonism between autonomy and authority. This chapter provides the reader with possible ways of reconciling the classical tradition on practical reason and the Kantian view on autonomy. This reconciling project goes beyond the scope of both this chapter and the book, however. The chapter does, nevertheless, provide a clear framework for understanding how practical reason and intentional action are intertwined and will therefore clarify to the reader the structure of the rest of the book. A detailed explanation of the relationship between the structure of practical reason and intentional action is provided in Chapter 4.

1.2 IMPLAUSIBILITY OF PERFORMING A COMPLEX ACTION: *BECAUSE AN AUTHORITY HAS SAID SO*

Let us imagine the following two scenarios:

Scenario 1 ('Registration'): you are asked by a legal authority to fill in a form that will register you on the electoral roll.

Scenario 2 ('Assistance at a car accident'): you are asked by an official to assist the paramedics at the scene of a serious traffic incident (ie by helping injured parties into the ambulance and by providing reassurance and basic first aid).

The scenario in 'Registration' involves the performance of a simple action, ie completing a form as clearly instructed. The scenario in 'Assistance at the car accident' involves performance of a more complex series of actions: it requires awareness of the situation and the possible dangers of moving the injured in one way rather than another and it requires providing emotional and physical assistance to others. It also requires to overcome obstacles in order to succeed in the purpose of saving the lives of the victims and therefore complying with the command.

According to Wolff' the model of authority (in both scenarios) can be formulated as follows:

X performs an action p-ing because *Y has said so.*[6]

In the case of 'Registration' we could say that the agent has filled in the form *because the legal authority has said so*; in the case of 'Assistance at the car

---

[6] RP Wolff, *In Defense of Anarchism* (New York and London, Harper Torchbooks, 1970) 9.

accident', the agent has also performed a series of action, *because* the legal official or authority *has said so*.

At first glance this seems to be a sound characterisation of 'authority' but
closer inspection reveals discrepancies. That an agent acts in a particular way
because they are directed to do so by a legal authority is, I will argue, an implausible
formulation that does not grasp the depth and richness of what is truly
happening in cases like 'Assistance at a car accident' which involves the
performance of a complex series of actions. It might explain simple cases such
as 'Registration' but it cannot account for complex ones. To act 'because
someone has said you should do so' means that you are acting because of an
empirical fact that is presented to you. But we have previously noted that to
perform that action requires awareness of the situation and its dangers; it
involves engaging and directing the will towards the action; and it involves
making judgments about how to succeed in the action. The question that
arises is how a mere empirical fact, ie the order or command to do something,
can engage the will in the complex performance of the action. I believe that
many different factors are entailed and demonstrate this in Chapters 2, 3 and
4. My aim in this chapter is simply to make the point that a mere empirical
fact cannot engage our will in cases where we perform complex actions.

A first (and charitable) reading of the empirical account will suggest something like the following: the legal command or directive is an empirical fact
that *causes the* agent to act in a certain way by virtue of the agent having certain
beliefs and desires. Sanctions or threats, in particular, *cause* an impulse or
desire in the agent to act in a certain way. I consider this view, however, to be
implausible because it entails that for each movement there is a compulsive
desire or impulse in the agent that causes each of the actions and series of
actions. I argue that legal commands as merely empirical and contingent cannot guarantee the continuity and direction that characterises the performance
of complex actions (sections 2.3, 2.4, 3.2, 3.3, Chapter 4, section 5.3). The
diachronic structure of future-directed intentions in action requires *rational
governance* within discrete times and simple empirical causation cannot guarantee such continuity. A second, more interesting, reading is that the intention
of the official is grasped by the agent's mental state and the agent's mental
state *causes* performance of the action. In this case we also have a notion of
causation between a mental state and the complex action and again the
appearance of deviation in the causal connection cannot be avoided. This
account is more promising because it directs our attention to the role that
intention plays in practical reasoning, but it is limited because it conceives
intention within the restricted model of mental states and empirical causation
(see for further discussion Chapter 2, and sections 3.2, 3.3, 5.3, 10.3).

With these preliminaries clarified, we can now concentrate on Wolff's anarchist account and the antagonism between authority and autonomy.

The argument that Wolff presents us with is the following:

(1) If I perform an action *because someone says so*, then I am not acting according to my own will.
(2) If I do not act according to my own will, then I do not act autonomously.
(3) Most cases involving the authority of a state involve (1).
(4) I cannot act according to (1) because the authority of the state undermines my autonomy.
(5) Therefore the authority of the state cannot be legitimate.

In the following section I concentrate on premise (2).

1.3 AUTONOMY VERSUS HETERONOMY: A QUICK GLANCE AT THE ACCOUNTS OF AUTONOMY IN WOLFF AND KANT

Wolff advocates the Kantian view which presupposes that we are metaphysically free because we ascribe responsibility for actions to ourselves and others.[7] This view does not demonstrate that we *are* metaphysically free, merely that this is presupposed. Being 'responsible' involves the task of deciding what we ought to do; it involves resisting impulses and desires; and it entails engaging ourselves with what we believe to be worth pursuing and achieving, and disengaging ourselves from our desires, moods, traditions and practices. (This means that I am the only judge of the maxims or principles that will determine my actions.) According to Wolff, and in a Kantian vein, autonomy is the capacity that all human beings have to legislate for themselves and create maxims in the form of imperatives that guide their actions: 'He may do what another tells him, but not because he has been told to do it. He is therefore, in the political sense of the word, free'.[8] If a man performs an action because another man has told him to do so, then the man has refused to engage in moral deliberation and therefore has refused to be autonomous. Wolff concludes that 'for the autonomous man, there is no such thing, strictly speaking, as a command'.[9]

But what does it mean to say that human beings ought to 'legislate for themselves'? Does it mean that human beings are the *authors* of their own moral laws and therefore that self-legislators impose on themselves the principles and maxims that they have authored? This existentialist and romantic interpretation of Kant's notion of autonomy has been rejected by Kantian

---

[7] ibid 12.
[8] ibid 14.
[9] ibid 15.

scholars[10] who criticise those interpretations of autonomy in which human beings behave as gods, creating their own moral world and imposing upon themselves their own principles and rules of conduct. There are, however, some passages in Kant that lend themselves to such an interpretation.[11] This kind of interpretation is, moreover, suggested in the tension that arises in Kant's formulation of autonomy and self-legislation. Kant's self-legislative thesis appears on a number of occasions in his *Groundwork for the Metaphysics of Morals*. See, for example, the two following extracts: 'the supreme condition of the will's harmony with universal practical reason is the Idea of the will of every rational being as a will that legislates universal law';[12] and, 'The will is therefore not merely subject to the law, but subject in such a way that it must be considered as also giving the law to itself and only for this reason as first of all subject to the law (of which it can regard itself as the author)'.[13] Kant advances the view that we need to regard ourselves as having the *idea* of legislating universally. The emphasis is on the perspective taken: we *regard* ourselves as the authors of the law[14] and this does not mean that we are *actually* the authors of the law, merely that we *consider* ourselves to be such.

Some authors, like Wolff, reject this interpretation and ask the following: if we have sovereignty of our actions, how can we be subject to external law and regard ourselves as legislators without truly and effectively creating our own law? For Wolff, we are the creators of the law and this explains our submission to it and our motivation to obey it. Kant's argument, however, is that because we have engaged in a deliberative process of creating the law, our created laws are intelligible to us and therefore (we have acquired the intelligibility of our 'created' law and therefore) we are motivated to act according to them. In the case of moral laws we have created them independently of our interests and desires and therefore we submit to them unconditionally (are able to impose it on ourselves categorically and not conditionally). As an agent, I will the moral law and it is imposed on me as a practical necessity, regardless of my desires and wants. Heteronomous deliberation opposes autonomous deliberation. In the former I am driven by my desires, interests and wants and in some sense they are external to me. The reasons and rules that guide my actions are derived from desires and wants. They might be presented as mere impulses, eg my desire to drink a glass of water if I am thirsty, or they might

---

[10] See A Wood, *Kantian Ethics* (Cambridge, Cambridge University Press, 2008) and O O'Neill, *Constructions of Reasons* (Cambridge, Cambridge University Press, 1989) 75–76.

[11] I Kant, *Groundwork for the Metaphysics of Morals* (Thomas R Hill and Arnulf Zweig (eds), Arnulf Zweig (trans), Oxford, Oxford University Press, 2002).

[12] ibid 4:431

[13] ibid 4:431.

[14] This interpretation is also advocated by A Reath, *Agency and Autonomy in Kant's Moral Theory* (Oxford, Clarendon Press, 2006) and Wood (n 10).

be manifested as more sophisticated desires, eg if I want to be rich then I need to study the stock market to learn to invest my money appropriately. In autonomous deliberation, the maxim that is part of the major premise of the practical syllogism[15] becomes a universal principle, because it is what every rational human being wills, independently of the contingencies of human nature (such as different desires, inclinations, characters, ways of life, social conventions, traditions, and so on). Subjective maxims, therefore, can become objective and universal principles and can ground our moral actions. Because the agent is the one who engages in this deliberation, he or she is motivated to act according to it.

For Wolff, however, an inescapable tension arises in Kant's thoughts on autonomy. If we are subject to objective standards in which sense do we legislate and in which sense are we the creators of moral laws? We are not free to decide how the law will be, and we cannot shape moral laws according to our conceptions and worldviews. On the contrary, autonomy entails that we are determined as rational beings to engage in the *right* process of moral deliberation whose result will be universal objective standards. There is no room for subjective worldviews or creative conceptions of moral law. The conflict is now between legislation which involves creation and subjectivity, and moral law that involves universality and objectivity. Wolff believes that this tension cannot be resolved and that, therefore, one of these ideas needs to be abandoned. He advocates the view that we need to give up the idea that there are objective standards that determine moral law.[16]

It is now apparent what motivates Wolff in his adherence to an existentialist or romantic reading of Kant's notion of autonomy. To take seriously autonomy, freedom and responsibility, we need to abandon the idea that there are constraints in terms of absolute and objective standards. In this way we are truly sovereign and the authors of moral laws. The price of this, however, is the abandonment of an important Kantian insight, ie the view that there are objective standards to evaluate the moral law. Alternatively, if we take seriously that reading of sovereignty and legislation in which we merely *consider or regard* ourselves as creators of the law, then a more plausible form of diminished autonomy emerges. Let us scrutinise this interpretation. Can we say that because the *source* of the principle or value that will guide our actions is not *created* by us (ie it is an objective standard in either natural or non-natural elements) then we are autonomous in a diminished form? Let us examine what this diminished form of autonomy might look like.

Imagine the following scenario ('Appearance of an angel'): you are a young adult who is trying to decide whether to go to university, travel around the

---

[15] For criticism of this interpretation of 'practical syllogism' see section 4.2.1.
[16] RP Wolff, *The Autonomy of Reason* (New York, Harper Torchbooks, 1973).

world, or find a job. You are sitting on the balcony of your house at midnight trying to decide what to do with your life. A luminous figure appears and you believe it is an angel. She says to you: 'Knowledge is valuable' and then adds, urgently, in an imperative voice: 'you ought to go to university'. Suddenly you grasp the value of knowledge and the truth in the command, and consequently you decide to go to university instead of finding a job or travelling around the world. If you are asked *why* you have taken the decision to go to university you will answer that it is because an angelic figure *told you to do so*. If you are asked why you should obey an angelic figure you will reply, 'because the command is grounded in the idea that knowledge is valuable'. The story sounds both incomplete and absurd because it does not explain *how* the agent grasps the value of knowledge. It might be argued, however, that this is self-evident.[17] Thus, in the same way that we grasp that the law of excluded middle in logic is true, we grasp that 'knowledge' is a value. Furthermore, to assert that knowledge is not a value is self-refuting, therefore to be coherent in my assertions about the world I need to accept the value of knowledge. But this comparison between theoretical reason, ie how it is self-evident that knowledge is a value that ought to be pursued, and how it is self-evident that knowledge is an objective value, is misleading. The comparison mistakenly characterises practical reason as theoretical reason *plus* volition. It encourages a conception of practical reason as operating along the lines of theoretical reason. It is then believed that something needs to be 'added' to guarantee the performance of an action. The additional element is a volitional element. It is a mystery, however, how the volitional element can be 'added' or 'stuck' to the theoretical reasoning of the agent. This way of understanding practical reason will be criticised in a subsequent chapter (see sections 4.1 and §.2). For now it is sufficient to assert that practical reason should be understood as a diachronic process rather than as a static theoretical process *plus* volition. The dynamic and diachronic process of practical reason is unfolded by the exercise of the actuality of reason in action (see Chapter 4). It is an actuality which all human beings have the capacity to engage in and involves the idea that reason is manifested in action. It also entails belief, but it is the content of the belief that determines the action.[18]

[17] A version of this argument can be found in J Finnis, *Natural Law and Natural Rights* (Oxford, Clarendon Press, 1980).

[18] This point has been emphasised by Jonathan Dancy, *Practical Reality* (Oxford, Oxford University Press, 2002). In contemporary debates this conception was first advanced by Joseph Raz, see *Practical Reason and Norms* (Oxford, Oxford University Press, 1999; originally published Hutchinsonn & Co, 1975) 17. However, Dancy takes the view that because we are not dealing with beliefs, but with the content of the belief, then reasons for action are only about the content and therefore normative. He severs the relationship between reasons for actions and the process of practical reason, where reasons for action are manifested.

For Kant, practical reason also has a structure and involves a process: that process of assent of the will.[19] The major premise of the practical syllogism is a subjective maxim that if it is universalisable, it becomes an objective principle that guides action. Our rational nature guarantees the result of the process of practical reason which is the objective and universal principle that will guide the action. I am not the author of the principle, rather I discover,[20] construct[21] or re-construct[22] the principle by engaging in sound practical reasoning. Because I have engaged in this process of practical reasoning I can *regard myself* as the creator of the law, as a *legislator*. I can reasonably consider myself as a creator of the law and am now bound by my 'as if a legislator' own creations. I am satisfied and can be proud of my task because I have followed a rational procedure engaging my full capacities as a rational human being. I can r*egard myself* as a *good* or *right creator* of the moral law because I did not create the law through arbitrary processes according to my moods and psychological constitution. Arguably, the source of the objective principles is *external* to me, but because I have engaged in a process of deliberation I can regard myself 'as if I am the legislator of the law'.

Let us now go back to our example 'Appearance of an angel'. The creator of the objective value or principle is the angelic authority, but the agent can *regard* herself or himself as if he or she were the creator of the law because he or she would have engaged in the process of practical deliberation, and possibly moral deliberation.

Legal authority involves both freedom and submission. It involves freedom because we are responsible if we do not obey legal directives and rules, or if we follow them wrongly. For example, if I am asked by the local authority to recycle my rubbish and do not do so, or do so wrongly, then I can be held to be at fault and subject to penalties or other sanctions. If we assume a purely

---

[19] See especially M Frede, *A Free Will: Origins of the Notion in Ancient Thought* (AA Long and D Sedley (eds), Berkeley and Los Angeles, CA, University of California Press, 2011) and A Dihle, *The Theory of Will in Classical Antiquity* (Berkeley and Los Angeles, CA, University of California Press, 1982) for illuminating historical accounts of the emergence of the idea of the will.

[20] See Wood (n 10) for a critique of the constructivist reading of Kant.

[21] See Reath (n 14); C Korsgaard, *Creating the Kingdom of Ends* (Cambridge, Cambridge University Press, 1996) and Rawls for a constructivist reading of Kant; J Rawls, *A Theory of Justice* (Cambridge, MA, Harvard University Press, 1971) and 'Kantian Constructivism in Moral Theory' (1980) 77 *Journal of Philosophy* 515.

[22] Wood argues that Kant's view concerning the objectivity of principles should be understood along realist lines. By engaging in practical reason, we only discover principles that are independent of our desires, beliefs, social practices, conventions or impulses. Wood believes that Kant was a metaphysical realist. By contrast, Korsgaard and Reath argue that Kant's principles are the result of a process of moral deliberation. We do not discover such principles but rather construct them. Arguably, a third position could be defended: principles are objective and independent of our desires, beliefs, social practices, conventions or impulses, but the determination of such principles in action can only be achieved through practical deliberation. Through engaging in moral deliberation we therefore re-construct the objective principles of morality that are already there.

empirical perspective and assert that your actions are only determined by your mental state of fear of punishment, then our notion of responsibility is weakened. Thus, if you fail to adopt the adequate mental state that will cause the action, ie the belief and desire to organise your rubbish according to the instructions of the local authority, we can only say that you are responsible for not having the mental state necessary to cause the appropriate actions. The question that arises is how can we force ourselves to acquire specific (determinate) mental states? How can we control our mental states? Is it our responsibility or the responsibility of an authority to ensure the adoption of the requisite mental states? Furthermore, when we do not comply with legal rules or directives, or when we follow them wrongly, we do not consider that we have failed to acquire the requisite mental states. We say that we are free to act in certain ways and that we are responsible because we have a certain scope of freedom. But how should submission be conceived and explained if we need to leave room for freedom? The strategy is to reduce the gap between freedom and submission. The idea of self-legislation 'as if' we were the creators of the law, enables us to explain how something that is external to the agent, such as a legal directive or rule, can be part of the agent through his or her engagement in practical deliberation.

If we accept this reading of 'as if' self-legislation in the domain of law, then we see that the antagonism between legal authority and autonomy is mitigated. We also see that Wolff's 'anarchist' conclusion is not granted and that a sound understanding of the nature and structure of practical reason can illuminate both legal authority and normativity.

1.4 A FIRST APPROACH TOWARDS A HARMONISING PROJECT

The conception of the classical tradition, ie that found in Aristotle and Aquinas, is not too far from Kant's notion of practical reason.[23] As discussed in Chapters 3 and 4, for Aristotle and Aquinas the possibility of grasping what is of value and worth pursuing as a guide for our actions can only be achieved by engaging in practical reasoning. The exercise of our reasoning capacities in the unfolding of action over time enables us to discover and determine what is good and valuable (both apparent and genuine, see Chapter 9), and to be guided by it. For both views practical reason is a process and has a structure. But differences between Kant's conceptions of practical reason and those of the classical tradition remain important. The core difference lies in understanding the distinction between the legislative and executive levels of practical

---

[23] See especially S Engstrom, *The Form of Practical Knowledge* (Cambridge, MA, Harvard University Press, 2009).

reason. For Kant the task of pure practical reason[24] is at the legislative level. It engages with the determination of objective and universal moral principles *before* the action and organises and *imposes a form* on the materials of our choice which are determined by our desires and interests. The following example helps to illustrate the point. Let us suppose that you wish to travel to South America with a friend who asks you to make the travel arrangements for both yourself and her. By engaging in purely practical deliberation you identify the objective and universal principle that you will only what you are willing to endorse universally. You take as a principle the idea that your friend wishes to travel comfortably and that she will want accommodation that affords a degree of privacy. The objective principle of respect and dignity in travelling, which you are willing to endorse universally, guides you in your choices about the means of travel, the specification and determination of your choices. As soon as purely practical reason identifies the objective moral principle and its application, it is the task of empirical practical reason to execute the action. O'Neill, for example, argues that objective principles and maxims underlie our intentions in action.[25] It is not clear, however, what the exact role of pure practical reason is in the execution of the action and how something that belongs to a non-causal domain can impose conditions on empirical causality.[26]

By contrast, for Aristotle, Aquinas and, more recently, Anscombe the task of practical reason involves both the exercise of legislative and executive functions *at the same time.* You perform an action because the end appears to you as having good-making characteristics and this constitutes the reason for your series of actions. The good-making characteristic gives form to, organises and justifies the series of actions that are performed by the agent. The action involves both legislative and executive moments throughout the performance of the action. The legislative function shapes the executive function and vice versa. There is no such a thing as a simple execution or application of principles or valuable ends. The good-making characteristics of the end guide the action, but there is need for judgment and an assessment of the actions that will lead to the end, and this requires the exercise of the legislative function. Consequently, the action is explained and justified by the reasons for actions as good-making characteristics. In the example above I begin to organise the

---

[24] Kant distinguishes between pure practical reason and empirical practical reason. In the former case, reason is engaged with the moral law and the categorical imperative which is independent of our interests, desires, traditions or conventions. In the latter case, reason is conditioned by our interests, desires, inclinations, traditions or conventions.

[25] O'Neill, (n 10) 151.

[26] The interaction between pure practical reason and empirical practical reason is made even more unclear by the fact that the latter is part of the empirical world of causality whereas the former is part of the domain of intelligibility and transcendental freedom where the laws of empirical causality do no apply. For criticism of the interaction of the intelligible and transcendental and empirical and causal see Wolff (n 16).

trip to South America for me and my friend. Our aim is to enjoy each other's company, and to learn about South American people and cultures and each other. The values and good-making characteristics of the end guide my actions. Therefore I choose accommodation where my friend will have comfort, privacy and respect. The results of my actions are similar to those in the Kantian account, but the advantage of the classical account is that it is able to explain *how* the action is controlled by the agent in its performance or execution, and how values and principles as good-making characteristics are embedded in the execution of the action. Furthermore, it can also explain evil actions as the performance of actions that are guided by 'apparent' good-making characteristics.

We now have a broad and familiar philosophical framework for understanding the stance of the book. In subsequent chapters I will show how the structure of practical reason can be seen in the diachronic process of intentional action and how, therefore, agents engage in intentional action and show their engagement with practical reason when they comply with legal rules. Consequently, legislators and judges as creators of the law need to advance formulations of the law that make possible this practical engagement, if they wish their legal rules to be followed. This is especially true when legal rules require the performance of complex actions over time. Judges and legislators as creators of the law need to formulate legal rules as based on reasons for actions as good-making characteristics, or so this book will argue. I will also show how the three main legal theories on legal authority and normativity, ie those of Hart, Kelsen and Raz, have misdiagnosed the deeper structure of the relationship between legal authority, normativity and practical reason. Finally, the book will show how the model of 'law under the guise of the good' can provide a powerful explanation for the deeper structure of legal authority and normativity.

2

Law as an Actuality

2.1 THREE QUESTIONS

T HE INTELLECTUAL INTUITION behind the idea that law is at once a social activity and normative is that the source of the normativity of law is an internal act of the will; an act of endorsement or avowal. Our rational capacities enable us to endorse or commit ourselves to following the law and law is only an expression of these *personal* normative commitments. The common belief is that we decide and we choose collectively to be regulated by law and therefore this act of endorsement creates reasons to follow the law. This view is too simple, but it contains a grain of truth. If normativity lies within the domain of what possibly could or should be done, then the active self plays an important role. Therefore there must be something active, such as the will, that determines how we are bound to what is normative. If this view is sound how can this *internal* act of the will also be *social?* This chapter concentrates on understanding the relationship between reasons and rules and advances the substantive view that legal rules are grounded on reasons as good-making characteristics which we avow in order to comply with legal rules.

Three questions arise concerning the relationship between reasons and rules: (1) Do legal rules have a reason-giving character? (2) How can legal rules be reason-giving and part of the practical reasoning of the addressees of legal rules *preserving* the addressees' deliberative point of view? (3) If legal rules have a reason-giving character should they not be formulated in terms of good-making characteristics?

The following analysis will refine the formulation of and the relationship between these questions.

2.2 LESSONS TO LEARN FROM TWO CONCEPTIONS OF INTENTIONAL ACTION: ACTION IN TERMS OF THE TWO-COMPONENT VIEW *VERSUS* ACTION ACCORDING TO THE 'GUISE OF THE GOOD' MODEL

Reflections on the nature of law often focus on either the concept of law,[1] the functional kind of law,[2] the common denominator or property that constitutes

---

[1] HLA Hart, *The Concept of Law*, 2nd edn (Oxford, Clarendon Press, 1994).
[2] M Moore, 'Law as a Functional Kind' in RP George (ed), *Natural Law Theory: Contemporary Essays* (Oxford, Clarendon Press, 1992) 188–242.

what law is,[3] or a set of propositions[4] about law in general[5] or the laws of a specific legal system. These scholarly engagements give priority to a theoretical understanding or explanation over the practical nature of law. This ensures that law acquires the status of scientific-theoretical or interpretive-theoretical knowledge or at least something close to it.

It is the view of this book that law should paradigmatically be understood as the *actuality*[6] of our practical reasoning capacities. Furthermore, I argue that the structure of practical reason and the exercise of this capacity can be understood through the structure of intentional action.

But questions arise: how can we unify the theoretical knowledge of law and the view that law is an actuality, and what is the sound explanation of the relationship between intentional action, reasons for actions and legal rules?

The view predominant in contemporary jurisprudence is to assimilate the idea of practice and human action with a theoretical understanding. Legal philosophers have, therefore, assumed a theoretical conception of intentional action which divides intentional action into two components (the 'two-component model'). First, intentional action is explicitly or implicitly understood as a mental state. The psychological properties of mental states are analysed in terms of other related notions such as acceptance, belief, motive or desires. Secondly, intentional action is also examined in terms of its results, which means that the theorist needs to look at what has been caused by the action. Therefore, for example, the action (a) 'she is legislating' is examined as a two-component model (sections 5.3, 6.4.1): 'she wants to legislate' and 'she has enacted a statute'; or the expression (b) 'she (the judge) is deciding a legal case' is composed of two components: 'she accepts to apply the law' and 'she has reached a legal decision'; or (c) 'he is following a legal rule' is divided into 'he believes he is following the rule established by the Road Traffic Act 1975' and 'he has stopped at the red light'; or (d) 'he is obeying the rule that vehicles are not allowed in Holland Park' is examined as 'he accepts the rule' and 'he has avoided parking his vehicle in Holland Park'. This understanding of intentional action overlooks an important aspect of action, which is prior to and more basic than other more sophisticated explanations, and which is

---

[3] H Kelsen, *The General Theory of Norms* (M Hartney (trans), Oxford, Oxford University Press, 1991). Cf J Finnis, 'Law and What I Truly Should Decide' (2003) *American Journal of Jurisprudence* 107, 115. Finnis points out: 'A complete and fully realistic theory of law can be and in all essentials has been worked out from the starting point of the 100 percent normative question, what should I decide to do and, equivalently, what kind of person should I resolve or allow myself to be. I can think of no interesting project of inquiry left over for a philosophical theory of law with any different starting point'.

[4] B Zipursky, 'Practical Positivism versus Practical Perfectionism: the Hart-Fuller Debate at Fifty' (2008) *New York University Law Review* 1170, 1199.

[5] R Dworkin, *Law's Empire* (Cambridge, MA, Harvard University Press, 1986) 31–35.

[6] For full clarification of this term see Chapter 4.

represented by the progressive or imperfect form of verbs. The expressions (a) 'she is legislating', (b) 'she is deciding a legal case', (c) 'he is following a rule' and (d) 'he is obeying the rule that vehicles are not allowed in Holland Park' have a prior and more *naïve* or basic connotation and this is expressed in the progressive form of the verbs 'is legislating', 'is deciding', 'is following' and 'is obeying'. Thus, that someone is legislating is different from the mental state 'she wants to legislate' or the resultant action 'she has enacted a statute'. The action is presented as continuous stages of series of actions or, to be more precise, as an *actuality* (see Chapter 3 and Chapter 4). But how should we understand the *actuality* that is conveyed in the progressive or imperfect form of verbs? The progressive form emphasises an aspect of the practice, action and human agency that is not grasped by the two-component model of intentional actions.

When one attempts to understand an intentional action one must ask the agent *why* he or she is Φ-ing, the response, after being invited to reflect, is not *primarily* because 'I accept', 'I believe' or 'I want'; the response, indicating that the agent is in a specific mental state, is a sophisticated explanation that is parasitic on a much more naïve or basic explanation. The question *why* aims to elucidate the *reason* for the action which is the intention of the action and invites the agent to reflect on her or his actions.

The notion 'intention of an action' conveys three core cases: an expression of an intention, the intentional action and the intention with which the action is performed. For example, let us suppose that I intend to make tea and I put on the kettle; you ask me why am I putting on the kettle; I respond that I am boiling water; you ask me why am I boiling water; I respond that I intend to pour it into a cup; you ask me why am I pouring the boiling water into a cup and I respond *because* I intend to make tea. To the question *why* I am making tea, I answer that it is *because* tea in the mornings give me comfort and energy to begin the day. At last the inquiry as to *why* I am making tea stops as the reasons for action have been elucidated by my series of answers which finishes with an end formulated in terms of good-making characteristics. The purpose of my action 'to make tea' is to obtain comfort and gain energy. It is a description that the agent herself advances in respect of her own actions. The core aspects of intentional action are present in the example. An agent expresses an intention, performs an intentional action and has an intention with which the action is performed. The view is not that I do have mental states such as desires or motives, ie the desire to have a cup of tea in the morning, which can explain my intentional action. Rather the position that I aim to defend is that there is a more basic explanation of action. Intentional action is explained in terms of other actions and this explanation is prior to other kinds of explanations, ie psychological features, and so on. In our example the agent provides the description of the action in terms of other actions and in terms of an end as a good-making characteristic and the latter makes intelligible the action.

The description of the action is from the point of view of the person who performs the action; this is called the deliberative point of view.

The *why-question* methodology (section 3.2 and Chapter 4) enables us to reflect on and elucidate the *reasons in the action or reasons for the action*. A theorist, however, might say that the agent has a mental state, ie intention, that causes her to put on the kettle, boil and pour water and that there is a cup of tea that is the result of the action. However, this explanation does not grasp the practical character or the deliberative point of view where the deliberator or agent does not observe or assess his mental states in order to act, rather he looks outward to the world, ie to the kettle, the plug, the on/off button, the boiling water, the tea bag, the cup, and so on (sections 3.3 and 5.3.1).

2.3 LEGAL RULES, REASONS AND THE ASYMMETRICAL VIEW

Law is not only a concept, but is also an *actuality* in the aforementioned sense (see Chapter 3 and Chapter 4), it is an *actuality* like 'making tea' with a successive series of actions performed by officials and citizens. But in what sense can we say that law is an *actuality*? When one follows the law, one follows a set of publicly ascertainable legal rules; law imposes on us certain behaviour and one does not choose to act as one chooses to make tea. There is, arguably, an element of intentional action when one follows the law and it *might* seem very different from other intentional actions such as 'making tea'. It is, however, not too different or so I will argue.

Let us think about a legal example. To the question *why* are you turning the wheel of your vehicle, the man might answer that he is turning his car around in search of a parking space. To the question *why* are you looking for a parking space, the man might answer that he intends to avoid parking in Holland Park; to the question *why* he is avoiding parking in Holland Park, the answer might be *because there is a rule that prohibits vehicles parking in Holland Park.*[7] In our example of 'tea-making' the action is divided into a successive series of actions and the totality of these stages constitutes a process that finds unity in the final end or *reason for action*. In the legal example of 'avoiding parking the vehicle in Holland Park', the action is also divided into stages that find unity in *a rule*.

---

[7] The example is taken from the Hart-Fuller debate. For a fine discussion of the example and the different positions of Hart and Fuller, see N Lacey, 'Philosophy, Political Morality, and History: Explaining the Enduring Resonance of the Hart-Fuller Debate' (2008) *New York University Law Review* 1059; F Schauer, 'A Critical Guide to Vehicles in the Park' (2008) *New York University Law Review* 1109; J Waldron, 'Why Law: Efficacy, Freedom or Fidelity' (1994) *Law and Philosophy* 259; J Waldron, 'Positivism and Legality: Hart's Equivocal Response to Fuller' (2008) *New York University Law Review* 1135. See also P Cane (ed), *The Hart-Fuller Debate in the Twenty-First Century* (Oxford, Hart Publishing, 2010). For an illuminating discussion on Fuller's inner morality of law see N Simmonds, *Law as a Moral Idea* (Oxford, Oxford University Press, 2007) 69.

However, the similarity between the two kinds of activity only goes so far. In the case of the intentional action of making tea, the final end makes intelligible the series of actions, but in the case of the intentional action of avoiding parking a vehicle in Holland Park, the deliberator has expressed his view that 'it is *because* of a rule'. To say 'it is because of a rule' is different than saying 'because of X as a good-making characteristic'. What is the good-making characteristic of a rule? How can it make intelligible the action? One might assert that the answer 'because there is a rule' is satisfactory and that the question *why* one ought to follow such a rule is a question *external* to the 'game' of following rules within a legal system. According to this view, the theorist perspective should prevail and actions as following rules should be explained according to the two-component model.

A similar theoretical answer has been provided by Hart. According to Hart, there is an analogy between the rules of a game and following the rules of law. One accepts the rules of games when one plays them (chess, cricket, and so on) and there is a variety of underlying reasons for such acceptance.[8] Therefore, when one follows legal rules, one accepts the rules or at least accepts a rule of recognition that establishes their validity and the fact that they should be followed. The legal philosopher, following Hart and using the two-component model of intentional action, will say that 'he is turning the wheel and avoiding parking in Holland Park, because he *believes or accepts* that there is a *valid* rule which states that vehicles are not allowed to park in Holland Park'. On the other hand, the action caused by the intention, which is conceived as a mental state, of avoiding parking in Holland Park can be observed. Therefore, it can be the subject of theoretical understanding. Within the two-component model, the answer to the question '*why* are you Φ-ing?', ie turning the wheel, reversing the vehicle and avoiding parking in Holland Park, makes perfect sense *because* there is a rule which says that 'vehicles are not allowed to park in Holland Park', therefore I 'avoid parking in Holland Park'. Yet this response is only *partially* intelligible. According to this view, the deliberative point of view needs to be explained and unpacked and it is explained either as an *acceptance* or as the *belief* that there is a rule. Any inquiry about the *validity* of such a rule is an external question. We do not need, therefore, the description provided from the deliberative point of view to understand the aspect of the law characterised as an *actuality*. The deliberative point of view collapses into a theoretical point of view. In other words, the point of view of the person who performs the intentional action collapses into the point of view of the person who aims to theorise or explain the action.

I reject this latter view and aim to defend the idea that the point of view of the person who performs the action is irreducible and has priority over the

---

[8] Hart (n 1) 198.

point of view of the person who theorises, explains or interprets the actions. Furthermore, it is argued that there are limitations to the 'theorising' of the deliberative point of view. The latter therefore remains primitive and *asymmetrical* with respect to the theoretical viewpoint.

The description of an action in terms of reasons for actions as good-making characteristics which is a response to the question *why*, is the core tenet of the 'guise of the good' model. It is a *naïve explanation* of intentional action. I advance arguments that support the priority of the 'guise of the good' model of intentional action to explain the phenomenon of legal rule-following, and show that we follow legal rules, in the paradigmatic case, only because we are following the grounding reasons for actions as good-making characteristics of legal rules.

2.4 'FOLLOWING LEGAL RULES' AS NAIVE EXPLANATION OF INTENTIONAL ACTION

Let us suppose that two people are playing a game of chess. The players have been instructed about the rules of the game and explain their actions in terms of the rules of the game. Their actions are intelligible to us *because* of the rules of the game. Let us imagine three explanatory perspectives on a game of chess: (A) the perspective of the players; (B) the perspective of the person who has just entered the room, understands well the rules of chess and explains the actions of the players to another observer; (C) the perspective of someone who has just entered the room, who has never seen chess before, who does not understand the rules at all and wishes to explain the players' actions. For reasons of simplicity, let us call (B) 'the rule-knowing observer' and (C) 'the rule-ignorant observer'.

The perspectives of B and C are theoretical in the sense that neither 'the rule-knowing observer' nor the 'rule-ignorant observer' are performing the action, rather they aim to explain the action. How can we proceed to an understanding of the perspectives of the players without 'theorising' their perspectives? An invitation to the players to reflect on their actions seems to be the best available strategy. We begin with asking the question *why*. This consequently obliges the players to reflect on what they are doing. The ensuing dialogue between us and them might be as follows:

Dialogue A.1

Enquirer: *Why* are you moving the knight?

Player 1: Because I intend to move my queen into the space currently occupied by my knight.

Enquirer: Why do you intend to move the queen?

Player 1: Because I aim to put my opponent into checkmate.

Enquirer: Why do you intend to do so?

Player 1: Because this is the main rule of the game. You need to put the other player into checkmate in order to win.

From the point of view of the 'rule-knowing observer' the explanation of the actions of Player 1 might not differ substantially from Dialogue A.1. The theorist may therefore state: 'he is moving his knight, so that he may move his queen in order to put his opponent into checkmate. This is *because* these are the rules of the game of chess'. From the point of view of the 'rule-ignorant observer' fewer options are available. One option is to take the 'hermeneutical' or 'interpretive' point of view and understand the actions of Player 1 from the point of view of the player. However, this latter approach tends to collapse into the two-component model. The *verstehen* point of view is a mental state as *interpreted or theorised* by the theorist, ie a belief or a desire. Thus, the formulation of his explanation of the player's action will be something like this: 'he wishes to play a game and knows, accepts and follows the rules of such a game. He is playing a game' (for a criticism of the interpretive view see section 10.6).

The interesting and intriguing question that I wish to investigate is why the explanation from the deliberative point of view, ie the point of view of the person who performs the action, and the point of view of the 'rule-knowing observer' *appear to be the same*. The explanation from the point of view of the agent who performs the action *following a rule* and the explanation of the 'rule-knowing observer' *appear* to be the same and this might enable us to say that if we can understand and explain the *internal aspect* of games, ie rules, then we can understand the intentional action of following rules *as if* it were from the deliberative point of view. I will call this position the 'symmetrical view' since it considers that the deliberative viewpoint and the point of view of the 'rule-knowing observer' are symmetrical. According to this view, it seems that the theorist can replicate, study, describe and analyse successfully the perspective of the deliberator or agent. Yet the explanation from the point of view of the agent or deliberator and the explanation from the point of view of the 'rule-ignorant observer' differ in *many* cases. The solution provided by the 'symmetrical view' seems very appealing, especially when one compares it with the situation of the 'rule-ignorant observer' who will in *many cases* provide mistaken views of the *internal* aspect of games as he can only *infer* the internal aspect, ie the rules of the game. He needs to *infer* such knowledge from his different beliefs and observations of the behaviour of the players.

However, the symmetry between the 'rule-knowing observer' and the deliberative point of view is an illusion. Let us suppose that I am running in the Park and you ask me, with the intention of eliciting the reasons for my actions, why am I running in the Park. Our dialogue might be as follows:

Dialogue A.2

Enquirer: Why are you running?

Runner: To catch the bus.

Enquirer: Why are you catching the bus?

Runner: To go to my office.

Enquirer: Why are you going to your office?

Runner: I intend to do my job.

Enquirer: Why do you intend to do your job?

Runner: Because I ought to earn money.

The difference between the case of the runner and the case of the chess player is that in the latter case the rules which provide the end of the action and make intelligible the successive series of actions are *transparent* to both the 'rule-knowing observer' and the agent who performs the action. We say that the chess player has formulated, as the end of his action, the rules of the game of chess. Outside restricted and *transparent* rules, reasons for actions rather than rules prevail and the understanding of intentional action gains complexity. The reason for action is only transparent to the person who performs the intentional action. In the case of the runner, the description of the successive and progressive series of actions is provided by his own account or description, and the inquiry as to why he is doing the action is stopped by the end of his action which constitutes the reason for action. The reason for action as a good-making characteristic, ie earning money, unifies the successive stages of the action (ie running, crossing the street, jumping onto a bus, paying the fare, getting off the bus, entering an office) and consequently the reason for action as a good-making characteristic is the *form* of the action, enabling us to make intelligible the action. Prior to the runner giving his description of his actions (in the best possible case) we can at best only have a *theoretical* account of actions in terms of his beliefs and desires, ie intentional actions as mental states; his desire to go to work and his belief that the bus will get him to work; but in the case of the runner, the asymmetry between the deliberative and the theoretical description is very clear. The action is not mediated by rules.

According to the 'symmetrical view', for the case of actions that follow rules, the knowledge of the action from the perspective of the chess player (the deliberative viewpoint) and from the perspective of the 'rule-knowing observer' are completely symmetrical. Yet a closer look at the case shows that there is no such symmetry. I will argue that the case of following the rules of the game of chess is not different from the case of the runner. An asymmetry pervades between both the deliberator's point of view and that of the observer, and between the rule-knowing and the rule-ignorant observer. The inquirer, who aims to elicit the reasons for the chess player's actions, seems satisfied by the answer 'because it is a rule'. But why should this *specific* rule guide his action, why do players not create different rules? The standard answer is that if they accepted different rules, they would not be playing chess at all but another game. An answer to the question '*why* do they have to follow the rules of chess?' will be that these are the rules that are practised and they are the rules of chess. Whoever wishes to play chess, has to follow the rules of chess. Is this the answer that the agent will give, namely, that since he has *accepted* to have a game of chess, he must if he wishes to play chess, follow the rules of chess? This is certainly not the answer that the agent will *primarily* give after having been invited to reflect on his own actions by the question *why*. The *form* of the answer of the chess player *will not differ* from the answer of the runner. Let us again examine the dialogue between the enquirer and the player:

Dialogue A.3

Enquirer: *Why* are you moving the knight?

Player 1: Because I intend to move my queen into the space currently occupied by my knight.

Enquirer: Why do you intend to move the queen?

Player 1: Because I aim to put my opponent into checkmate.

Enquirer: Why do you intend to do so?

Player 1: Because this is the rule of the game.

Enquirer: Why do you follow the rule of the game?

Player 1: Because I intend to win.

Enquirer: Why do you intend to win?

Player 1: Because I am playing a board game and board games are about winning and losing.

Enquirer: Why are you playing a board game which is about winning and losing?

Player: Because it will entertain both my friend and myself.

For the agent there is no clear demarcation or border that separates the end of playing a game because of certain good-making characteristics from the rule. The rules of the game of chess make the game interesting and entertaining, and this is the good-making characteristic that provides the description of the agent's action of playing the game and following the rules of chess. His reasons are not the rules of the game. The rules of the game cannot describe his intentional action *unless* the rules are described in terms of good-making characteristics. Then, it is not the rules, but the *content* of the rules that guides the agent. It is not that the agent moves the knight to make space for the queen because the agent follows the rules of chess, rather it is that the agent moves the knight to make space for the queen *because he intends to put his opponent into checkmate, because he aims to win, because he finds it entertaining*.

Let us imagine the opposite case of a non-intentional action of playing chess. This thought experiment will show us, contrary to the view advocated by the 'symmetrical view', that the 'rule-knowing observer' is not able to distinguish between intentional and non-intentional actions of following rules. Imagine that you suffer regularly from sleepwalking but that your housemate is unaware of your sleep disorder. He is playing chess in the lounge alone when he sees you coming out of your bedroom; he believes you are awake but your are in fact sleepwalking. You sit and you both play chess. The sleepwalker follows the rules of chess without any anomaly. This is an unconscious behaviour. From the perspective of the 'rule-knowing observer' his housemate is playing chess because he moves the knight and the queen in the right way, the observer *infers* from *his* knowledge of the rules of chess and from the behaviour of the sleepwalker that he is trying to put his opponent into checkmate. But the action of the sleepwalker is not an intentional action. However, the 'rule-knowing observer' cannot distinguish between the intentional and the non-intentional action of playing chess. He cannot make such a distinction because he does not rely on the description provided by the agent (in this case the player) which unifies the successive and progressive steps of the intentional action. The 'rule-knowing observer' mistakenly believes the sleepwalker to be acting intentionally. A similar mistake will be committed by the observer who does not understand the rules of chess. For the 'rule-ignorant observer' the sleepwalker has the desire to play chess, accepts the rules of chess and believes that he is playing chess. Both the 'rule-ignorant' and the 'rule-knowing' observers are obviously mistaken. From the deliberative viewpoint there is no knowledge of the action, there is neither belief nor acceptance of the rules. If the sleepwalker is asked *why* he moves his knight in such way, he cannot reply as he did when he was reflecting on his actions. He is, after all, asleep.

2.5 THE PROMULGATION PUZZLE

For the chess player the justification of the rules and the practice of them is not especially problematic. The question why these rules, and not other rules, exist does not arise. He intends to play chess because it is entertaining. Playing chess is justified because he sees the *end of the action as good*. He does not raise questions about the promulgation of such rules because his will is directed to the end or grounding reason as a good-making characteristic of the rule. The end of his action as a good-making characteristic is to be entertained. What is entertaining? Are the rules or the game entertaining? We can say 'both' since the rules *are* the game. The chess player has, therefore, reasons to play the game and follow the rules. But who has made these rules, he might ask? Why not make other rules and subsequently create another game similar to chess, let us call it chess*, which will be even more entertaining? Apart from the difficulties of creating a new game and new rules that will guarantee an entertaining game, there are obvious advantages in playing by the current rules of chess rather than by the rules of chess*. For example, the existing rules have been practised over many centuries, it could create confusion if we tried to introduce new rules and we would, consequently, have to spend time teaching and writing down the new rules.

By contrast, in the case of the law, the puzzle of promulgation arises. Legal rules are created and imposed by officials, and officials themselves and citizens let their actions be guided by them. What does it mean to say that officials and citizens are guided by legal norms or rules? In this book, it is shown that to follow and comply with legal rules is an *actuality of our practical reasoning capacities* not very dissimilar from 'making tea' or 'running to catch a bus to work'.

If law is an actuality of our practical reasoning, how does this operate, how does it work? Hart, implicitly advocating both the 'symmetrical view' and the two-component model of intentional action, asserts that there is no need to examine and evaluate the grounding reasons as good-making characteristics of legal rules. This is so because the mental state of the *acceptance* of the rule of recognition or rules will guide us into *the internal aspect* of rules, and subsequently will enable us to understand, describe and explain intentional action and its *internal aspect*. Is the 'symmetrical view' false? My argument is that the naïve explanation of intentional action, namely the explanation of action from the deliberative point of view in terms of good-making characteristics, should have priority over the two-component or sophisticated explanation of intentional action. The naïve explanation of intentional action gives us access to an internal aspect of rules that cannot be grasped by the two-component model. The will of the chess player was engaged in the action, not because of the convergence, agreement, acceptance or common practice of the rules of chess, but *primarily because* it is entertaining, *because* there are grounding reasons as good-making characteristics of the rules. The chess player did not examine the acceptance, desire or agreement of the other player. He aimed at the good-making characteristic of the chess game.

Would the legal agent, the person who performs successive legal actions, need to identify the grounding reasons as good-making characteristics that will make intelligible his intentional actions in the context of the law? From the point of view of the agent, ie the legislator, the judge or the citizen, the question that arises is 'why should I be guided by these specific legal norms or rules?'. The Hartian answer 'because there is a rule of recognition that both is accepted from the internal point of view and gives validity to the other rules of the legal system', overlooks the fact that the notion of acceptance is parasitic upon the idea that the action is guided by reasons as good-making characteristics. If *qua* legislator 'I am legislating', *qua* judge 'I am deciding', *qua* citizen 'I am following and complying with legal norms', should not my intentional action in order to be intentional be guided by an end as a good-making characteristic of the *actuality* or process? In this respect, the most controversial legal process or *actuality* is neither the legal decision-making nor the legislating but rather the idea of following and complying with legal norms or rules. The book will concentrate mainly on the latter, but I envisage that the conclusions of this book can be extended to the activities of legislating and judging.

2.6 LEGAL NORMATIVITY AGAIN

The authoritative and normative nature of law obliges us to confront the nature of the will and intentional action. We see ourselves as active selves when we deliberate, decide and act. These functions are part of our active selves as opposed to our passive selves, ie when we are driven by our inclinations, feelings and desires. In the former case we are in control of our actions, but in the latter we have not chosen or decided anything; something just happens to us. The contrast between the two seems, at first glance, rather crude; only animal appetites are the plausible subjects of our passive nature since most of our desires are either subject to some kind of reflection or entail some type of cognition; for example, when we love someone we have a strong desire to be with them and are driven by this desire, even though we have the rational capacity to reflect on our desires.

This stark and crude opposition between our active and passive selves helps us to understand that there are happenings and doings, and that the latter require reasons for actions and agency. The opposition also explains another dichotomy: the internal and the external. When we act, we do, decide, choose and the result, ie actions, come from us, whereas happenings just happen to us and come from outside; in some sense they are external to us. Law, however, enjoys a peculiar nature; we act as citizens according to the law of a state, but law is external to us. Law has a directive nature since it guides our actions. Furthermore, when law make claims on us: requests, demands or commands, we are bound by these requests and we say that law is normative because it has a force on us. However, to preserve our active nature, this force must come from us rather than be external to us. The crucial question is whether law can request, demand or command us to do certain things whilst we are being active selves. How can something that is external to us have a normative force upon us? In other words, in what sense is law's normativity compatible with our self-conception as active selves since positive law is something that is imposed on us rather than something we decide or choose to endorse.

Some authors have argued that in the legal context our self-reflective and active nature plays no role at all. This view has been advocated, indirectly, by sanction-based explanations such as that advanced by Austin. We, citizens of a state, Austin argues, do not choose to act according to the law, we are merely coerced by sanctions. The idea of law's force can be explained by the idea that law exercises coercion on us. Therefore, law's force comes from outside us and the problem of the compatibility of law's force, ie law's normativity, with our active and self-reflective nature is an illusory problem. There is no normative dimension; there are only facts, ie sanctions. However, our self-understanding as law-abiding citizens, in clear contradiction to the Austinian approach, is in terms of legal rules that create duties and impose obligations on us, ie we ought to pay taxes, fulfil our contractual promises, and so on. If I sign a mortgage contract with a lender, the contract has created an obligation for me to repay my mortgage according to the terms agreed in the contract. The capacity of legal rules to create duties and impose obligations on us, if these duties and obligations are genuine, involves the idea that our active selves must play some role.

However, we have seen that the *form* of intentional actions, typically of processes such as 'legislating', 'deciding cases' and 'following legal rules', where there are successive series of actions, is given by the description provided by the deliberator or agent himself. The I-concept or the first-person perspective plays a primary role in understanding legal activities. Psychological or social facts cannot fully grasp *this* internal aspect of law, in other words, the deliberative viewpoint. We are faced, therefore, with the puzzling conflict between our self-understanding as active selves and the authoritative and normative character of law. This conflict has been called the moral puzzle of legal authority.

The moral puzzle states that there is a conflict between the authoritative and normative character of the law (a heteronomous force on the agent) and the reasons for actions that the agent from the deliberative viewpoint has.[9] Why should the agent surrender his/her judgement to a normative power? What some authors have called the 'Possibility Puzzle' of legal authority[10] is a corollary of the 'Moral Puzzle'. Authority seems impossible because norms are the outcome of human will since they are a human creation and they cannot,

---

[9] RP Wolff, *In Defense of Anarchism* (New York and London, Harper Torchbooks, 1970).
[10] See S Shapiro, *Legality* (Cambridge, MA, Harvard University Press, 2010).

therefore, confer legitimate power to obligate. If we assume that there is a basic authoritative norm that confers power on legitimate authorities, we enter an infinite regress as it could similarly be assumed that there is a more basic norm that gives power to the basic norm. As Shapiro describes it, we get the egg-chicken paradox.[11]

We have learned, above, that the theoretical point of view cannot fully grasp the active features of ourselves. If the theoretical point of view is to play a role in the understanding of the authoritative and normative power of law, then it will be as parasitic upon the deliberative perspective. We need therefore to engage in an investigation of the nature of the will and intentional action.

2.7 THE PROBLEM OF GUIDANCE

If our actions are guided by legal rules, they need to guide us in the temporal unfolding of the successive steps of the action and it is only through their grounding reasons or *logos* that this is possible. We guide and control our actions.[12] When the agent follows legal rules, he needs to make compensatory adjustments to the facts and state of affairs of the world to fulfil the intentions expressed in the legal rules; only through the adjustment of his actions guided by the grounding reasons of legal rules can the agent perform the action required by the legal rule. Let us suppose that we are climbing a mountain guided by an expert. Before we start climbing, he gives us a set of basic safety rules such as 'do not pull the rope', 'do not pass the person who is ahead of you', and so on. We begin climbing and do what he tells us to do, he shouts 'throw the rope', 'put on the harness', 'small and steady steps, please', 'don't look back'. We follow the successive steps of the action 'climbing the mountain' following the safety rules. But whilst doing the actions my harness breaks and I need to adjust my conduct. I take my scarf off and make a harness with it. If I am asked *why* did you do that? The naïve or basic answer is 'I needed to

---

[11] See my chapter 'The Moral Puzzle of Legal Authority: A Commentary on Shapiro's Planning Theory of Law' in G Pavlakos and S Bertea (eds), *Normativity in Law and Morality* (Oxford, Hart Publishing, 2012).

[12] The idea of control involves a different emphasis which is not on the antecedent cause of the action, but on the mechanism that makes possible the action. Frankfurt puts this as follows: 'The state of affairs while the movements [of a person's body] are occurring is far more pertinent [than the causes from which they originated]. What is not merely pertinent but decisive, indeed, is to consider whether or not the movements as they occur are under the person's guidance. It is this that determines whether he is performing an action. Moreover, the question of whether or not movements occur under a person's guidance is not a matter of their antecedents. Events are caused to occur by preceding states of affairs, but an event cannot be guided through the course of its occurrence at a temporal distance' (H Frankfurt, 'The Problem of Action' (1978) *American Philosophical Quarterly* 157, 15).

be safe'. To be safe when one climbs is the grounding reason or *logos* of the set of rules for climbing safely. Therefore, what guided me in my actions was not the rule, but a set of facts about the world together with a grasping of the grounding reasons as good-making characteristics of the rules, ie it is good to be safe. The two-component model of intentional action cannot explain how legal rules guide us. I did not pull off my scarf and made a harness because I was in the mental state of 'accepting' the set of rules on climbing, nor *primarily* because I was in the mental state of desiring to follow the rules. I did not, either, look at my mental state of accepting, desiring, believing, and so on; rather, I looked at my scarf, my broken harness, the angle of my rope and made a harness (section 3.3).

Guidance and control should not be understood independently.[13] If something can guide me, so to speak, it is because I can exercise control over it. We say that rules guide us, but this is inexact. I am the agent and therefore I guide and control my actions and if I follow rules I guide and control my actions according to the rules. In order to control and guide my action in following rules, I need to have knowledge of the grounding reasons of the rules. This knowledge is not empirical, it is rather non-observational or practical (section 3.3). As the previous example shows, I cannot say that I am acting intentionally under, for example, the description 'following the safety rules for climbing mountains' without acting intentionally under the description 'following the grounding reasons for the safety rules for climbing mountains'. In other words, if I mistakenly understand the grounding reasons for actions of the specific rule, then I am neither guided *by the rule* nor exercise control over my actions *because of the* rule. The control that we exercise when we act for reasons is not control in the weak sense that *I* am the agent who acts, but in a stronger sense; I *direct myself* to the end as described by the grounding reasons for actions as good-making characteristics of the legal rules. This does not mean that we cannot follow legal rules and merely act *according to* the rule, but in these cases we are not *guided by* the rule. Let us say that I follow the rule of taking my hat off in church. I do it because others are doing it, but I cannot grasp the grounding reason of the rule, which, we might say, from the perspective of the non-believer is to show respect to the people in the church and their beliefs. I follow what others do, therefore I am not guided by the rule, I am guided by what others are doing, the movements of their bodies and gestures, and *my inferences* about these observational data.

The grounding reasons or *logos* of rules *guide* me because they constitute the reason for my intentional action of following the rule. They also enable me to *control* my action towards the end of the rule formulated as a reason for action. However, if I do not grasp or avow their grounding reasons, they cannot

---

[13]   J Hornsby, *Action* (London, Routledge, 1980) chs 1–3.

guide me and I cannot direct myself towards its ends. Let us go back to our example of the climber. If I am able to make a harness out of my scarf and follow the rule, it is because I understand the grounding reasons for the set of safety rules for climbing. Let us suppose that I mistakenly believe that the grounding reason for the rules of climbing mountains is for the climber to be more comfortable. This means I believe, mistakenly of course, that the grounding reason of the rules of climbing is comfort. Then we can say that I do not understand the safety rules for climbing mountains. Can we still be guided by the legal rules? Can I, in other words, exercise control over my behaviour and develop compensatory adjustments? Let us suppose that my harness breaks whilst I know that I have a scarf, I also know that I have a (feeble) plastic bag in my pocket which, I think, would make a more comfortable harness than a harness made out of a scarf. In this case, one might say that the rule cannot guide me as I do not grasp correctly its grounding reason.

This is the paradigmatic case of 'legal rules-following'. In Chapter 8, we discuss the possibility of following legal rules just because we think that the authority is a good sort of thing. This gives us a reason to accept the legal rules issued by the authority. We act intentionally on our *presumption* of the goodness of the authority (section 8.6).

We can have guidance and control only when we act intentionally which means acting for reasons.[14] This is why in our exploration of how and why we follow legal rules and their bearing on reasons for actions, we take intentional action as the paradigmatic example of action. Only through understanding our expressions of intentions, the notions of intentional action and of an intention with which we act can we explain our exercise of practical reasoning, reasons for actions and reasons *in* actions and their connection to legal rules. Finnis, following Aristotle and Aquinas, has advanced the view that law has its principal intelligibility as a guide to choice, proposed to a community of choosers by the choice of that community's law-makers.[15] An understanding of intentional action as a goal-directed action, and of rule-following whose content is a *logos* or grounding reason, enables us to understand how we are choosers of legal rules and how law is created as a guide to choice.

---

[14] Finnis emphasises that T Aquinas, *Summa Theologica* (Latin and English text, paperback edn, Thomas Gilby (trans), Cambridge, Cambridge University Press, 2006) I–II prol and q1a1 makes central the mastery of one's own acts and that this should not be understood as if 'a ghost or homunculus were controlling the part of some body (and their movements) "from within", but is rather one's being in a position to adopt, and adopting, a proposal for action – one's own action – in preference to some alternative action(s) (of one's own) that one has envisaged and been interested in'. J Finnis, '"The Thing I Am": Personal Identity in Aquinas and Shakespeare' (2005) *Social Philosophy and Policy* 250.

[15] J Finnis, *Natural Law and Natural Rights* (Oxford, Clarendon Press, 1981).

3

The Guise of the Good Model

3.1 THE GUISE OF THE GOOD MODEL

IN CHAPTER 2, I presented a view of rules that is strongly interconnected with the idea of reasons for actions as good-making characteristics[1]
and showed that there is an asymmetry between the first-person and the
third-person perspectives concerning a description of an action that follows
legal rules. Thus, when the person who is performing the action of following a
rule is asked *why* he has carried out an action, the response is in terms of the
reasons for actions as good-making characteristics whereas when we describe
the action of following a rule from the third-person perspective we can (intelligibly) answer that it is 'because of the rule'. It is also argued that the two-
component model of intentional action cannot explain this puzzling
asymmetry. By contrast, 'the guise of the good' model can provide a satisfactory explanation of this asymmetry.

In this chapter, a detailed explanation and a defence of the 'guise of the
good' model is advanced together with an elucidation of the relationship
between reasons for actions, good-making characteristics and intentional
action.

3.2 THE WHY-QUESTION METHODOLOGY

We take intentional action as the paradigm of action and we have said that we
cannot understand how legal rules are binding on the will without understanding in the first place what intentional action is and how the will operates
in relation to action.

The first question that requires our attention is whether there is a distinction between an intention to act, where my will is active and involved in the

---

[1] For Anscombe there is an interdependence between learning to use words such as 'has to',
'must', 'should', etc and reasons or the *logos* that ground such words. The game of stopping and
forcing modals is learned together with reasons for actions or *logos* (E Anscombe, 'Rules, Rights and
Promises' in *Ethics, Religion and Politics* (Oxford, Blackwell, 1981) 101, 102). See also a discussion of
this point in R Teichman, *The Philosophy of Elisabeth Anscombe* (Oxford, Oxford University Press,
2008) 98–101.

action, and a voluntary action. Let me clarify. Actions can be voluntary or involuntary. Examples that illustrate the latter are the movements of my stomach, the respiratory functions of my lungs, and so on. Walking, talking, lifting my arms, etc all exemplify the former. But is it the case that for all voluntary actions intention is involved? Let us imagine two different cases. In the first, I move my arm but my foot moves instead. In the second, I move my arm and my arm moves. In both cases my actions are voluntary. However, in the first case my action is not intentional as my will, ie the moving of my arm, is not satisfied. Let us now suppose that you are observing what I am doing, ie you are observing my foot moving and then my arm moving. How do you know whether my will is satisfied in one case and not in the other? *We can assert that a volitional act is one initiated by a person whereas a wilful act is a volitional act performed with an intention.* But can we know this distinction by merely *observing* from the third-person perspective what a person is doing? The only thing you can *observe* is that I move my foot and arm, but you cannot observe, so to speak, my will; you cannot *observe* that I have moved my arms *intentionally*. The only way to identify whether or not the will is involved in the action is to understand the action as described by the agent.

This is one of the few commonalities between Davidson's account and the 'guise of the good' model as advanced by Anscombe. It is because Davidson relies on some of Anscombe's ideas and because of the inherent difficulties in understanding Anscombe's work, which does not rely on a general theory or system, that it was assumed that Anscombe and Davidson were saying the same thing concerning intentional action.[2] Davidson explains intentional actions in terms of the reasons that the agent provides when explaining what he did. The aim is to *rationalise* the action. The agent has a reason whenever he can be characterised as (a) having a pro-attitude toward the action and (b) believing (or knowing, perceiving, noticing, remembering) that his action is of that kind.[3] The belief/desire pairing is called a primary reason and Davidson asserts that 'a primary reason for an action is its cause'.[4]

Davidson argues that beliefs and desires can cause action because they are mental events.[5] Thus the action 'my flipping the switch is caused by my desire to flip the switch and my belief that this action is of that kind'. We can observe the result of the action, ie the flipping of the switch. However, Davidson

[2] See J Annas, 'Davidson and Anscombe on the "Same Action"' (1976) *Mind* 251. On related aspects of Anscombe's work such as 'practical knowledge', see K Falvey, 'Knowledge in Intention' (2000) *Philosophical Studies* 21; K Setiya, 'Knowledge of Intention' in A Ford, J Hornsby and F Stoutland (eds), *Essays on Anscombe's Intention* (Cambridge, MA, Harvard University Press, 2010); K Setiya, 'Practical Knowledge Revisited' (2009) *Ethics* 388; T Grunbaum, 'Anscombe and Practical Knowledge of What is Happening' (2009) *Grazer Philosophische Studien* 41.

[3] D Davidson, 'Actions, Reasons and Causes' (1963) 60 *Journal of Philosophy* 685.

[4] ibid.

[5] ibid.

denies that there are psychophysical laws that connect actions and reasons, he says that if there are laws they ought to be neurological, chemical or physical.[6]

Davidson's view on intentional action has been extremely influential in the last 40 years. The tendency has been to assimilate practical reasoning into intentional action as a mental state.[7] This assimilation has two main important advantages over other competing views such as the 'guise of the good' model. First, it has enabled neo-Humeans[8] to explain in a more sophisticated form the Humean view that our pro-attitudes or desires are the key motives for and explanation of our intentional actions. Secondly, it is compatible with a scientific explanation of action as caused by our mental states. However, we show that the major flaw of this view is that it cannot ensure that the causal connection between a reason and the action is of the *right sort*[9] (sections 5.3.2, 10.3). Davidson's legacy is palpable in a number of contemporary explanations of what an intention is. For example, Bratman[10] follows Davidson, but he develops a richer psychological picture of desires and beliefs and, consequently, for Bratman, intentions seem to commit the agent in a way that desires cannot commit him or her.[11] Intention then is a very elusive concept and we need to

---

[6] ibid.

[7] For example, Jay Wallace in the entry 'Practical Reason' in the *Stanford Encyclopaedia of Philosophy* points out: 'Practical reasoning gives rise not to bodily movements *per se*, but to intentional actions, and these are intelligible as such only to the extent they reflect our mental states. It would thus be more accurate to characterise the issue of both theoretical and practical reason as *attitudes*; the difference is that theoretical reasoning leads to modifications of our beliefs, whereas practical reasoning leads to modifications of our intentions'.

[8] See G Harman, *Change in View* (Cambridge, MA, MIT Press, 1986); G Harman, 'Willing and Intending' in Richard Grandy and Richard Warner (eds), *Philosophical Grounds of Rationality* (New York, Oxford University Press, 1986) 363–80; S Blackburn, *Ruling Passions* (Oxford, Clarendon Press, 1998); M Smith, *The Moral Problem* (Oxford, Blackwell, 1994).

[9] Some scholars denied that intentional actions are causes (J Dancy, *Practical Reality* (Oxford, Oxford University Press, 2000)). Others attempt to develop a notion of causation closer to the Aristotelian notion of causation as opposed to the empiricist or Russellian. The Aristotelian notion of causation relies on the idea of a process whose actuality is required to produce what should be achieved for the agent's intended ends to be achieved (R Stout, *Action* (Buckingham, Acumen, 2005) 88–98). The underlying idea is the Aristotelian and Thomist view that one knows the nature of things by its capacities, and its capacities by its activities.

[10] M Bratman, *Intentions, Plans and Practical Reasons* (Cambridge, MA, Harvard University Press, 1987) 4–5. However, for Bratman intentions are mental states (119). Bratman criticises Davidson (see his article 'Davidson's Theory of Intention', reprinted in *Faces of Intention* (Cambridge, Cambridge University Press, 1999) 209–24), but still continues to think that intentions are mental states. However, Bratman separates the idea of 'intention' from the notion of 'desire'.

[11] It seems that this commitment is the result of a conception of personhood. For a critique of Bratman, see R Moran and M Stone, 'Anscombe on Expression of Intention' in C *Sandis (ed), New Essays in the Explanation of Action* (London, Palgrave McMillan, 2010) 132–68. See S Shapiro, *Legality* (Cambridge, MA, Harvard University Press, 2010) for the application of Bratman's conception of intentional action to the understanding of law. Cf V Rodriguez-Blanco, 'From Shared Agency to the Normativity of Law' (2009) *Law and Philosophy* 59 and V Rodriguez-Blanco, 'The Moral Puzzle of Legal Authority' in G Pavlakos and S Bertea (eds), *Normativity in Morality and Law* (Oxford, Hart Publishing, 2011). For a criticism of Bratman's notion of intention and its relationship to coordination see T Pink, 'Purpose Intending' (1991) *Mind* 343.

avoid the temptation of thinking of intention to act as a mere 'state'. Velleman[12] criticises Davidson's view and aims to show the limitations of this theory. However, he endorses the desire/belief pair and modifies it in terms of a reflective justification in which the agent is involved. Thus, being reflective is being disposed to do what is justified in terms of what makes sense to oneself.

There are other problems that affect the two-component model in its more sophisticated form. An intention to act involves the view that something will be carried out and that I can control my action and make adjustments to my behaviour, that there are successive steps towards an action and that it has a beginning, a middle and an end. However, if an intention to act is a mental state, it entails that I can remember my mental state, I can reflect on it, but it seems that the memory or reflection on my intention as a mental state vanishes. Wittgenstein points out:

> For a moment I meant to . . . That is I had a particular feeling, an inner experience; and I remember it. And now remember *quite precisely*! Then the 'inner experience' of intending seems to vanish again. Instead one remembers thoughts, feelings, movements, and also connections with earlier situations. It is as if one had altered the adjustment of a microscope. One did not see before what is now in focus.[13]

If intentions are *purely* mental states, they can vanish, we might not remember them correctly, they might not endure, and then our intentional action might also vanish. Imagine a man who sits down to write a lecture which has to be delivered in three days' time. He needs to work continuously in a focused manner. He opens his books, makes notes, and then gets distracted by the thought of a great meal he had the night before; now his intention stops as he is in another mental state. To continue in his intentional action, he needs to re-remember his intention; he needs to remember that he has three days to prepare a lecture and that he intends to do so. His memory comes back, but in the following three days he sleeps, has lunch and talks on the phone, among other things. Does he need constantly to remind himself about his intention? Does he have to explore his inner sense and mental states to check for his intention? An intention can be carried out on any day and at any time but a mental state might be forgotten or vanish altogether.[14]

[12] D Velleman, *Practical Reflection* (Princeton, NJ, Princeton University Press, 1989) and *The Possibility of Practical Reason* (Oxford, Oxford University Press, 2000). In spite of his more sophisticated account, Velleman advocates the two-component model in which the agent's desires and beliefs jointly cause an intention to act, which, in turn, causes the corresponding movements of the agent's body. D Velleman, 'What Happens When Someone Acts', reprinted in *The Possibility of Practical Reason* (Oxford, Oxford University Press, 2000) 123–43. *For Velleman*, the intention tends to cause an outcome by representing itself as tending to cause it.

[13] L Wittgenstein, *Philosophical Investigations* (E Anscombe (trans), Oxford, Blackwell, 1953) para 645.

[14] For a discussion on this point see R Sheer, 'The "Mental State" Theory of Intentions' (2004) *Philosophy* 121.

As already mentioned, the only way to identify the will and whether it is involved in the action is to understand the action in terms of the description provided by the agent himself. We elicit such a description when we ask '*why*'[15] such and such an action is performed. This way of eliciting the description of the action is called the why-question methodology and is Anscombe's central device in *Intention* for elucidating the connections between the different parts of an action and (our) practical reasoning.[16] There are a number of considerations that need to be taken into account to fully grasp this methodology:

(a) an intentional action is, paradigmatically, a successive series of actions directed towards the final end of the action;

(b) we know that the explanation finishes because the last step is described in terms of good-making characteristics that make intelligible and illuminate as a coherent whole the successive steps of the action;

(c) we do not have different actions but only one action unified by the final intention as a reason for action formulated in terms of good-making characteristics;

(d) it is a reason that is given to *others* in a genuine way within a framework of justification, but it is also the reason that the agent gives to *her/himself*.

Taking these considerations into account, let us now explain the why-question methodology.

Anscombe begins *Intention* by stating that the subject of the book should be studied under three headings: expression of an intention, intentional action and intention in acting[17] and that all these should be understood as interdependent.

---

[15] Moran and Stone explain the why-question methodology as follows: 'Hence all psychic forms are performance modifiers: insofar as they are employable in action-explaining answers to the question "why?", they express forms of being on-the-way-to-but not-yet having Φ-ed, of already stretching oneself toward this end'. See R Moran and M Stone, 'Anscombe on Expression of Intention' in *New Essays in the Explanation of Action* (n 11) 148.

[16] E Anscombe, *Intention*, 2nd edition (Cambridge, MA, Harvard University Press, 2000, originally published in 1957). Anscombe's exposition follows very closely Aquinas' explanation of intentional action. A Kenny, *Aristotle's Theory of the Will* (New Haven, CT, Yale University Press, 1979) points out that Aquinas' model should be understood more as a *Gelstat* psychology. Recent work on Anscombe emphasises the point that acting intentionally should be interpreted as a series of successive steps towards an action. See Moran and Stone, 'Anscombe on Expression of Intention' (n 11) and M Thompson, *Life and Action* (Cambridge, MA, Harvard University Press, 2008) 85–119.

[17] Moran and Stone in 'Anscombe on Expression of Intention' (n 11) explain the transformation of these three headings in the post-*Intention* literature. Most of the authors ignore the heading 'expression of an intention' and conflate the other two sub-headings: intentional action and the intention with which the action was committed. Consequently, intention becomes a mental state. 'Given the possibility of "pure" intending, it becomes hard to see how this category could fail to designate a mental state, attitude or disposition of some kind. So the divisions of "intentions" now take shape around the philosophical polestar of the division between mind and world: two notions of intentions find purchase only where there is behaviour causing things to happen; a third refers to a mental state, attitude or disposition which, though in some way is present in such behaviour, is also abstractable from it and capable of existing on its own' (137).

Thus, an expression of an intention cannot be understood as a prediction about my future acts nor as an introspective explanation of an intention such as desires, wants, etc. Anscombe tells us, however, that people formulate expressions of intentions that are about the future and that *they turn out to be correct*.[18] How is this possible? In order to answer this question, she tries to understand how we can identify intentional actions and demarcate them from non-intentional actions. The logical step is to understand what it means to say that 'I have acted with an intention'. Anscombe identifies acting intentionally with acting for a reason or 'reasons for actions' and such acting involves the view that the question *'why'* applies.[19] In other words, when we act for reasons, we act intentionally and therefore we are sensitive and responsive to a justificatory framework. If we perform an action Φ and the answers are genuine, for example, any of the following: 'I did not know I was doing Φ', 'I was not aware I was doing Φ', then we neither have an intentional action, nor an action performed and guided by reasons; we might have a voluntary action, but not an intentional one.[20] But if the response has, for example, any of the following forms: 'in order to Φ', 'because Φ', then we might have a *prima facie* case for an intentional action or an action done for reasons. In other words, reasons, so to speak, show themselves in intentional action and indicate, by 'showing themselves', how they are able to operate and be part of the agent's practical reasoning.

Do we have any control over the truthfulness of the answer given by the question 'why?'? Anscombe points out that we have a set of contextual conditions that enable us to say whether or not the person has expressed his genuine intentions.[21] For example, if someone is poisoning a river with toxic substances and we ask him 'why are you doing this?', his response might be 'I am just doing my job'; we can verify whether this is part of his routine job, but if it is not we have reason to think that his response is not genuine.

As explained in Chapter 2, intentional action or an action done for reasons involves a successive number of steps or actions and subsequently a successive number of reasons that explain each step, but when do we know that the explanation provided by the agent can stop? Anscombe tells us that the explanation and justification stop when the end of the action is described in terms of what is good or desirable. The final end of the action is something, ie a state of affair, events, facts, objects that *seems or appears* to be good or desirable to the agent. The state of affairs, event, fact or object is believed to be a good sort of thing by the agent. In some ways, this is the most common sense and *naïve* explanation of our actions.

---

[18]   E Anscombe, *Intention* (Oxford, Blackwell, 1957, 2nd edn, 1963) paras 3–4.
[19]   ibid paras 4–6.
[20]   ibid para 17.
[21]   ibid para 25.

For example, when I collect you at the train station, I do not say that I collect you because I am in the mental state of desiring to collect you at the train station and have the mental state of believing and remembering that this is that kind of action; similarly, when I follow the legal rule 'vehicles are allowed to park in the Park', I do not *say* that I did not park my vehicle in the Park because I was in the mental state of desiring or accepting to follow the legal rule and have the belief that this is the kind of action that involves not parking in the Park. On the contrary, *in order to pick you up at the train station*, I start my car, drive down the road, park my car at the train station and get out of my car and enter the train station. The successive steps of action find unity and intelligibility in my *reason* as a good-making characteristic that, for example, you are my friend and it is good to welcome friends at the train station. In the second example above, I might say that I turn my car around and park my car in a parking space some metres away from the Park because of the grounding reason of the rule 'vehicles are not allowed to park in the Park' which is that it is good to keep the peace in the Park.

The core motivation behind the why-question methodology is to pay attention to the structure or articulation of an intentional action.[22] The action is *not given* and therefore the matter is not to discover the propositional attitudes, ie beliefs and desires, that will explain the action. The issue is to unveil the structure of the intentional action to understand whether there is an action or not.

In Anscombe, evaluation and motivation do not come apart. I ask the deliberative viewpoint '*what* should I truly do?' and '*why* should I this or that'? The answers to these questions involve both an apprehension and an evaluation of the state of affairs or facts of the world and this entails, so to speak, a theoretical engagement with the world. In some way, we might say that the question is formulated from the deliberative point of view, but the answer should be given as if it were a theoretical question (section 9.1).

3.3 TRANSPARENCY CONDITION AND PRACTICAL KNOWLEDGE

In the previous section I showed that the idea of reasons for action is linked to the idea of intentional action and that, therefore, the participation of the will is engaged in deliberating and choosing the action. We have said that the agent knows the reasons for his actions without observation. This means that the reasons for actions are transparent to the agent (sections 3.3 and 5.3.1). The phenomenon of transparency is clear from the example of the man who goes shopping for butter in Chapter 5 (section 5.3.1). An expression of an

---

[22] C Vogler, 'Anscombe on Practical Inference' in E Millgram (ed), *Varieties of Practical Reasoning* (Cambridge, MA, MIT Press, 2001).

intention, according to Anscombe, is not mainly from the third-person perspective.[23] The knowledge that we have about our body's position is not known *mainly* by observation; it might be *aided* by observation, but I do not need to take a theoretical or observational stance to know that my legs are crossed whilst I sit typing on my laptop. Anscombe tells us that intentional action is a sub-class of non-observational knowledge.[24]

Gareth Evans in *The Varieties of Reference* refers to the phenomenon of 'transparency' that characterises beliefs:

> In making a self-description of belief, one's eyes are, so to speak, or occasionally literally, directed outward – upon the world. If someone asks me 'Do you think there is going to be a Third World War?', I must attend, in answering him, to precisely the same outward phenomena as I would attend to if I were answering the question 'Will there be a Third World War'? I get myself in a position to answer the question whether I believe that *p* by putting into operation whatever procedure I have for answering the question whether *p*.[25]

Wittgenstein asserts:

> 477. What does it mean to assert that 'I believe p' says roughly the same as 'p'? We react in roughly the same way when anyone says the first and when he says the second; if I said the first and someone didn't understand the words 'I believe', I should repeat the sentence in the second form, and so on.

> 478. Moore's paradox may be expressed like this: 'I believe p' says roughly the same as 'p'; but 'Suppose I believe that p' does not say the same as 'Suppose p'. . . .

> 490. The paradox is this: the *supposition* may be expressed as follows: 'Suppose this went on inside me and *that* outside'; but the assertion that this is going on inside me asserts: this is going on outside me. As suppositions the two propositions about the inside and the outside are quite independent, but not as assertions.[26]

For both Evans and Wittgenstein, answers about whether I 'believe p' are outward-looking. I cannot answer the question whether I believe that it is raining, for example, without looking through the window, or reading the weather forecast. To answer such a question in terms of my introspective states seems absurd. We do not need to look inward at our states of mind to know whether or not it is raining.

Moran also advocates the 'transparency condition' but goes a step further in arguing that when I answer a question from a deliberative standpoint I

---

[23] Anscombe, *Intention* (n 18) paras 2–3.
[24] ibid para 8.
[25] G Evans, *The Varieties of Reference* (Oxford, Oxford University Press, 1982) 225. See also R Edgeley, *Reason in Theory and Practice* (London, Hutchinson and Co, 1969).
[26] L Wittgenstein, *Remarks on the Philosophy of Psychology* (E Anscombe (trans), Oxford, Blackwell, 1980).

need to 'make up my mind' and this entails self-constitution. Following in the steps of Evans and Wittgenstein, Moran explains transparency as follows:

> With respect of belief, the claim of transparency is that from within the first-person perspective, I treat the question of my belief about P as equivalent to the question of the truth of P. What I think we can see now is that the basis for this equivalence hinges on the role of deliberative considerations about one's attitudes. For what the 'logical' claim of transparency requires is the deferral of the theoretical question 'What do I believe?' to the deliberative question 'What am I to believe?'. And in the case of the attitude of belief, answering a deliberative question is a matter of determining what is true. When we unpack the idea in this way, we see that the vehicle of transparency in each case lies in the requirement that I address myself to the question of my state of mind in a *deliberative* spirit, deciding and declaring myself on the matter, and not confront the question as a purely psychological one about the beliefs of someone who happens also to be me.[27]

For the purposes of this book we do not need to engage with this dispute about the connection between self-knowledge and self-constitution.[28] We can take the idea of transparency and see how it applies to reasons for actions. If I act intentionally I act according to reasons for actions, therefore I *believe*[29] that I am acting intentionally for reasons as good-making characteristics, but if the transparency condition is sound, I do not to look at my mental state to know whether I have the belief in my intentional action for reasons that for *me* are good-making characteristics, I just look outward to the facts, objects and state of affairs of the world. In this way, my belief that I am acting intentionally and that I have reasons for acting as good-making characteristics is transparent. The transparency condition establishes the following:

> **(TC for reasons for actions) 'I can report on my own reasons for actions, not by considering my own mental states or theoretical evidence about them, but by considering the reasons themselves which I am immediately aware of'.**

In an example provided by Anscombe (for further details see section 5.3.1), a man goes shopping and a detective is following him. The detective makes a description of the man's actions and his statements are true or false in terms of what the man is doing, whereas if the man fails to do what he intends to do, ie,

---

[27] R Moran, *Authority and Estrangement* (Princeton, NJ, Princeton University Press, 2001) 62–63.

[28] On this debate see S Shoemaker, 'Self-knowledge and Inner-sense' (1994) *Philosophy and Phenomenological Research* 249 and *The First Person Perspective and Other Essays* (Cambridge, Cambridge University Press, 1996); P Boghossian, 'Content and Self-Knowledge' (1989) *Philosophical Topics* 5; A Byrne, 'Introspection' (2005) *Philosophical Topics* 79.

[29] Setiya defines the connection between belief and acting intentionally as follows: 'When someone is acting intentionally, there must be something he is doing intentionally, not merely trying to do, in the belief that he is doing it'. K Setiya, *Reasons Without Rationalism* (Princeton, NJ, Princeton University Press, 2010) 41.

to select from the shelf the items that are on his list, we do not say that the proposition 'he intends to φ-ing' is false, rather we say that there is a mistake in performance. This is what Anscombe calls the Theophrastus principle,[30] which states that in intentional action the mistake is not in judgement but in performance. Anscombe puts this as follows:

> As when I say to myself 'Now I press button A' – pressing button B – a thing which can certainly happen. This I will call the *direct* falsification of what I say. And here, to use Theophrastus' expression again, the mistake is not one of judgement but of performance. That is, we do *not* say: What you *said* was a mistake, because it was supposed to describe what you did and did not describe it, but: What you *did* was a mistake, because it was not in accordance with what you said.[31]

Thus, when I say that I intend to get up at six o'clock in the morning tomorrow to drive you to the train station because you are my friend and one should always help friends even in little ways, I know that I intend to act for such reasons. I do not need to look at my mental state to know that I have such reasons, I look outward to the world, my car, your presence in my house and the fact that it takes 10 minutes to drive to the train station from my house. I have *groundless* knowledge of my reasons for action. It is not incorrigible.[32] Let us suppose that I discover that you are not truly my friend and that, therefore, my reason for driving you to the station because you are my friend is a mistaken one. However, the way I attain knowledge of my reasons for action does not depend on an inference from my observations or other data about myself. This entails that we have certain capacities, not only conceptual, but also practical. In the case of rules, we can say that we learn rules and their grounding reasons for actions simultaneously. Our practical and conceptual capacities enable us to learn rules in the context of grounding reasons as good-making characteristics.

I am also able to exercise control over my actions because I can direct myself towards the end of my action as described by the reasons for actions as good-making characteristics and I can change the movements of my body if I discover, aided by observation, that I am not doing what I intended to do (Theophrastus principle). Thus, let us suppose that I am making an espresso and mistakenly I find myself about to pour milk into the cup, then I do not say 'I am not making an espresso after all, I am actually making a latte, that's all

---

[30] See Teichman (n 1) 22–26 and also M Alvarez, *Kinds of Reasons* (Oxford, Oxford University Press, 2010) 70–71.

[31] Anscombe, *Intention* (n 18) paras 32–33.

[32] KS Donnelan, 'Knowing What I am Doing' (1963) 60 *Journal of Philosophy* 401, 403, argues that there is a difference between our knowledge of having a headache, being in anger, in pain, and practical knowledge that is non-observational. In the latter case, the knowledge is corrigible whereas the former not. We revise the statements of our intentions and we can make mistakes about them. However, observation is not the basis of our knowledge, we cannot *infer* from our observations our intentions. What we correct is the *result* or purpose of our intentions.

right'. On the contrary, I change my movements and stop my action of pouring the milk into the cup. The world fits my intentions, I transform the state of affairs through my actions to fit what I intend and am committed to perform, whereas in theoretical knowledge my beliefs fit the world. In this way, I do not need observational knowledge to know that I intend to make an espresso, but I can be aided by observation to know the results of my intention.

Groundless knowledge of our reasons entails not only the capacity to act for reasons, but also includes a *knowing how* to act intentionally according to reasons for actions in the specific context. Following legal rules entails *know-how* about how to follow the legal rules because of their grounding reasons. But this does not mean that this groundless knowledge is not factive. On the contrary, it is knowledge about the world. Anscombe put this as follows:

> Say I go over to the window and open it. Someone who hears me moving calls out: What are you doing making that noise? I reply 'Opening the window'. I have called such a statement knowledge all along; and precisely because in such a case what I say is true – I do open the window; and that means that the window is getting opened by the movements of the body out of whose mouth those words come. But I don't say the words like this: 'Let me see, what is this body bringing about? Ah yes! the opening of the window'.[33]

Our practical knowledge is also factual. When I intend to open the window and make the necessary movements with my hands, I know that I am opening the window and that I am actually opening the window.

Can we understand what we are doing *because* we *observe* what we are doing? If we take a theoretical stance towards our own actions, then we might argue that there is a kind of alienation concerning the identity of ourselves and our actions;[34] in one sense the action is lost, because we do not look at the goal or object towards which our actions are directed, but we look at ourselves doing the action. We do not look outwards, but inwards, and we lose the object or goal that we aim to bring about. Imagine that I am making an espresso and begin to reflect on the movements of my hands; the way the coffee flows into the cup, I see myself putting the coffee beans into the espresso machine and smile at the thought of a fresh coffee. At some point it seems that I will lose the action of 'making an espresso'. It is impossible to be Narcissus. O'Shaughnessy asks whether this impossibility is really about the impossibility of doing two things at the same time, rather than a matter of the character of practical knowledge because, if this is the case, then it is a quantitative matter and trivial. O'Shaugnessy argues that it is a matter of logic: '*Just as I cannot be going*

---

[33] Anscombe, *Intention* (n 18) paras 28–29.
[34] Moran (n 27) explores the nature of this theoretical stance towards our deliberative understanding of our actions. He makes an important connection between the Sartrean notion of 'bad faith' and the theoretical stance that we might take towards our actions (77–83).

north and south at the same time, so I cannot be reading a book and playing tennis at the same time.[35] Thus, pathological cases are explained as the separation of the acting and the observing self.[36]

3.4 A DEFENCE OF THE GUISE OF THE GOOD MODEL

Plato in the *Republic* asserts 'Every soul pursues the good and does whatever it does for its sake' (505e).[37] Aristotle in *Nichomachean Ethics*[38] states:

> Absolutely and in truth the good is the object of volition; but for each person what appears to him good. That which is in truth the object of volition is the object of the good man's volition . . . the good man judges each class of things rightly, and the truth is what appears true to him. Each state of character differs in what it finds noble and pleasant, and perhaps the most important difference between the good man and others is that he sees the truth in each class of things, being as it were the standard and measure for each of them. (1113a25–33)

Aristotle in *De Anima*[39] points out 'it is always the object of desire which produces movement, [and] this is either good or the apparent good' (433a27–29), and in *Eudemian Ethics* he establishes:

> The end is by nature always a good and one about which people deliberate in particular, as a doctor may deliberate whether he is to give a drug, or the general where he is to pitch his camp; in these there is a good, an end, which is the best without qualification; but contrary to nature, and by perversion, not the good but only an apparent good may be the end. (1227a19–22)[40]

How can values actualised in particulars provide reasons for actions? When we begin to deliberate about what to do, we begin with judging whether something, ie an object, state of affairs or an event, is good or not. We engage in valuing and we start to desire that this something obtains. Values are instantiated by the good-making characteristics of objects and states of affairs and they become reasons for actions. Pure desires, by contrast, are passive and do not engage in valuations. Pure desires are a pure state of the mind without object. For example, the pure desire for pleasure does not aim at a

[35] B O'Shaughnessy, 'Observation and the Will' *(1963) Journal of Philosophy* 380.

[36] See L Bortolotti and MR Broome, 'Delusional Beliefs and Reason-Giving' (2008) *Philosophical Psychology* 821.

[37] Plato, *Republic* 505e (A Waterfield (trans), Oxford, Oxford University Press, 1993).

[38] Aristotle, *Nichomachean Ethics* (H Rackham (trans), Cambridge, MA, Harvard University Press, 1934).

[39] Aristotle, *De Anima* (DW Hamlyn (trans), Oxford, Clarendon Press, 1968).

[40] Aristotle, *Eudemian Ethics*, Loeb Classical Library (H Rackham (trans), (Cambridge, MA, Harvard University Press, 1952). See also T Aquinas, *Summa Theologica* (Latin and English texts, T Gilby (ed), Cambridge, Cambridge University Press, 2006) 1a2ae,8,1.

specific object, but at its own satisfaction or fulfilment, but also at *eliminating* itself. When making valuations, we aim at the object and the satisfaction of attaining the object. *Desires are mute on the question of what is good.*[41] These are two independent sources of motivation.[42]

Let us imagine two drug addicts: a licentious and a compulsive one. The former values being in a permanent state of dreamlike unconsciousness, he thinks about the best strategy for obtaining drugs and for staying, as long as possible, in a numb and unconscious state. By contrast the compulsive drug addict does not value being in a state of dreamlike unconsciousness, he fights against his addiction and tries to avoid meeting friends who will encourage him to take drugs; he always succumbs, however. The problem is that what he most desires or values is not actually what he wants (as pure desire). The compulsive drug addict does not value or want being an addict, contrary to the licentious one whose values and desires are in harmony; the compulsive addict wishes to *get rid* of his wanting or pure desire, and he does want to and value ridding himself of his addiction. It is usual, however, to conflate the two ideas: wanting (as pure desire) and valuing (desiring as valuing). We can have pure desires without valuing what we desire. In the example of the two drug addicts, one of them desires the drug and values it, and the other merely desires it without valuing it. He desires it in spite of himself. Can we say that cases of pure desire are just urges or impulses? Watson[43] thinks not and clarifies his view as follows. There is no reason why we cannot think about a persistent and pervasive desire that constantly dominates the individual, in spite of himself. All addictions, ie sex, alcohol, drugs, are a good example of this. The distinction does not lie in the content of the desire or the object of our valuing, but in our structure of wanting and ends. The same object, state of affairs or event can be the object of wanting or valuing. For example, I desire food because it relieves my anxiety (pure desire) or because I value the enjoyment of a good meal with friends and family. Of course, pure desires can gain value. For example, I may attend dinner parties with people I do not (even) like and eat and drink a lot to relieve my anxiety. With time I can learn to appreciate and value their company. An agent may ask himself, 'what should I do in terms of my values, and not just in terms of my desires?'. The question is not which desires should I *eliminate* or *get rid of*, which is a question about *me*, but what should I truly do, and this question involves examining the different options and valuing them. Pure desires are independent of my internal value system and they do not form part of the question 'what should I do?'. They

---

[41] G Watson, 'Free Agency' (1975) *Journal of Philosophy* 205, 208.

[42] See ibid for a contemporary defence of this Platonic distinction between two sources of motivation. See also Plato, *Phaedrus* 237e–238e in J Cooper (ed), *Plato Complete Works* (A Nehamas and P Woodruff (trans), Indiannapolis, IN, Hackett, 1997).

[43] Watson (n 41) 210.

play a role only when I value something such as an object, a state of affairs or event, and when subsequently I desire it.

Most of the examples given against the 'guise of the good' model are examples of pure desire as opposed to examples of desiring as a result of valuing. The 'guise of the good' model is about deliberative and intentional action according to the latter. By contrast, in the former case, there is no full agency as I am dominated by pure desires without valuing.

A number of contemporary philosophers have defended the 'guise of the good' model,[44] but important criticisms have also been raised against its core tenets.

Akrasia or incontinence is one key criticism that needs to be addressed by the 'guise of the good' model. The *akratic* agent judges all-things-considered that A is better than B; however, he performs B instead of A. He acts against what he considers good. One possible explanation of his actions is that the agent, even though he knows that A is better than B, re-describes B so that B is also presented as having a good-making characteristic. In other words, B is good from some other perspective. The desire for B wins over A, according to the agent's objective understanding. This is not a motivational failure, but a cognitive one.[45] Tenenbaum tells us that acquiring self-control is '*finding a clear and obvious way to present something that one abstractly and perhaps vaguely conceives to be good all things considered*'.[46] This theme is vast and, whilst important, I cannot do complete justice to it here. I will concentrate instead on the criticism that says that agents *do not* take their actions as good.

In a recent challenge to the 'guise of the good' model, Setiya has argued that we can act for reasons and even for reasons the agent considers good, but the explanation of the action is not always intelligible. He puts the following example:

> imagine someone who is relentlessly and indiscriminately rude. He seems to have no sense whatsoever of the effect of his brusque approach on others, and when he is aware of it, he could not care less. If he one day decides to tone down his complaints in order to spare my feelings, because he believes he should do so, I am liable to find his action unintelligible, even though it is done for a reason he sees, suddenly and inexplicably, under the guise of the good. His behaviour makes no sense.[47]

In the example, we know that the agent has in the past behaved rudely and is now acting politely and toning down his complaints *because* he aims to spare the feelings of others, but the response that is missing is 'why does he intend to

[44] Anscombe, *Intention* (n 18); J Raz, 'Agency, Reason and the Good' in *Engaging Reasons* (Oxford, Oxford University Press, 1999); S Tenenbaum, *Appearances of the Good* (Cambridge, Cambridge University Press, 2007).
[45] Tennenbaum (n 44) 279, 288.
[46] ibid 279.
[47] Setiya (n 29) 63.

do so?'. Setiya tells us that it is for a reason that the agent considers good. What can that reason be? It might be that he has realised that his reputation as a rude person is damaging to him in the long run, or that he has realised that Setiya can be a good ally for the future, and so on. Let us suppose that the agent responds, 'I don't know what the reason is, I think hard but I find no reason; this is just how I am – moody'. If his response is genuine, we can say that his action is voluntary but not necessarily intentional.[48] Setiya's example fails to be an example of an action for a reason (intentional action).

Stocker[49] also raises important criticisms of the 'guise of the good' model. He begins his essay 'Desiring the Bad' with the following phrase *'desiring the bad and not desiring the good are ordinary features of our ordinary life'*. Stocker advances the view that motivation and evaluation usually come apart because of our complex psychological structures. Thus, our moods, interests and energy play an important role in our valuing. Stocker challenges the distinction between valuing and pure desiring and aims to provide a general argument to undermine the distinction and, consequently, the 'guise of the good' model. Stocker considers two versions of the 'guise of the good' model. First, the weak one which asserts that only the attractive act or act-feature is believed good in some respect or over-all, or even best. By contrast, the stronger version asserts that the acts or features are believed absolutely good, ie with no aspects that are believed bad or neutral. Stocker tells us that the weak version of the thesis is uninteresting but he advances no arguments to support this assertion! I suggest that the 'guise of the good' model should be understood in its weak version for reasons that will become apparent in the following paragraphs. For example, if I eat an orange to boost my immune system, I would not think that it is good in an absolute way. On the contrary, an orange can be bad if you have an upset stomach. But Stocker does not think that he needs to rely on the weak/strong distinction to show his point that the (believed) bad can attract the agent.

Stocker argues that we usually fail to seek the good due to spiritual or physical tiredness, weakness of the body, illness, despair, apathy or inability to concentrate, and he points out that *'a frequent added defect of being in such "depressions" is that one sees all the good to be won or saved and one lacks the will, interest, desire, or strength'*.[50] But in the instances suggested by Stocker above, it seems to me that we are not acting intentionally and that there is, subsequently, no full agency. We lack an engaging will directed towards an end. We are acting, however, voluntarily. Stocker's characterisation is closer to the characterisation of the compulsive drug addict who is dominated by passive pure desires and who does not have the will to engage in valuing. Stocker reinforces his

[48] Anscombe, *Intention* (n 18) para 17.
[49] M Stocker, 'Desiring the Bad: an Essay in Moral Psychology' (1979) *Journal of Philosophy* 738.
[50] ibid 744.

arguments as follows: '*more generally, something can be good and one can believe it to be good without being in the mood or having an interest or energy structure which inclines one to seek or even desire it*'.[51] This is not a case of intentional action, not even of an action, and therefore not a case where evaluation and motivation come apart. In this case there is appraisal but, of course, I do not act on all that is the subject of my positive appraisals. Thus, as agents, we evaluate our surroundings, we grasp the beauty of a sunset, flowers, or a musical tune, we value a mathematical theorem, and so on. However, if I intend to go to bed before sunset because I have an exam the following morning, I close the windows to block out noises from outside, I draw my curtains to block out the light, and I turn off my radio. Similarly, if I intend to become a good philosopher I do not engage in solving mathematical theorems. The guise of the good thesis does not state that we should act upon everything that we value. Rather, it states that if we act, it is because we value the end of our action which we *have chosen*.

In the final part of his attack on the guise of the good model, Stocker aims to show that '*we have desires and appetites for the (believed) bad*'.[52] Stocker puts the example of a man who wants to and succeed in burning himself to see if he can emulate the famous Roman. He does this because of his desire for self-knowledge. Stocker argues that knowledge can be harmful or bad and then he advances the following reasoning: '*But, I contend, some knowledge is bad or harmful, some is simply not worth having, the desire to know some things is shameful and so on. (This is so even if some knowledge is good in itself.) Thus, it seems that we can take the desire or appetite to know as having proper objects which are (believed) good, bad, or neutral*'.[53] Stocker's argument, I will argue, is not sound. In the first part of the argument he agrees that some kinds of knowledge are not good and are even painful or harmful. Thus, if I prick myself with a needle in order to know what it feels like to be pinched by a needle, then, *in spite of* my belief in the good-making characteristic of my act, ie the knowledge of the pain, the act is harmful to my health. In other words, contrary to my belief in the goodness of my act, I am mistaken. The guise of the good model precisely asserts this, although the action is done because of the (believed or hypothetical) good-making characteristic of the action, the agent is mistaken in his or her understanding. However, in the second part of the argument, Stocker concludes that we can have a desire for knowledge that is (believed) good, bad or neutral and therefore we can desire the bad. But this is a *non-sequitur*. I did not put the needle in my skin because I believe it is a bad sort of thing; on the contrary, I believe it is good sort of thing, but I was mistaken; the action is actually harmful and therefore has mainly bad-making characteristics. Stocker could alternatively have said, '*Thus, it seems that we can take the desire or*

[51] ibid 745.
[52] ibid 747.
[53] ibid 747.

appetite to know as having proper objects which are good, bad, or neutral. But then, this will support the 'guise of the good' model, because the guise of the good model maintains that the action is done for the (believed) good even though the agent might be mistaken in his valuation.

The guise of the good model does not aim to establish that we always evaluate correctly what is objectively good, it merely states that we evaluate and that we can make mistakes (and we often do!) in such evaluations.

Stocker also argues that when, for example, we harm another person, we do not do it for an ulterior purpose, ie to exercise control or domination, for pleasure, and so on. We harm others, he says, for the sake of harming. Let us use the why-question methodology to see whether in this case the action is an intelligible and intentional action. Let us suppose that I see you putting a needle in the skin of your enemy who is tied up and cannot move. I ask you why are you doing that and you respond that you intend to harm him, I ask you 'why?' and your answer is that it is for the sake of inflicting pain. This is unintelligible. From such a response, I could infer two possible interpretations. First, I might think that you do not know the reasons for your actions and, if that is the case, then your action might not be intentional. It is voluntary, but it might be just an impulse or simply the result of a pure desire to cause harm. Your behaviour is merely compulsive. Secondly, I might think you are not honest about your true intentions, ie your reasons for actions, or that you prefer to be silent about them. In this case, we imagine that there *might be* a justification and therefore reasons for your actions. We might imagine, for example, that it is because he is your enemy and you are taking revenge on him because he broke your rib.

We have emphasised the fact that the 'guise of the good' model does not entail that we do not make mistakes when we engage in evaluation. The thesis does not involve the view that human beings always choose what they should choose, and what is of true value.[54]

Velleman has also raised important challenges to the 'guise of the good' model. According to Velleman, truth and correctness are constitutive of belief, but goodness and correctness are not constitutive of desire as the 'guise of the good' model aims to show. If the 'guise of the good' model were sound, Velleman tells us, then perverse desires would be impossible.[55] He complains that Anscombe's arguments in favour of the 'guise of the good' model make of perverse figures like Satan a sappy figure who just aims to do the good. Velleman quotes the following passage from Anscombe's *Intention*:

---

[54] Raz correctly puts this as follows: 'The thesis does not express optimism about human nature. It is meant to accommodate not only mistakes, even gross mistakes about what is of value, but also anomic conduct in defiance of value': 'On the Guise of the Good' in S Tenenbaum (ed), *Desire, Practical Reason and the Good* (Oxford, Oxford University Press, 2010) 116.

[55] Velleman, *The Possibility of Practical Reason* (n 12) 118.

'Evil be thou my good' is often thought to be senseless in some ways. Now all that concerns us here is that 'What's the good of it?' is something that can be asked until a desirability characterisation has been reached and made intelligible. If then the answer to this question at some stage is 'The good of it is that it's bad', this need not be unintelligible; one can go on to say 'And what's good of its being bad?' to which the answer might be condemnation of good as impotent, slavish and inglorious. Then the good of making evil my good is my intact liberty in the unsubmissiveness of my will.[56]

For Velleman, Anscombe's Satan is purporting to get things right and aims at correctness on what is of value. He rejects the good because it is slavish and inglorious and this puts Satan as a searcher of valuable things. Anscombe, for Velleman, has portrayed us a sappy Satan, a minor and sweeter beast than the legendary evil and perverse characters of history and literature. Anscombe's picture makes impossible perverse actions. But is this what the 'guise of the good' model involves? The underlying idea that good-making characteristics are constitutive of desire as truth is constitutive of belief is not that the agent is trying to 'obtain what is good'. In the example of Satan, Satan is aware that evil is *not* good, but he finds good-making characteristics in evil. It can bring him power and glory, in spite of knowing that perverse acts are not good. The problem in understanding this lies in the asymmetry between belief and desire. It is not an exact characterisation of the 'guise of the good' model to assert that belief aims at truth as desire aims at the good. Rather we should say that 'desire aims at good-making characteristics' whereas beliefs do not aim at 'truth-making characteristics'. On the contrary, beliefs aim at truth *simpliciter*. States of affairs, objects or events can be evil but can at the same time have good-making characteristics from the point of view of a certain agent. In other words, actions are different from statements about the world, states of affairs, objects or events. For Satan, to torture children is an evil action, but this action enables him to be powerful and this is the good-making characteristic that constitutes the intelligible reason for his action. There is no paradox in asserting 'To torture children is absolutely evil, but this act *also* involves glory and power and therefore I desire it'. Satan would reject helping and being generous with others because it is slavish and inglorious, rather he prefers perverse acts such as torturing children because, in spite of believing that it is truly and perfectly evil, he sees the (hypothetical or believed) good-making characteristic of such an act, ie glory and power. Thus, Anscombe's Satan is not sappy. On the contrary, Anscombe's Satan is *truly* perverse, but in one sense, he aims to get it right as he is convinced that glory and power are *truly* good-making characteristics.

---

[56] Anscombe, *Intention* (n 18) para 39.

4

Understanding the Nature and Structure of Practical Reason: Excavating the Classical Tradition

4.1 PRIORITY OF THE FIRST-PERSON PERSPECTIVE OR DELIBERATIVE POINT OF VIEW AS MANIFESTING THE FORM OR STRUCTURE OF PRACTICAL REASONING

IN CHAPTER 2 it was shown that there is an asymmetry between the first-person and the third-person perspectives in making intelligible the legal rule-compliance phenomenon. The agent can assert that she performs an action because of a rule but this does not answer the question 'why does the rule cause you to perform the action?', and subsequent 'why?' questions only cease when the agent responds in terms of a reason as a good-making characteristic.

We have also discussed the two-component view of intentional action construed as a mental state represented by the belief/desire pairing that causes the action. This is an alternative conception to the classical notion of intentional action construed as diachronically directed intention towards an end. In contemporary philosophy of action, the two-component view and its reliance on causation is the predominant view. In both the classical tradition and the contemporary view, however, there is the recognition that the description of the action is the key element to identify the action *qua* intentional action. We have argued that the central description comes from the first-person or deliberative point of view since it is the perspective that truly grasps the action as intentional. But how should we understand the first-person or deliberative point of view that reveals itself through a chain of answers that attempt to satisfy the question 'why?'? What happens if we simply just explain the desires and beliefs of the agent without considering the possible revelations arising from the first-person or deliberative point of view advanced in response to the 'why' chain of questions? The danger in doing this is that we miss the structure of practical reason that is manifested in the answers to the 'why?' chain of questions and that reveal whether there is an intentional action or not. At the heart of the matter is the idea that the structure of practical reason and the structure of intentional action run parallel and that we cannot access the latter without accessing the former. In other words, the form or structure of intentional action is the midwife of the form or structure of practical reason. If we fail to understand the form or structure of intentional action and intentions and reasons in action, then we fail to identify the form of practical reason. Thus if, in answer to the question 'why are you eating mud'?, the agent responds 'for no reason', this means that there is no ordering of reason in the action and therefore no practical reasoning. Consequently, we can confidently assert that the action is neither intentional nor is there an intention with which the agent has acted.

But this is still very cryptic. Are we saying that we aim to reveal the form or structure of practical reason *via* the form or structure of intentional action? The difficulty is that we do not understand how the form or structure of intentional action is able to reveal the form or structure of practical reason.

We need to dig deeper into Aristotelian metaphysics to scrutinise practical reason. The Aristotelian metaphysical view is that we are creatures of a certain nature who possess a power or capacity and that among these powers practical reasoning is the most important. We are structured by powers or capacities, but we are unable to either 'observe' this key feature of our constitution by empirical methods or to rationalise it (eg through taking a theoretical view of our actions; for more on this see Chapter 10). Capacities or powers can only be grasped when we are active. But what does it mean to say that these capacities are 'active' or are *actuality*?[1] The core argument of this chapter is that the Aristotelian distinction between actuality and potentiality provides the general framework for understanding the idea of capacity-change that underlies the view of practical reason as a capacity or power that changes and manifests itself in different ways.[2] What is required, therefore, is an understanding of the actuality/potentiality distinction to grasp *how* practical reason as a capacity is able to work, operate, manifest itself and shape our intentional actions. In section 4.2 I explain the actuality/potentiality distinction and how it illuminates the notion of practical reasoning capacity and capacity change.

---

[1] I use this term as Kosman and Coope interpret it from Aristotle's *Physics, Books III and IV*, Clarendon Aristotle Series (E Hussey (trans), Oxford, Clarendon Press, 1983). This means, the change that acts upon something else so that this something else becomes F, ie the fulfilment of a potentiality. For example, the building of a house by a builder so that the house becomes built. See LA Kosman, 'Aristotle's Definition of Motion' (1969) *Phronesis* 40 and U Coope, 'Change and its Relation to Actuality and Potentiality' in G Anagnostopoulos (ed), *A Companion to Aristotle* (Oxford, Wiley-Blackwell, 2009) 277.

[2] This interpretation is also advanced by M Frede, 'Aristotle's Notion of Potentiality' in T Scaltsas, D Charles and M Gill (eds), *Metaphysics θ', Unity, Identity and Explanation in Aristotle's Metaphysics* (Oxford, Clarendon Press, 1994). See also S Makin's commentaries on Aristotle in *Aristotle, Metaphysics Book θ*, Clarendon Aristotle Series (Oxford, Clarendon Press, 2006) 133; cf WD Ross, *Aristotle's Physics: A Revised Text with Introduction and Commentary* (Oxford, Oxford University Press, 1995).

In section 4.3 I analyse the implications of this view for the central inquiry of the book which is an explanation of the legal-rule compliance phenomenon.

4.2 UNDERSTANDING *ENERGEIA*: AN INTERPRETATION OF THE WHY-QUESTION METHODOLOGY

4.2.1 Key features of intentional action

In her book *Intention*, Elisabeth Anscombe engages with the task of explaining intentional action along the lines of the philosophical tradition of Aristotle and Aquinas and identifies a number of key features that characterise intentional action. These features include the following.

(a) Former Stages of an Intentional Action are 'Swallowed Up' by Later Stages

Intentional action is composed of a number of stages or series of actions. For example, if I intend to make a cup of tea, I first put on the kettle *in order* to boil water, I boil water *in order* to pour it into a cup of tea. While I am making tea, however, there are many other things that I am doing that are irrelevant to my intentional action and to what is happening as intentional. For example, I sneeze, I look through the window, I sing, and so on. Similarly, many other things are happening in the world that are irrelevant to what I do intentionally. Thus, the kitchen has a specific location, the flowers in the garden are in bloom, the wind is blowing and blows open the window, and so on. Because my action of making tea is intentional, I impose an order on the chaos of the world and this order is the order of reasons. Thus I put on the kettle *in order* to boil water and I boil water *in order to* pour it into a cup. This is how I understand the sequence of happenings in the world that I, as an agent, *produce or make happen*. But, arguably, there could be an infinite number of series of actions; there could be a continuous infinite, or ceaseless, seamless web of actions. The question 'why?' can always be prompted: 'why are you making tea'? and the agent might reply, 'because it gives me comfort in the morning'. There is, however, an end to the 'why?' series of questions and the end comes when the agent provides a characterisation of the end or *telos* as a good-making characteristic. The action becomes intelligible and there is no need to ask 'why?' again. The end as the last stage of the 'why?' series of questions swallows up the former stages of the action and makes a complete unity of the action. Intentional actions are not fine-grained, they are not divisible into parts. Thus, parts of series of actions are only intelligible because they belong to an order that finds unity in the whole.

(b) Intentional Action is Something Actually *Done, Brought About according to the Order Conceived or Imagined by the Agent*

Intentional action is not an action that is done in a certain way, mood or style.[3] Thus, it is not an action plus 'something else', ie a will or desire that is directed towards an action. Intention is not an additional element, eg an interior thought or state of mind, it is rather something that is *done* or *brought about* according to the order of reasons that has been conceived by the agent. Consequently, if the question 'why?' has application to the action in question, we can assert that the action is intentional. The prompting of the question 'why?' is the mechanism that enables us to identify whether there is an intentional action. Intentional action is neither the mere movements of our body nor the simple result of transformations of the basic materials upon which agency is exercised, eg the tea leaves, kettle, boiling water. It is a doing or bringing about that is manifested by the expression of a future state of affairs and the fact that the agent is *actually* doing something or bringing it about according to the order of reasons as conceived or imagined by the agent.[4]

(c) Intentional Action Involves Knowledge that is Non-observational, but it Might be Aided by Observation

If I am an agent that acts in an intentional way, I know that I am bringing about something and I know this without the need to observe every single step of my series of actions to verify that (effectively) I am acting.[5] In performing my action I might be aided by observation, but I know *what* is the order of the series of actions and *why*. This is the essence of practical knowledge. You do not need a theoretical stance towards yourself, a verification and observation of the movements of your body to know that you are performing an intentional action and bringing about *something*. Following the previous example, you do not need to observe that 'you are making tea' to know that you intend to 'make tea' and that you are bringing this about. You put on the kettle and boil the water, you do not ask yourself, 'let me see what my body is up to, let me observe what I am doing', and then infer from the movements of your body that you are actually bringing about 'making tea'. Of course you can be aided by observation, you need your sight to put the kettle in the right position and to pour the boiling water without spilling it. But you do not use your observation and inferences from the observational data to know that you are making tea. On the contrary, the more you need this verification or theor-

---

[3] E Anscombe, *Intention* (Cambridge, MA, Harvard University Press, 2000, originally published 1957) 20.
[4] ibid paras 21–22.
[5] ibid paras 28–29.

etical stance towards yourself, the more likely it is that your action is not intentional, you are not controlling the action and you are not guided by the order of reasons. You are not an agent on this occasion, rather something is happening to you.

The state of affairs that you intend to bring about is at a distance, it might not be within your sight.[6] Imagine a painter who intends to make a painting. He has an idea about what the painting will look like, eg how the colours will be distributed across the canvas, and what topics and concepts will be at work in the painting. The painting is at a distance and the painter does not need to observe the movements of his body and the motion of the brushes to know *what* he is painting and *why* he is painting what he is painting. Certainly, his sight will help him to find the adequate colour at the correct time and to shape the figures at the right angle, but his intentional action is not what he observes; it is not the result of his painting but what he is actually doing. We do what happens.

(d) In Acting Intentionally, We Exercise our Practical Knowledge. We Can Understand Practical Knowledge if We Understand the Structure of Practical Reasoning

Intentional action is not in the mind, it is not primarily a mental state, it is not an internal thought.[7] Rather it manifests itself publicly and within the public reasons that we share as creatures with certain constitutions and belonging to a particular time and place. For example, we eat healthy food because it is good to survive, we look after our family because we love them, we avoid harm because we aim to enjoy pleasant things, and so on. Similarly, we know that to make a cake you need flour, sugar, eggs and milk. If I see you mixing grass and earth and you tell me that you are making a cake, then I can assert, if I consider that you are in sound mind (your full capacities), that there might be a mistake in your performance or that you do not understand what it is 'to make a cake'.

According to Anscombe, Aristotle establishes a strong analogy between practical and theoretical syllogism and this has led to misinterpretations about what practical syllogism is.[8] Like theoretical syllogism, practical syllogism is often systematised by Aristotelian interpreters as having two premises, ie major and minor, and a conclusion. It is said that, as in the case of theoretical syllogism, the practical syllogism is a proof or demonstration. The typical form might be as follows:

---

[6] ibid paras 29–30.
[7] ibid paras 21–22, 25, 27–28.
[8] ibid paras 33, 33–34.

Vitamin X is good for all men over 60
Pigs' tripes are full of vitamin X
I am a man over 60
Here are pig's tripes

But in this case nothing seems to follow about doing anything. Furthermore, the practical syllogism is sometimes interpreted as having an ethical or moral character and establishing a way to prove what we ought to do. Following the previous example, the conclusion might be 'I should eat pigs' tripes'. Anscombe rejects this view since Aristotle's examples are not in ethical contexts, ie 'dried food is healthy', 'tasting things that are sweet' that are pleasant. Additionally the word 'should' (*dei*) as it appears in the Aristotelian texts has an unlimited number of applications and does not necessarily refer to the ethical or moral context.[9]

Aristotle insists that the starting point of any intentional action is the state of affairs or something that the agent wants and is wanted because it is presented to the agent as having good-making characteristics or as being valuable (see Chapter 3). For example, the man wants to have vitamin X because it is healthy. Furthermore, the practical syllogism is not limited to two premises and a conclusion, there can be many intermediate instances that are part of the syllogism. After a close analysis, the analogy between practical and theoretical syllogism breaks. Unlike theoretical syllogism, practical syllogism is not a proof or demonstration of a true proposition, nor is it a proof or demonstration of what ought to be done or what we ought to do. It is a form of *how* and *why* we are bringing something about when we are *actually* bringing it about.

Anscombe presents us with an alternative analysis to the practical syllogism and a different way to understand practical reasoning. Thus, the series of responses to the question 'why?' manifests or reveals the practical reasoning of the agent and enables us to identify whether the action that the agent is performing is intentional or not. However, she warns us, the why-question methodology is as 'artificial' as the Aristotelian methodology of practical syllogism.[10] When we act intentionally, we are exercising a kind of reasoning which is not theoretical and which is grounded on a desire for that which seems to the agent to be constituted by good-making characteristics. You know the thing or state of affairs that you are bringing about because you desire the thing or state of affairs that you are bringing about, and you are able to desire the thing or state of affairs that you bringing about because you know *practically* the state of affairs. Your desire arises because you represent the thing or the state of affairs to be brought about as valuable or good. Volition and

---

[9] ibid para 35.
[10] ibid paras 41–42.

knowledge do not fall apart.[11] For example, if you are a painter, you know how and why the shapes and colours on the canvas are what they are, it is because you desire and value the painting you will produce that it should be such and such a colour and shape. But it is also true that because you desire and value *this* and *not that* arrangement of colours and shapes, that you are able to know it *practically*. Consequently, moral approbation is irrelevant for practical reasoning and for our practical engagement with the world.[12] This does not mean that there are no instances of objectively justified reasons for actions. On the contrary, in Chapter 9, we aim to defend the possibility of objectively justified values or goods that ground reasons for actions and legal rules.

Whatever strategy we follow to show the structure of intentional action, whether we take the Aristotelian practical syllogism or the Anscombian series of actions revealed by the question 'why?', we are able to grasp the mechanism of practical reasoning in its different manifestations.

In this section I will argue that if Anscombe is right and both strategies are 'artificial' ways of understanding,[13] then a deeper and more 'natural' way of understanding practical reasoning is by grasping the nature of the capacity that is exercised by the agent. *In other words, the answers to the 'why?' questions show a capacity that the agent is exercising when acting.* In the next section, I will show that the Aristotelian potentiality/actuality distinction sheds light on understanding the exercise and nature of our practical reasoning capacities. Furthermore, the potentiality/actuality distinction illuminates each of the key features of intentional action ((a), (b), (c) and (d)) and their interplay as identified by Anscombe.

4.2.2 Aristotle's Distinction Between Actuality and Potentiality

Contra Parmenides who has argued that motion is impossible since something cannot come from nothing, Aristotle advances the idea that motion or change is possible if there is an underlying nature or constant feature that does not change. To explain this, Aristotle resorts to the distinction between potentiality and actuality. In *Metaphysics*, book θ, Aristotle uses the analogical method to show that particular instances of the scheme or idea of potentiality and actuality have a pattern.[14] Thus he begins with the particular instances of capacity/change and matter/form to explain the common patterns that will

---

[11] ibid para 36.
[12] ibid paras 37–38.
[13] ibid paras 41–42.
[14] I follow the interpretation of Aristotle's *Metaphysics Book θ* advanced by Frede (n 2) and Makin (n 2).

illuminate the general scheme of potentiality/actuality. However, since our purpose is to elucidate the character of practical reasoning which is a power or capacity, and I have argued that the general scheme of potentiality/actuality will help us to clarify the nature of practical reason, it is circular to resort now to the particular instance of capacity/change to explain potentiality/actuality. I will, therefore amend the Aristotelian argumentative strategy and explain the general scheme of potentiality/actuality. I will then proceed to explain the particular instance of exercising our practical capacities as the actuality of a potentiality.

Capturing what 'motion' is, is difficult and many definitions of 'motion' tend to use terms that presuppose motion (for example, 'a going-out from potency to act which is not sudden', but 'going-out' presupposes motion and 'sudden'[15] is defined in terms of time which is also defined in terms of motion). Therefore, this kind of definition is discarded by Aristotle for being circular and unhelpful. Nor can we define motion in terms of pure potency, because if we say that 'bronze is potentially a statue', we are merely referring to the piece of bronze which has not yet been changed and therefore there is no motion. You can neither refer to motion nor to change as what is actual. For instance, you cannot refer to what has been built or transformed, eg a building or statue, because it is not being moved, but has *already* moved. In the example of a building, the bricks, wood, clay, cement of the building have been already moved; and in the case of a statue, the bronze has already been transformed. Thus, Aristotle defines motion as a kind of actuality which is hard to grasp. In other words, *the actuality of what exists potentially, in so far as it exists potentially.*[16] Motion is an actuality that is incomplete. It is hard to grasp and the tendency is to say that motion is the actuality. In the example of the house, it is the house that has been built. The other tendency is to say that motion is the privation of something, ie the going from nothing to something; from not being a house to being a house. Finally, the tendency is also to think that motion is what exists before – potentiality – eg the bricks, steel, wood, cement, and so on. Contrary to these tendencies, Aristotle insists that motion is what happens exactly at the *midpoint*, neither *before* when nothing has been moved and is mere potentiality, and neither *after*, when something *has* been moved. Furthermore, motion is not privation, it is rather constitutive actuality. For example, if the baby has not learned to speak English, we say that the baby is potentially a speaker of English; when a man knows how to speak English and is in silence, he is also potentially a speaker of English; and finally, when the man is speaking English, we say that he is actually an English speaker speaking English. However, the potentiality of the baby (p1) is different from the

---

[15] Aristotle's *Physics* (n 1) 284.
[16] ibid III.1.201a9–11.

potentiality of the man in silence (p2), and motion is located in the second potentiality (p2), when the man is in silence, but begins to pronounce a sentence to speak English. Motion is midway and is not privative, but rather constitutive. We do not say that the man speaking English went from being a non-speaker of English to a speaker of English, we say that he spoke English from being in silence (he knew how to speak English, but did not exercise his capacities).

The previous example locates us in the domain of the particular instance of capacity and change as exemplified by the potentiality/actuality distinction. Aristotle argues that there are many different types of capacity, ie active/passive, non-rational/rational, innate/acquired, acquired by learning/acquired by practice, and one-way/two-way capacities. Two-way capacities are connected to rational capacities, whereas one-way capacities are linked to non-rational capacities. For example, bees have a natural capacity to pollinate a foxglove flower in normal circumstances,[17] ('normal' circumstances might include a healthy bee in an adequate foxglove, and the absence of preventive circumstances). In the case of two-way capacities there ought to be an element of *choice or desire* to act, and the rational being can exercise her capacity by producing or bringing about 'p'. Furthermore, she also knows how to produce or bring about 'non-p'. The paradigmatic example used by Aristotle is medical skill. The doctor knows how to make the patient healthy (p) and how to provoke disease or illness (non-p). Therefore the doctor can bring about two opposite effects.[18] For Aristotle, to have a rational capacity is to have an intellectual understanding of the form that will be transmitted to the object of change or motion. Thus, the doctor will have an understanding of what it means to be healthy and without illness, but also of what it means to be ill. Let us suppose that a doctor is producing illness in enemies through prescribed drugs. She needs to understand the order of the series of actions that will result in sickness for the enemies and she needs to possess knowledge about the necessary drugs to make the enemies collapse. Her action will be directed to produce illness. But the doctor can choose otherwise, eg she can choose to make the enemy healthy.

In the exercise of practical reason we choose to act[19] and this choosing activates the action and directs the capacity towards the series of actions that will be performed. By contrast, a non-rational capacity is non-self-activating, its acts are necessary. If the bee is in good health and there are no obstacles, it will pollinate the foxglove flower. By contrast, rational agents need to *choose or decide* to act to produce a result.

---

[17] See Makin (n 2) 43.
[18] Aristotle's *Metaphysics Book Q* (n 2) 1046b4–5, 6–7.
[19] Aristotle, *Metaphysics Book Q* (n 2) book Q 5, 1048a10–11.

When we say that the medical doctor has the rational capacity to change the unwell patient into a healthy human being, we say that she has the 'origin of change'. She is curing the patient and therefore she is in motion because she actualises her practical reasoning capacities to bring about the result as she understands it. She has an order of reasons that connects a series of actions and a knowledge of how to produce changes.

She is the origin of change because her medical know-how explains why certain changes occur in situations involving that object, eg the patient who suffers chickenpox has fewer spots and less fever. For example, when a teacher intends to teach and starts to say some sentences on the topic of 'Jurisprudence' to her pupils, we say that she is teaching. She is the origin of change in the pupils who are the objects of change. Thus, the students begin to understand the topic and have a grasp of the basic concepts.[20] Similarly, when legislators create the law and judges decide cases, they establish rules, directives and principles and these rules, directives and principles can be found in statutes and case reports. Can we say that legislators and judges have reached the end of the process? No, we cannot: statutes and case reports do not represent the end of the process since citizens need to comply with the legal rules and directives and perform the actions as intended by the legislators and judges. We say that legislators and judges are the origin of change because they know how and have an order of reasons that enables citizens to comply with legal rules and directives. The order or reasons as good-making characteristics ground the rules, decisions and legal directives. In parallel to the situation of the teacher, I cannot say that I am teaching unless my pupils begin to understand the topic that I am teaching. Thus, the legislator cannot say that she is legislating and the judge cannot say that she is judging, in paradigmatic cases, unless there is some performance of their actions by the addressees as they intend.

The distinction between potentiality/actuality clarifies the structure of practical reason as a capacity that is actualised when we act intentionally. We can now understand that the features of an intentional action identified by Anscombe can be illuminated by the potentiality/actuality distinction. The idea that the former stages of an intentional action are swallowed up by the later stages is explained by the idea that motion is constitutive and not privative. It is not that when I begin to act I do so as an irrational or a-rational being, and that when I finish acting I am a rational being, or that I go from non-intentional to intentional action, but rather that I go from being a rational being and *potentially* intentional action to being a rational being and *actual* intentional action. Later stages begin to actualise something that was potentially there. My practical reason was always there *potentially* and the intentional action

---

[20] Makin argues that the teacher analogy is intended to show that the teleological perspective is equally appropriate for other-directed capacities and self-directed capacity (n 2) 198.

actualises an order of ideas provided by my practical reason. For Anscombe, intentional action is something *actually* done, brought about according to the order conceived or imagined by the agent. If practical capacity is understood in the light of the general scheme of actuality/potentiality, then intentional action involves knowledge that is non-observational, but it might be aided by observation. In acting intentionally, I am exercising my practical reasoning capacity and this capacity is in motion. This motion is represented at the midpoint; *after* I potentially have an intention to act and *before* I have reached the result of my intentional action. It is not that the forming of an intention from nothing to something is a *magical* process. *It is rather that I potentially have the power to intend which in appropriate circumstances can be exercised.* As being in motion, I am the agent who knows *what* she is doing and *why* she is doing what she is doing, but if I observe myself doing the action, then I have stopped the action. There is no action. There is no more motion and no exercise of my capacities. Finally, Anscombe asserts that in acting intentionally, we exercise our practical knowledge. Because we are the kind of creatures that we are, we can *choose* or *decide to bring about* a state of affairs in the world and we do this according to our order of reasons. Practical knowledge is potentially in all human beings and when we decide to bring about a situation or do certain things, then we actualise this potentiality. We can direct our actions to produce either of two opposing results, eg health or illness, ignorance or knowledge, as opposed to non-rational creatures who can only produce one result under normal circumstances and with no impeding conditions, eg the bee pollinating the foxglove. It should be noted that to have an actual capacity, such as practical reasoning and the capacity to act intentionally, does not mean that A can F, nor that A will F if there are normal conditions and no impending elements. Instead it means that *A will F unless she is stopped or prevented.* Thus, once our practical reasoning capacity begins to be actualised, it will strive to produce or do what A (she) has conceived. Once A (she) decides or chooses to act, then a certain state of affairs will be produced unless she is prevented or stopped. Intentional action and practical reasoning are not dispositions like being fragile or elastic, nor are they possibilities that something will be done. They are powers.

Now that we have grasped the idea of potentiality/actuality as the general scheme for explaining the structure of practical reason, we can turn to the rule-compliance phenomenon which raises a different set of difficulties that will be dealt with in the next section.

4.3 LAW AND *ENERGEIA*: HOW CITIZENS COMPLY WITH LEGAL RULES?

So far we have argued that an intentional action is the bringing about of things or states of affairs in the world. We can argue, too, that there are different kinds of bringing about. Human beings can produce houses, clocks, tables, tea cups, and so on, but we can also produce rules of etiquette, rules for games, and legal directives, rules and principles. Legislators create legal rules and directives and judges create decisions according to underlying principles and rules. These legal rules and directives are directed to citizens for them to comply with. They are meant to be used in specific ways. When a legislator creates a rule or a judge reaches a decision that involves rules and principles, she creates them exercising her practical capacities with the intention that the citizens comply with them. But how is this compliance possible? How do legislators and judges create legal rules and directives that have the core purpose of directing others' intentional actions and of enabling them to engage in bringing about things and states of affairs in the world? In other words, how do other-directed capacities operate? This is the question that we aim to explore in this section.

In Chapter 1 (section 1.2), I gave two examples of authoritative commands to highlight the distinction between different kinds of authoritative rules:

> Scenario 1 ('Registration'): you are asked by a legal authority to fill in a form that will register you on the electorate roll.

> Scenario 2 ('Assistance at a car accident'): you are asked by an official to assist the paramedics in a car accident, eg to help by transporting the injured from the site of the accident to the ambulance, to assist by putting bandages on the victims, to keep the injured calm, and so on.

We have asserted that the performance required by the addressee is more complex in the latter example than in the former since the latter requires the engagement of the will and the performance of a series of actions over a certain period of time, and it requires that the addressee should circumvent obstacles to achieve the result according to what has been ordered. It requires that the addressee exercises her rational capacity in choosing *this* way rather than *that* way of proceeding. While the addressee executes the order she needs to make judgements about how to do *this or that*. Successful performance as intended entails knowledge about how to proceed at each step in order to perform the series of actions that are constitutive of what has been commanded. This cannot be done unless our practical reasoning and intentional action are involved in the performance. In other words, the successful execution of the order requires the engagement of practical reasoning and therefore of our intentions. Furthermore, it requires an understanding of the *telos* or end as a good-making characteristic of what has been commanded. In the case of 'Assistance at a car accident', it requires engagement with the health and well-being of the victims of the accident. Thus, the addressee needs to know that the bandage ought to be applied in *this way* and not *that way in order* to stop the bleeding, and she knows that she needs to stop the bleeding *in order* for the victim to have the right volume of blood in his body. The victim needs a certain volume of blood in his body in order to be healthy and being 'healthy' is something good and to be secured.

Because our practical reasoning capacity is a two-way capacity (section 4.2.2) the agent needs to *decide or choose* to actualise this capacity which, prior to actuality, is mere potentiality. As in our previous example (section 4.2.2) the speaker needs to *decide or choose* to speak in order to actualise her potentiality of speaking English. Then the exercise of her capacity to speak actualises according to a certain underlying practical knowledge, eg the order of the sentences, grammar, style, and so on. It is not the case that as a bee pollinates a foxglove without any decision or choice by the bee, the agent will speak English and actualise her potential capacity to speak. In the case of legal rules, the question that emerges is how a legislator or judge can produce or bring about something that will engage the citizens' intentions so that they comply with legal rules or directives that are constituted by a complex series of actions. The core argument is that legislators and judges intend that citizens comply with legal directives and rules, and this intention is not merely a mental state that represents a way of cooperating and laying plans to achieve an aim.[21] On the contrary, for the legislators' and judges' intentions (ie to engage the citizens' practical reasoning) to be successful, they need to exercise their own practical reason. It is not that they interpret or construct the citizens' mental states and interior thoughts so that their values and desires can constitute the ground that enables legislators, judges and officials to construct the best possible rules, directives or legal decisions according to the citizens' values as represented in their beliefs. On the contrary, they will look outward to *what* is of value and *why* certain states of affairs and doings are valuable (see the discussion on the transparency condition at sections 3.3 and 5.3.1, see also the discussion on Dworkin at section 10.6). Reasons for actions as values and goods that are the grounds of legal rules and directives will engage others' practical reason, therefore the citizens' practical reasoning power or capacity become an *actuality*. If, as I have argued, our intentional actions become *actuality* by an order of reasons in actions and for actions that are ultimately grounded on good-making characteristics, then legislators and judges need to conceive the order of reasons as good-making characteristics that will ground their legal rules, legal directives and decisions. Judges and legislators would hence take the first-person deliberative stance as the privileged position of practical reasoning to disentangle *what* good is required and *why* it is required (see also section 10.6). In other words, if as judge or legislator you intend that your legal rule or directive is to be followed by the addressees and, *arguendo*, because these legal rules and directives are grounded on an order of reasons, then you cannot bring about this state of affairs, ie rule-compliance, without

---

[21] See S Shapiro, *Legality* (Cambridge, MA, Harvard University Press, 2011) for an attempt to show that legal systems are created by collective intentions of planners (legislators and judges).

thinking and representing to yourself the underlying order of reasons. Let me give a simple example. You are writing an instruction manual on how to operate a coffee machine. You need to represent to yourself a series of actions and the underlying order of reasons to guide the manual's users. If you are a person of certain expertise, eg a manufacturer of coffee machines, then the practical knowledge that entails the underlying order of reasons is actualised without much learning and thinking. The required operating instructions are actualised as a native English speaker speaks English, after being in silence. By contrast, if you have only just learned to write instruction manuals for coffee machines, then you need to ask yourself 'why do it this way'? (see Chapter 3 and Chapter 4) at each required action to make the machine to function. This process guarantees understanding of the *know-how* to operate the machine, and the success of the manual is measured by the fact that future buyers of the coffee machine are able to operate it. When legislators and judges create legal directives and legal rules they operate like the writers of instruction manuals, though at a more complex level. They need to ensure that the addressees will decide or choose to act intentionally to comply with the legal rules or directives and thereby bring about the intended state of affairs. But they also need to ensure that the order of reasons is the correct one so that the intended state of affairs will be brought about by the addressees. We have learned that the early stages of an intentional action are 'swallowed up' by the later stages and ultimately by the reason as a good-making characteristic that unifies the series of actions. Thus, for addressees with certain rational capacities and in paradigmatic cases, understanding the grounding reasons as good-making characteristics of the legal rules and legal directives will enable them to decide or choose to comply with the rule and will guide them through the different series of actions that are required for compliance with the rules and directives.

Legal rules and directives do not exist like houses, chairs, tables or cups of tea. We need to follow them for them to exist. But we create legal rules and directives as we create houses, chairs, tables. We bring these things about by exercising our practical capacity and we are responsive to an order of reasons as good-making characteristics that we, as creators, formulate and understand. Thus, builders create houses that are either majestic or simple, elegant or practical, affordable or luxurious. To achieve the intended features of a house, builders need to select specific materials and designs, hire skilled workers, and so on. Similarly, legislators, officials and judges create legal directives and rules to pursue a variety of goods, eg to achieve safety, justice, the protection of rights, and so on. Legislators, officials and judges actualise their practical reasoning by creating an order of reasons in actions that will ground rules so that we are able to comply with them because we actualise our practical reasoning. Like builders, legislators, officials and judges need to choose values, goods and rights that will be fostered or protected by their rules or directives.

Likewise, they need to formulate legal rules and directives that will have appropriate sanctions, are clearly phrased and follow procedures for their publicity. In this way, they make the addressee of a directive choose or decide to actualise their potential practical reasoning capacity to comply with legal rules and directives. The addressees of a legal directive or rule are not like bees, who without decision and, given normal conditions and the absence of impediments, will pollinate the foxglove. As addressees of legal directives and legal rules, we need to choose or decide to bring about a state of affairs or things which are intended by the legislator, official or judge. This is precisely why I say in Chapter 8 that legal authority operates under the guise of an ethical-political account since it needs to present legal rules and directives as grounded on reasons for action as good-making characteristics.

We now see that the model of authority formulated by Wolff is implausible. The model is as follows (section 1.1):

X performs an action p-ing *because Y has said so.*

As rational creatures, we are responsive to reasons as grounded in good-making characteristics, but if this is truly the case, then how do mere expressions of doings as brute facts such as 'because I said so' make *actual* our practical reason? In fact this is only possible if 'because I said so' involves reasons in action that are grounded in good-making characteristics, eg 'I am the authority and compliance with the authority has good-making characteristics' (see Chapter 7 and Chapter 8). For example, compliance with authority is a secure way that some goods – apparent or genuine (see Chapter 9) – will be achieved. The potentiality/actuality and capacity/change discussion shows that as intellectual and rational beings, we need to apprehend the 'form' that underlies the brute fact 'because I said so' in order to be able to comply with legal directives and rules. The 'form' takes the shape of goods and values that are intended to be achieved by legislators, officials and judges. If it were a matter of facts, and we were able to apprehend the brute fact of 'because I said so' by our senses, then how could we control and direct the doings and bringing about that are intended by legislators and judges? Some stages of the action will *seem* this and other stages will *seem* that. There is no way to bring about *this* and not *that*. Let us take the example of 'Assistance at the car accident'. I assist the official at the car accident *because he has said* so. I have no reason to assist him at the car accident; my action is only *caused* by my fear of sanction, ie a psychological impulse in me. But now as I am merely guided by my senses, it *seems* to me that I need to put the bandage on in this way rather than that way, but my sight says that, *not* it is rather *that* way, or better this. Since I am guided by my eyes and other senses, I do not know *why* I should apply the bandage or *how* I should apply the bandage. Furthermore, how can we attribute responsibility as we cannot be blamed for not 'seeing' or 'hearing' appropriately? By analogy, mere scribbles on the board by the teacher cannot make the pupil understand the topic that the teacher is teaching. The teacher needs to make transparent the premises and conclusions of her arguments so that the pupils can 'grasp' the form of the argument and can *themselves* infer its conclusion.

There is an alternative strategy to showing how 'because I said so' operates as a fact. This view is that the legal authority – by positing legal rules and directives and by saying 'because I said so' – triggers a dormant reason for action which is represented by a belief in the agent who will comply with the rule because there is a causal nexus between the agent's belief and the action. I reject this view in section 10.3. But we have also learned that the causal nexus is not how we primarily understand how intentional actions operate and work (Chapters 2 and 3).

The classical model of practical reasoning and intentional action also laid out the view that for an action to be controlled and guided by the agent, the reasons need to be in the action and therefore transparent to the agent (see sections 3.3 and 5.3.1). The answers to the question 'why'? provide the order of reasons that guarantees successful compliance with the legal rules and directives by the agent. They are the *reasons in action* that the agent has. But if the order of reasons is opaque, how can there be an action as intended by the legislator or judge as an order of reasons? If the reasons are opaque and you do something 'because someone says so' you do not know under which description you are performing the action. Therefore, the action is non-intentional (see section 8.5). Furthermore, one might assert, the legislator, judge or official is not the origin of change and the origin of change is in external empirical factors, eg the fear *mechanism* that acts within the agent, psychological processes in the agent, and so on.

Aquinas[22] tells us that when you command, it is an act of reason for something to be *done*. He also adds that an act of will can be commanded. In the intra-personal case, you are able to command yourself to do x-ing, but you need to command it to yourself, *to will it*. In other words, you need to engage in thinking about why x-ing is good or to be pursued. Why is this not the same for inter-personal cases? Legal authorities command as an act of reason a command to do x-ing, but legal authorities command it to will it. Therefore, legal authorities ought to present legal rules and directives as grounded on good-making characteristics.

In the previous three chapters I gave a detailed explanation of the 'guise of the good' model. In the following chapters, we will see how this model enables us to solve difficulties concerning the nature of legal normativity and authority.

---

[22] T Aquinas, *Summa Theologica* (Latin and English text, Thomas Gilby (trans), Cambridge, Cambridge University Press, 2006) Q17, 5.

5

*A Defence of the Parasitic Thesis: A Re-examination of Hart's Internal Point of View**

THE PARASITIC THESIS aims to show that conceptions of legal normativity based on the social or psychological features of agents are parasitic on the 'guise of the good' model. This chapter will concentrate on Hart's notion of the internal point of view whilst Chapter 6 will look at Kelsen's notion of legal normativity.

5.1 HART'S MODEL OF INTENTIONAL ACTION AND THE PARASITIC THESIS

HLA Hart in his book *The Concept of Law*[1] advanced an important idea that aimed to solve fundamental problems in our understanding of the normative character of law: the internal point of view. The internal point of view might be seen as a promising explanation of how rules provide reasons for actions to legal participants and, consequently as a promising explanation of legal obligation and the duty-imposing character of law. If the internal point of view is thought to provide a satisfactory explanation of how law creates duties and imposes obligations, this should mean the triumph of legal positivism over natural law conceptions, as the internal point of view would be able to show that there is no need to postulate a common good as mysteriously metaphysical[2] that is only realisable through the law to explain the normativity of law. Legal positivism would also triumph over empirical views of the law as it would show that there is something more to the law than merely power or predictable facts such as the mental states of judges and citizens. Yet the notion of the internal

---

* This chapter relies on material published in 'Social and Justified Normativity: Unlocking the Mystery of the Relationship' (2012) 25 *Ratio Juris* 409 © Blackwell Publishing Ltd.
[1] HLA Hart, *The Concept of Law, 2nd edn* (Oxford, Clarendon Press, 1994).
[2] ibid 82.

point of view remains obscure and confusing.[3] I have traced elsewhere[4] the historical roots of Hart's idea of the internal point of view and show the inherent tensions between a social and publicly ascertainable conception of the internal point of view and the demands of a much more robust normative conception. Central to Hart's internal point of view is the idea of 'acceptance' and intentional action. If officials' actions *are guided* by legal rules, their actions must be both intentional and voluntary. But how should we understand Hart's conception of intentional action? This chapter aims to disentangle the underpinning conception of intentional action that Hart's internal point of view would need to presuppose for it to be intelligible. Reaching an understanding of his underpinning conception of intentional action might enable us to look more favourably upon his attempt to lay out an intermediate realm between empirical-predictive theories of law and natural law views. In the 1980s a number of criticisms were levelled against Hart's idea of the internal point of view. John Finnis[5] advanced the view that the 'internal point of view' is an unstable position, Joseph Raz[6] put forward the view that Hart's practice theory of legal rules cannot explain how legal rules provide reasons for actions and impose obligations and duties on citizens and officials, and Ronald Dworkin[7] adumbrated the view that there needs to be 'an interpretive stance' toward the end or point of our practices, and that the best possible interpretation of what our legal practices are ought to satisfy the two criteria of fitness with our past legal materials and moral soundness. All of these criticisms are illuminating but they do not explain *why* the *internal point of view* as formulated by Hart cannot per-

---

[3] In the last 10 years, there has been an important body of literature that discusses Hart's idea of the 'internal point of view'. See S Shapiro, 'What is the Internal Point of View?' (2006) 75 *Fordham Law Review* 1157; S Shapiro, 'The Bad Man and the Internal Point of View' in S Burton (ed), *The Path of Law and Its Influence: The Legacy of Oliver Wendell Holmes, Jr* (Cambridge, Cambridge University Press, 2000) 158–96; J Coleman, *The Practice of Principles* (Oxford, Oxford University Press, 2001); B Zipursky, 'Legal Obligations and the Internal Aspect of Rules' (2006) 75 *Fordham Law Review* 1229; S Perry, 'Hart on Social Rules and the Foundations of Law: Liberating the Internal Point of View' (2006) 75 *Fordham Law Review* 1171; S Perry, 'Interpretation and Methodology in Legal Theory' in A Marmor (ed), *Law and Interpretation* (Oxford, Clarendon Press, 1995) 97; S Perry, 'Holmes versus Hart: The Bad Man in Legal Theory' in S Burton (ed), *The Path of Law and Its Influence: The Legacy of Oliver Wendell Holmes, Jr* (Cambridge, Cambridge University Press, 2000) 158; D Patterson, 'Explicating the Internal Point of View' (1999) 52 *Southern Methodist University Law Review* 67; F Schauer, 'Fuller's Internal Point of View' (1994) 13 *Law and Philosophy* 285; M Adler, 'Social Facts, Constitutional Interpretation and the Rule of Recognition' in M Adler (ed), *The Rule of Recognition and the US Constitution* (Oxford, Oxford University Press, 2009) and R Holton, 'Positivism and the Internal Point of View' (1998) 17 *Law and Philosophy* 567.

[4] V Rodriguez-Blanco, P Winch and HLA Hart, 'Two Concepts of the Internal Point of View' (2007) *Canadian Journal of Law and Jurisprudence* 453.

[5] J Finnis, *Natural Law and Natural Rights* (Oxford, Clarendon Press, 1980).

[6] J Raz, *Practical Reason and Norms* (Oxford, Oxford University Press, 1999, originally published in 1975).

[7] R Dworkin, *Taking Rights Seriously* (London, Duckworth, 1977) and *Law's Empire* (Cambridge, MA, Harvard University Press, 1986).

form the task of explaining the normative character of legal rules.[8] John Finnis provides some guidance to elucidate this point in the first chapter of his book *Natural Law and Natural Rights*. He argues that law should be understood from the deliberative point of view – in his terminology the point of view of the man who possesses practical reasonableness – and not from the internal point of view. Using the Aristotelian notion of central analysis or focal meaning, Finnis purports to show that the deliberative point of view is the central or paradigmatic case to determine the nature of law. In my view, the Aristotelian notion of the central case does not sufficiently assist us in showing the primary role of the deliberative point of view[9] that Finnis aims to defend. The argumentative strategy of this and proceeding chapters is, following the Finnisian line of thinking, to adumbrate arguments to show the primary role of the deliberative point of view in understanding the nature of law. I show that the notion of intentional action as outward-looking towards an end as a good-making characteristic is *primary* to the inward notion of intentional action that relies on the desires/beliefs coupling.

Contrary to the view advocated by Hart's critics, Hart did not think that the internal point of view could explain how legal rules can impose duties and obligations. On the contrary, Hart aimed to explain the *beliefs* of legal participants who *recognise* that law imposes duties and obligations.[10] In other words, Hart aimed to explain the social normativity of law. Arguably, Hart was not interested in the justified character of the normativity of law whereby the law-abiding citizen is guided by legal rules as providing reasons for actions and imposing genuine obligations. Hart aimed to describe the behaviour of participants when they *accept* rules which they *believe* are duty-imposing and reason-giving. However, the social normativity of law is merely a *partial* explanation of the normative character of the law and this is, perhaps, the target of Hart's critics. They are dissatisfied, rightly in my view, with the notion of social normativity if it is presented as a *comprehensive* explanation of the normativity of law.

This chapter aims to defend the thesis that Hart's notion of social normativity is *parasitic* on the notion of justified normativity (*the parasitic thesis*). The arguments adumbrated in this chapter do not purport to show that Hart's notion of social normativity is false. Rather, the point of the chapter is more subtle; it aims to show that justified normativity *is prior to* and more important than the social normativity of law adumbrated by Hart. Furthermore, the intelligibility of the latter depends on the intelligibility of the former.

---

[8] Raz criticises Hart because, he says, the notion of practice cannot explain the normative character of law. However, he does not explain why Hart's internal point of view cannot provide a satisfactory explanation of this character. See Raz, (n 6) 53–58.

[9] See my article 'Is Finnis Wrong?' (2007) *Legal Theory* 257.

[10] E Pattaro, *The Law and the Right: A Reappraisal of the Reality that Ought to be* (Dordrecht and New York, Springer, 2005).

The chapter is divided into three parts. The first part examines Hart's underpinning notion of intentional action and its relation to his idea of the internal point of view. The second part shows the limits and paradoxical nature of Hart's notion of intentional action. The third part considers some possible objections to the *parasitic thesis*.

5.2 HART'S NON-COGNITIVIST ACCOUNT OF INTENTIONAL ACTION AND THE INTERNAL POINT OF VIEW

5.2.1 Some Textual Analysis

Contrary to Kelsen, who only aims to explain the regulative role of law, Hart aims to explain the guiding role of legal rules. He emphasises the view that rules should be examined not only from the point of view of the legal official who applies them, or the legal scientist who aims to know and explain them, but also from the point of view of the man who wishes to be *guided* by such legal rules. For Hart a legal official, such as a judge, also uses the rule as his guide and the *breach of the rule as his reason and justification for punishing the offender*.[11] Apart from applying sanctions, legal rules guide the behaviour of citizens and officials. In his book *The Concept of Law*, Hart points out: '*The principal functions of the law as a means of social control are not to be seen in private litigation or prosecutions, which represent vital but still ancillary provisions for the failures of the system. It is to be seen in the diverse ways in which the law is used to control, to guide, and to plan life out of court*'.[12] Shortly after this Hart asserts:

> Rules conferring private powers must, if they are to be understood, be looked at from the point of view of those who exercise them. They appear then as an additional element introduced by the law into social life over and above that of coercive control. This is so because possession of these legal powers makes of the private citizen, who, if there were no such rules, would be a mere duty-bearer, a private legislator . . . Those who exercise these powers to make authoritative enactments and orders use these rules in a form of purposive activity utterly different from performance of duty or submission to coercive control.[13]

For the legal official and the citizen the predictive aspect of the legal rule is irrelevant, the judge does not say 'this man will breach the rule and then we will punish him', and the citizen does not say 'I will breach this legal rule, then the authority will punish me'. By contrast, Hart tells us, rules have terms such as 'ought', 'must', 'obligation', 'should' and a sound understanding of such terms cannot be achieved if we consider that legal rules have a merely predic-

---

[11] Hart (n 1) 10.
[12] ibid 39.
[13] ibid 40–41.

tive function. The terms 'ought', 'must', 'obligation' and 'should' are addressed to the legal community in order to determine what should be done and how affairs should be organised. Hart criticises Austin for reducing legal rules to commands and habits.[14] For Austin, law is conceived as a coercive order that creates a habit of obedience. Hart argues, however that portraying law in this way does not help us in distinguishing law from illegitimate situations of coercion. When we obey the law we say that we have an obligation, we do not say that we have been obliged. According to the Austinian theory of law, therefore, there is no distinction between the threats of the state and those of the gangster. Threats and coercion result in effective obedience to the law because there is a *belief* in the possibility of coercion.[15] But how many people must either (effectively) obey the legal rules or believe sufficiently in the threat to have a settled legal system? Hart raises doubts about the possibility that general habitual obedience to general orders backed by threats explains the *settled character and continuity which legal systems possess*.[16] Furthermore, as the above quotation demonstrates, criminal legal rules are just one specific type of rule; there are other kinds of rules, such as rules that confer powers to make wills or contracts, these rules are related to capacity and cannot be described as orders backed by threats.

But how does Hart account for the guiding function of legal rules without resorting to the idea of the common good or moral ideals?[17] Hart identifies the following key features possessed by social rules: criticism or deviation from the rules is regarded as legitimate or justified;[18] followers of social rules have a reflective critical attitude,[19] this means they regard rules as the standard according to which they adjust their behaviour; and they use normative language such as 'you ought to', 'I ought not to', 'you must do that', 'that is right', 'that is wrong'.[20] Where can we find an explanation of these features of social rules? Hart's answer is that social rules, as distinctive from habits, have an *internal aspect*.[21] The internal aspect is shown by acceptance and use of the rule. Thus, accepted rules are forward-looking, their aim is to regulate and guide future behaviour, not to predict behaviour. For Hart it is only required that officials *accept* legal rules from the internal point of view;[22] but how can this acceptance *be known or observed*? Hart argues that general acceptance is a

---

[14] ibid 18–25.
[15] ibid 23.
[16] ibid 24.
[17] See Finnis (n 5); I Fuller, *The Morality of Law*, 2nd edn (New Haven, CT, Yale University Press, 1969); N Simmonds, *Law as a Moral Idea* (Oxford, Oxford University Press, 2007).
[18] Hart (n 1).
[19] ibid 54.
[20] ibid 56.
[21] ibid 55–56.
[22] ibid 59.

complex phenomenon; officials may expressly say that they accept the fundamental rules of the legal system, and the legislators will make laws according to the rules. Thus, it is not required that the citizens accept the legal rules,[23] but in a healthy legal system citizens do show this acceptance. Through making their acceptance conspicuous, they contribute to the *existence* of the legal system.[24] According to Hart, the Austinian sanction theory of law does not show the a*ctive* aspect of identifying, applying and obeying the law. Hart puts this as follows: '*The weakness of the doctrine is that it obscures or distorts the other relatively active aspect, which is seen primarily, though not exclusively, in the law-making, law-identifying and law-applying operations of officials or experts of the system. Both aspects must be kept in view if we are to see the complex social phenomenon for what it actually is*'.[25]

But what does Hart mean by 'acceptance' of a rule? What is this *active* element that, for Hart, is so central to understanding what law is? We cannot understand how the rule of recognition can perform all of its complex functions without an understanding of the *active* element that Hart identifies. Hart recognises the important connection between rules and actions. He argues that there are two main kinds of rules: rules that confer powers, public or private, and rules that impose duties. Both kinds concern *actions* and the latter kind involve variation upon or the creation of duties and obligations.[26]

5.2.2 Hart's Non-cognitivism

There are a number of possible interpretative solutions that can be provided in answer to the questions 'what does Hart mean by "acceptance" of a rule? and what is this *active* element that for Hart is so central to understanding what law is?'. First, one can assert that Hart as a non-cognitivist[27] in relation to normative statements would assert that 'acceptance' of legal rules by officials and citizens is merely an expression or an attitude of approval towards these legal rules. It does not describe normative facts, values or what is good. Citizens and judges are not saying that legal rules are *obligatory* but merely that they are *judged* to be obligatory and that this is *expressed* by those who accept such rules. How are intentional actions to be interpreted as being non-

---

[23] ibid 59.

[24] ibid 59.

[25] ibid 60.

[26] ibid 79.

[27] Kevin Toh, 'Hart's Expressivism and his Benthamite Project' in (2005) 11 *Legal Theory* 75, has argued that Hart advocates a non-cognitivist theory of normative statements. See also his article 'Raz on Detachment, Acceptance and Describability' (2007) 27 *Oxford Journal of Legal Studies* 403.

cognitivist? According to non-cognitivists,[28] intentions are mental states and an adequate naturalistic psychological theory should be able to provide a full explanation of such states. However, there seems to be a tension between Hart's non-cognitivism[29] and his rejection of sanction-based and predictive theories of law.[30] There is an explanatory gap in Hartian texts on this issue. What kind of non-cognitivism did he advocate? What are the implications of his non-cognitivism for his understanding of intentional actions and practices in the context of the law and their relation to legal rules? This is a problem for Hart as plausible explanations of non-cognitivism are naturalist and therefore tend to sit well with 'scientific' theories of behaviour and intentional action. In spite of this tension, let us pursue the non-cognitivist reading of the notion of 'acceptance' of the legal rule. Alan Gibbard is one of the most sophisticated defenders of non-cognitivism or expressivism in morality and rationality. In his book *Wise Choices, Apt Feelings*,[31] he begins his inquiry with the question 'What is rational to do or believe?'. In other words, 'what does it make sense to do', and 'what ought we to do?'.[32] His answer, which has a Hartian flavour, is that 'to call something rational is to *express* one's acceptance of norms that permit it'.[33] Using Gibbard's analysis in the context of the law, we might say that 'when I say I ought to stop at the traffic lights I am *expressing* my acceptance of the legal norms'. Gibbard is aware of how cryptic his answer is and he subsequently asks 'What does it mean to accept norms?'. Gibbard distinguishes between *internalising* a norm and *being governed* by a norm. In the former case, we act by habit and mere adaptation such as, for example, when we have a conversation with friends or strangers and physically move nearer to or away from them. There is a set of social norms concerning degrees of intimacy or distance. In the latter case, we act by *acceptance*. We work out in our community how to think, what to do and how to feel,[34] we share our evaluations and accept norms on what to do. According to Gibbard, acceptance involves spontaneous and sincere avowal and consistency.[35] Gibbard proceeds

---

[28] See S Blackburn, *Spreading the Word* (Oxford, Oxford University Press, 1984); A Gibbard, *Wise Choices, Apt Feelings* (Oxford, Clarendon Press, 1990); D Dennet, *Intentional Stance* (Cambridge, MA, MIT Press, 1987).

[29] For descriptions of HLA Hart as a non-cognitivist see J Raz, 'HLA Hart (1907–1992)' (1993) 5 *Utilitas* 148. For Hart's own description of his non-cognitivism see HLA Hart, 'Legal Duty and Obligation' in *Essays in Jurisprudence and Philosophy* (Oxford, Clarendon Press, 1983) 159–60 and 'Commands and Authoritative Legal Reasons' in the same volume at 266–67.

[30] For an illuminating discussion of the tension between Hart's non-cognitivism and his criticism of the sanction-based and predictive theories of law and Hart's difficulties in explaining legal normativity, see Perry, 'Hart on Social Rules and the Foundations of Law' (n 3).

[31] Gibbard (n 28).

[32] ibid 6–7.

[33] ibid 7.

[34] ibid 72.

[35] ibid 74–75.

to move from mere *expression* to a *psychological* condition. He states: *'Normative governance by the norm is a tendency to conform to it. Accepting a norm is whatever psychic state, if any, gives rise to this syndrome of avowal of the norm and governance of it'.*[36] This move can be explained by the fact that from the first-person perspective to say '"I accept the norm" or "we accept the norm" is merely the way either I express myself or we express ourselves' is absurd. To make sense of the first-person perspective Gibbard needs to give a more *psychological* account and this account sits well with non-cognitivist approaches concerning what I or we ought to do. Gibbard rejects the view that there is such a thing as the 'faculty of reason'[37] that exercises 'rational control'. Our different capacities for governance of action, avowal and acceptance are called by Gibbard 'putative reason'. The connection that links 'putative reason' and 'what I ought to do' is *belief*. Gibbard puts this as follows: *'On the analysis I have proposed, the connection between rationality and the deliverances of putative reason is this. For a person's faculty of putative reason to permit something is for the person to believe that thing to be rational'.*[38]

We can reconstruct Hart's notion of 'acceptance' of a rule as the view that *beliefs* and *motives* are sufficient to establish the truth of the proposition that 'X accepts the legal rule'. The explanation will be that X has a pro-attitude, ie a desire, a motive to follow the rule and believes that this type of action is the one indicated by the rule towards which he has a pro-attitude.[39] Is this how we should understand the notion of 'acceptance'? Thus, the legal rule that 'vehicles should not park in the Park' *is accepted by* the citizen or the official if and only if he *believes* that the type of action that is commanded by the rule is the action that he favours, and he has a pro-attitude, ie a belief or desire, to act following the pattern of behaviour such as 'I *want* to follow this pattern of behaviour because it is beneficial for me'. We can formulate this as follows:

> *Acceptance thesis: C accepts the legal rule LR if and only if (a) he believes that the type of action or pattern of behaviour that is indicated by the rule is the one that he has a pro-attitude towards and (b) he has a pro-attitude (desire/ motives) towards the pattern of behaviour indicated by the rule.*

Thus, for example, in the case of the rules of chess, I have a desire to act according to the rules of the game of chess as I want to play chess and I believe that to move the queen and the knight in such-and-such a way are part of the pattern of behaviour indicated by the rules of chess. Similarly, *qua* legislator I desire to act according to the rules that regulate the process to

---

[36] ibid 75.

[37] ibid 81.

[38] ibid 81.

[39] Davidson has formulated these two conditions in 'Actions, Reasons and Events' in *Essays on Actions and Events* (Oxford, Clarendon Press, 1980) 3–19. This analysis is modified in his essay 'Intending' which is published in the same collection. However, he still maintains the causal account of intentions. For an illuminating critique of introspection or the inward approach see R Hursthouse, 'Intention' in R Teichman (ed), *Logic, Cause and Action* (Cambridge, Cambridge University Press, 2000) 83.

enact statutes, and I believe that to raise my hand to vote for the enactment of the statute is the type of action or pattern of behaviour that is indicated by the rule and the one that I have a pro-attitude towards.

At first glance, Hart seems to reject this interpretation:

> Thus not only is it the case that the facts about B's actions and his beliefs and motives in the gunman case, though sufficient to warrant the statement that B was obliged to hand over his purse, are not sufficient to warrant the statement that he had an obligation to do this; it is also the case that facts of this sort, ie facts about beliefs and motives, are not *necessary* for the truth of a statement that a person had an obligation to do something. Thus the statement that a person has an obligation, eg to tell the truth or report for military service, remains true even if he believed (reasonably or unreasonably) that he would never be found out and had nothing to fear from disobedience.[40]

It appears, in this paragraph, that Hart collapses the notion of 'a pro-attitude towards following a pattern of behaviour and the belief that the type of action indicated by the rule is the one that is favoured' with the idea that 'his pro-attitude is the fear of disobedience'. In other words, he collapses the sanction theory of law, the predictive theory of law and the belief/pro-attitude conception of intentional action. In other paragraphs, it is unclear whether the 'acceptance thesis' is the one that underlies his notion of the acceptance of a legal rule. Let us examine carefully the following paragraph:

> When we move a piece in chess in accordance with the rules, or stop at the traffic light when it is red, our rule-complying behaviour is often a direct response to the situation, unmediated by calculation in terms of the rules. The evidence that such actions are a genuine application of the rule is their setting in certain circumstances. Some of these precede the particular action and others follow it: and some of them are stateable only in general and hypothetical terms. The most important of these factors which show that in acting we have applied a rule is that *if* behaviour is challenged we are disposed to justify it by reference to the rule: and the genuineness of our acceptance of the rule may be manifested not only in our past and subsequent acknowledgements of it and conformity to it, but in our criticism of our own and others' deviation from it. On such or similar evidence we may indeed conclude that if, before our 'unthinking' compliance with the rule, we had been asked to say what the right thing to do was and why, we would, if honest, have cited the rule in reply. It is this setting of our behaviour among such circumstances, and not its accompaniment by explicit thought of the rule, that is necessary to distinguish an action which is genuinely an observance of a rule from one that merely happens to coincide with it. It is thus that we would distinguish, as a compliance with an accepted rule, the adult chess-player's move from the action of the baby who purely pushed the piece into the right place.[41]

[40] Hart (n 1) 81.
[41] ibid 136–37.

According to Hart, the acceptance of the rule is shown explicitly, ie through acknowledgement of the rule, or implicitly as (a) criticism when there is deviation; (b) justifying reason when one is challenged; (c) justifying reason when one is asked to reflect on one's actions. Are these all 'expressions' or 'attitudes' towards the rules? Let us imagine three different examples that reflect Hart's notion of acceptance of a rule:

> *(A) You are playing chess and the other player incorrectly moves the knight. You criticise her and ask her why has she broken the rules.*

> *(B) You are playing chess and the other player asks you why you are moving the queen in such a way (challenging mood). You respond that you are moving your queen according to the rules of chess.*

> *(C) You are playing chess and the other player asks you why are you moving the queen in such a way (reflective or justificatory mood). You respond because this is the rule of chess on how to move the queen.*

In all three cases, you have shown that you accept the rules of recognition. But *to whom* has it been *expressed* that *you* accept the rules of chess? It has been *expressed* to the other player and when we ask the other player, 'how do you know that your opponent accepts the rules of chess?' he has two possible answers. He can take an outward-looking approach and, seeking an understanding of the action, he could ask you, '*why* do you move your hands?'; the answer to this will be 'to move the queen'; he could then ask 'why did you move the queen?'; and the answer to this will be 'to play chess', but the enquiry could continue and he might ask 'why do you play chess?'; the response to this might be 'to win' or 'to be entertained'. The end of the action is presented as a good-making characteristic and you could infer that he accepts the rule. We could formulate this 'acceptance thesis*' as follows:

> *Acceptance thesis*: C accepts the legal rule if and only if (a) his actions are explained in terms of other actions and such actions are the core instance of what it is to follow the legal rule and (b) the purpose or end of the action is its reason and is formulated as a good-making characteristic.*[42]

The problem with the 'acceptance thesis*' is that it involves an *evaluation* and understanding of the end of actions that are instances of 'following a

---

[42] For a criticism of the idea that a reason for action ought to be presented as a good-making characteristic, see R Hursthouse, 'Arational Actions' (1991) 57 *Journal of Philosophy* 57–58; M Stocker, 'Desiring the Bad: An Essay in Moral Psychology' (1979) *Journal of Philosophy* 738 and K Setiya, *Reasons Without Rationalism* (Princeton, NJ, Princeton University Press, 2007) 62–67. Cf J Raz, 'Agency, Reason and the Good' in *Engaging Reasons* (Oxford, Oxford University Press, 2000) 22–45. For a helpful discussion of the idea of values as part of our actions see G Watson, 'Free Agency' (1975) *Journal of Philosophy* 205. See Chapter 4 for a full discussion of this criticism.

rule'. This means that in order to understand the action as intelligible, one needs to understand that the end or goal has a 'good-making' characteristic for the agent who performs the action. It has been proposed that one does not need to endorse the good-making characteristic of the action to be performed as it merely involves identifying the 'good-making' characteristics of the action *for the agent*. Raz has advanced this in a sophisticated form. He argues that there is a detached viewpoint from where we can make evaluations without endorsing them. We will discuss this view in later sections (5.3.4 and 5.4). It will be called 'the detached viewpoint on the "acceptance thesis*"'.

The second possibility is to argue that the other player knows that you accept the rules of chess because he has identified your beliefs and pro-attitudes, ie your desire to play chess and your belief that moving the queen is a pattern of behaviour indicated by the rules of chess. In other words, Hart advocates the 'acceptance thesis'.

In the next section, I will reject the view that the 'the acceptance thesis' and 'the detached viewpoint on the "the acceptance thesis*"' are independent from the 'acceptance thesis*'. First, I will argue that the 'acceptance thesis' presupposes that the player is able to take the theoretical viewpoint of the other player's agency and I will show that such a theoretical viewpoint is parasitic on a deliberative or first-person perspective.[43] I will adumbrate the 'social version of the acceptance thesis' and argue that this might be seen as the most plausible view advocated by Hart. However, I will also argue that the 'social version of the acceptance thesis' is also dependent on the 'acceptance thesis*'. In other words, I will show that (1) the 'acceptance thesis' and the 'social version of the acceptance thesis' are parasitic on the 'acceptance thesis*'; (2) that, contrary to appearances, 'the detached point of view of the "acceptance thesis*"' is a *theoretical* standpoint that depends on the *deliberative* viewpoint of intentional actions. In other words, 'the detached point of view of the "acceptance thesis*"' is parasitic on the 'acceptance thesis*'. These two core arguments constitute the 'parasitic conception' that I defend.[44]

---

[43] For an explanation of the 'deliberative point of view' see Chapters 2 and 4. See also J Finnis, 'Law and What I Truly Should Decide' (2003) 48 *American Journal of Jurisprudence* 107 and 'On Hart's Ways: Law as Reason and as Fact' in *The Legacy of H.L.A. Hart* (Oxford, Oxford University Press, 2008).

[44] The parasitic conception is endorsed by Finnis (n 5) 11–19 and 233–37, but he does not explain *how* this parasitic conception works. This is the task I have set myself.

5.3 WHY DID I PARK MY VEHICLE IN THE PARK?:
A DEFENCE OF THE PARASITIC CONCEPTION

5.3.1 The Practical Standpoint: the Distinction Between the Deliberative and the Theoretical Viewpoints

What is the distinction between practical and theoretical knowledge? Let us take a modified version of the example provided by Anscombe in *Intention*.[45] A man is asked by his wife to go to the supermarket with a list of products to buy. A detective is following him and makes notes of his actions. The man reads in the list 'butter', but chooses margarine. The detective writes in his report that the man has bought margarine. The detective gives an account of the man's actions in terms of the evidence he himself has. By contrast, the man gives an account of his actions in terms of the reasons for actions that he *himself* has. However, the man knows his intentions or reasons for actions not on the basis of evidence that he has *of* himself. His reasons for actions or intentions are self-intimating or self-verifying. He acts from the deliberative or first-person perspective. There is an action according to reasons or an intention *in doing* something if there is an answer to the question *why*. It is in terms of his own description of his action that we can grasp the reasons for the man's actions. In reply to the question '*why* did you buy margarine instead of butter?', the man might answer that he did so because it is better for his health. This answer, following Aristotle's theory of action[46] and its contemporary interpretations advanced by Anscombe, provides a reason for action as a desirability or good-making characteristic. According to Anscombe, the answer is intelligible to us and inquiries as to *why* the action has been commit-

---

[45] E Anscombe, *Intention, 2nd edn* (Cambridge, MA, Harvard University Press, 2000, originally published in 1957) para 32.

[46] Aristotle, *Nichomachean Ethics* I.i.2; III. V.18–21 (H Rackham (trans), Cambridge, MA, Harvard University Press, 1934). See also T Aquinas, *Summa Theologica* (Latin and English text, Thomas Gilby (trans), Cambridge, Cambridge University Press, 2006) Ia2æ.12, I. See also A Kenny, *Aristotle's Theory of the Will* (London, Duckworth, 1979); R Pasnau, *Thomas Aquinas on Human Nature* (Cambridge, Cambridge University Press, 2002); J Finnis, *Aquinas* (Oxford, Oxford University Press, 1998) 62–71 and 79–90. For contemporary formulations of the Aristotelian theory of intentional action see J Raz, 'Agency, Reason and the Good' in *Engaging Reason* (Oxford, Oxford University Press, 1999); W Quinn, 'Putting Rationality in Its Place' in *Morality and Action* (Cambridge, Cambridge University Press, 1993) 228–55; C Korsgaard, 'Acting for a Reason' in *The Constitution of Agency* (Oxford, Oxford University Press, 2008) 207–29); R Moran and M Stone, 'Anscombe on Expressions of Intention' in Constantine Sandis (ed), *New Essays on the Explanation of Action* (Basingstoke, Palgrave MacMillan, 2008) 132–68; M Thompson, *Life and Action* (Cambridge, MA, Harvard University Press, 2008). For the connection between the teleological view and the 'guise of the good' model see M Hanser, 'Intention and Teleology' in (1998) *Mind* 381 and M Boyle and D Lavin, 'Goodness and Desire' in *Desire, Practical Reason and the Good* (Oxford, Oxford University Press, 2010).

ted stops. However, in the case of the detective when we ask *why* did you write in the report that the man bought margarine, the answer is that it is the truth about the man's actions. In the case of the detective, the knowledge is theoretical, the detective reports the man's actions in terms of the evidence he has of it. In the case of the man, the knowledge is practical. The reasons for action are self-verifying for the agent. He or she does not need to have evidence of his own reasons for actions. This self-intimating or self-verifying understanding of our own actions from the deliberative or practical viewpoint is part of the general condition of access to our own mental states that is called the 'transparency condition'.[47] Its application to reasons for action can be formulated as follows:

> *(TC for reasons for actions) 'I can report on my own reasons for actions, not by considering my own mental states or theoretical evidence about them, but by considering the reasons themselves which I am immediately aware of*'.

The direction of fit in theoretical and practical knowledge is also different. In the former case, my assertions need to fit the world whereas in the latter, the world needs to fit my assertions. The detective needs to give an account of what the world looks like, including human actions in the world. He relies on the observational evidence he has. The detective's description of the action is tested against the tribunal of empirical evidence. If he reports that the man bought butter instead of margarine, then his description is false. The man, by contrast, might say that he intended to buy butter and instead bought margarine. He changed his mind and asserts that margarine is healthier. There is no mistake here.

---

[47] See G Evans, *The Varieties of Reference* (Oxford, Oxford University Press, 1982) 225; R Edgeley, *Reason in Theory and Practice* (London, Hutchinson and Co, 1969). The most extensive and careful contemporary treatment of the 'transparency condition' is in R Moran, *Authority and Estrangement* (Princeton, NJ, Princeton University Press, 2001). For discussions on Moran's notion of transparency, reflection and self-knowledge see B Reginster, 'Self-Knowledge, Responsibility and the Third Person' (2004) *Philosophy and Phenomenological Research* 433; G Wilson, 'Comments on Authority and Estrangement' (2004) *Philosophy and Phenomenological Research* 440; J Heal, 'Moran's *Authority and Estrangement*' (2004) *Philosophy and Phenomenological Research* 427; J Lear, 'Avowal and Unfreedom' (2004) *Philosophy and Phenomenological Research* 448; R Moran, 'Replies to Heal, Reginster, Wilson and Lear' (2004) *Philosophy and Phenomenological Research* 455; S Shoemaker, 'Moran on Self-Knowledge' (2003) *European Journal of Philosophy* 391; L O'Brien, 'Moran on Self-Knowledge' (2003) *European Journal of Philosophy* 375; R Moran, 'Responses to O'Brien and Shoemaker' (2003) *European Journal of Philosophy* 402; C Moya, 'Moran on Self-Knowledge, Agency and Responsibility' (2006) *Critica, Revista Hispanoamericana de Filosofia* 3; T Carman, 'First Persons: On Richard Moran's *Authority and Estrangement*' (2003) *Inquiry* 395. For a critical view on the transparency condition see B Gertler, 'Do We Determine What We Believe by Looking Outward?' in A Hatzimoysis (ed), *Self-Knowledge* (Oxford, Oxford University Press, 2008).

5.3.2 Problems with the 'Acceptance Thesis'

The 'acceptance thesis' presupposes an inward-looking approach to action as opposed to an outward-looking approach. The latter examines intentional actions as a series of actions that are justified in terms of other actions and in view of the purpose or end of the intentional action as a good-making characteristic, eg to put the kettle on in order to boil the water, in order to make tea *because* it is pleasant to drink tea. The former examines the mental states that rationalise the actions; however, at the ontological level, it is argued that these mental states cause the actions. The mental states consist of the belief/ pro-attitude towards the action. If the 'acceptance thesis' is the correct interpretation of Hart's central idea concerning the internal point of view towards legal rules, then criticisms that are levelled against inward-looking approaches of intentional actions also apply to the 'acceptance thesis'. The main criticism that has been raised against the idea that the belief/pro-attitude pairing can explain intentional actions is the view that it cannot explain deviations from the causal chain[48] between mental states and actions. Let us suppose that you intend to kill your enemy by running over him with your vehicle this afternoon when you will meet him at his house. Some hours before you intend to kill your enemy, you drive to the supermarket, you see your enemy walking on the pavement and you suffer a nervous spasm that causes you to suddenly turn the wheel and run over your enemy. In this example, according to the belief/pro-attitude view, there is an intentional action if you desire to kill your enemy and you believe that the action of killing your enemy, under a certain description, has that property. Ontologically, the theory would establish that you had both the desire to kill your enemy and the belief that this action has the property 'killing your enemy'. Thus, this mental state has caused the action and there is an intentional action. The problem with this view is that it needs to specify the 'appropriate causal route'. Davidson has made much effort to specify the 'attitudes that cause the action if they are to rationalise the action':[49]

> And here we see that Armstrong's analysis like the one I proposed a few pages back, must cope with the question *how* beliefs and desires cause intentional actions. Beliefs and desires that would rationalize an action if they cause it in the right way – through a cause of practical reasoning, as we might try saying – may cause it in other ways. If so, the action was not performed with the intention that we could have read off from the attitudes that caused it. What I despair of spelling out is the way in which attitudes must cause actions if they are to rationalize the action.

[48] The first person to discuss deviant causal chains was R Chisholm, 'Freedom and Action' in K Lehrer (ed), *Freedom and Determinism* (New York, Random House, 1976) 28–44.

[49] D Davidson, 'Freedom to Act' in *Essays on Actions and Events* (Oxford, Clarendon Press, 1980) 79.

In the following paragraph, Davidson seems to fear that the idea of attitudes causing action might lead to *infinite regress*:

> A climber might want to rid himself of the weight and danger of holding another man on a rope, and he might know that by loosening his hold on the rope he could rid himself of the weight and danger. This belief and want might so unnerve him as to cause him to lose his hold, and yet it might be the case that he never *chose* to loosen his hold, nor did he do it intentionally. It will not help, I think, to add that the belief and the want must combine to cause him to want to loosen his hold, for there will remain the two questions how the belief and the want caused the second want, and how wanting to loosen his hold caused him to loosen his hold.

Here we see Davidson struggling with his own proposal.[50] He asks *how attitudes must cause actions if they are to rationalise actions.* Davidson's model of intentional action does not help us to determine whether there is an intentional action, it only help us to determine the *conditions* that would explain the existence of an intentional action. The intentional action is already *given.* A similar criticism is applicable to the 'acceptance thesis' and to this we now turn.

Let us suppose that I intend to go to the Park in my car, however, I read a sign at the entrance of the Park that states 'Vehicles are not allowed to park in the Park'; I turn the wheel of my vehicle, reverse it and park a few streets away. You ask me why I turned the wheel of my vehicle, reversed and parked a few streets away from the Park, I answer that I carried out these actions because there is a rule that states 'Vehicles are not allowed to park in the Park'. According to the 'acceptance thesis', my desire to follow the pattern of behaviour indicated by the rule and my belief that turning the wheel of my vehicle, reversing it and not parking in the Park is the type of action or pattern of behaviour indicated by the rule. However, let us suppose that I desire to avoid parking in the Park and have the respective belief. In other words, I accept 'not parking in the Park'. On my way to the Park, however, whilst following directions to the Park, I take a wrong turning and end up parking just outside the Park entrance. Even though the two criteria of the 'acceptance thesis' have been met, this was not a case of following the legal rule by acceptance since I comply with the rule by accident.

The problem with the 'acceptance thesis' is that it does not consider the action from the deliberative point of view, ie as it is seen from the point of view of the agent or deliberator. When the agent explains his actions he does not examine his own mental actions, rather he looks outwards to the vehicle, the Park, the sign, and so on. The reasons for actions, ie turning the wheel to reverse the vehicle, then parking outside the Park to follow the rule, are self-evident or *transparent* to him. But then, an objector might advance, what is the

[50] For an illuminating discussion of this point see C Vogler, 'Modern Moral Philosophy Again: Isolating the Promulgation Problem' (2007) *Proceedings of the Aristotelian Society* 347.

good-making characteristic of a rule that, as in the example of the shopper who intends to buy margarine because is healthier, is the goal of the action of avoiding parking in the Park? My reply is as follows. When the driver is asked why he or she is turning the wheel and reversing the vehicle, his answer will be 'because it is the rule'. But this is still not completely *intelligible* unless we *assume* or *know* that the driver is a law-abiding citizen or that he believes in the general fairness of legal rules, etc. We can still ask him 'why, because of the rule, do you do this?'. His answer would need to be in terms of reasons as good-making characteristics for him, in order to make intelligible his intentional action. He will probably reply that he has reasons to follow the legal rule because it is the best way of preserving the peace of the Park, or that he has reasons to follow legal rules in general because it is the best way of preserving coordination[51] among the members of a community. In a nutshell, the agent or deliberator needs to provide the reasons for the action in terms of good-making characteristics and the end or reason of the action provides the *intelligible form of the action*. This explanation of action has also been called a *naïve* explanation of action as opposed to a more sophisticated explanation of action, ie in terms of mental states.

5.3.3 Social Version of the Acceptance Thesis

It could be argued that the 'acceptance thesis' is not what Hart aimed to convey when he asserted that the internal point of view and the acceptance of the rule is shown by criticism of or deviance from the following of a rule. Indeed, Hart rejected the view that mental states can cause actions as was apparent in his stern and implacable criticisms of the predictive and sanction theories of law. An interpreter might assert that we can recognise acceptance merely by observing social behaviour, including the linguistic behaviour of citizens and officials. Let us recall the example of the driver of the vehicle who wishes to follow the rule that prohibits vehicles from parking in the Park. Suppose that a friend is driving with him and *observes* that he is turning the wheel. His friend will interpret this action as meaning that the driver shares with him the social practice of following the rule 'vehicles are not permitted to park in the Park'. They both share 'the internal point of view' and the friend can see that the driver's convergence behaviour is the same as the social practice. The social version of the acceptance thesis can be formulated as follows:

---

[51] See E Anscombe, 'On the Source of Authority of the State' in *Ethics, Religion and Politics: Collected Philosophical Papers of GEM Anscombe* (Oxford, Blackwell, 1981) for an argument of authority as practical necessity.

Social version of the acceptance thesis (SVAT): X accepts the legal rule if and only if (a) there is a social pattern of behaviour as indicated by the legal rule and (b) the social pattern of behaviour is recognised as an instance of the common understanding of the content of such a rule as provided by social practice amongst the participants of a community.[52]

The problem with this definition, apart from being a mouthful, is that it does not say much about the description of the action provided by the agent himself. Thus, there can be a social pattern of behaviour as indicated by the rule 'vehicles are not allowed to park in the Park', and the recognition of such behaviour as an instance of our common understanding of the content of the rule 'vehicles are not allowed to park in the Park'. We can see a driver reversing his vehicle and avoiding parking in the Park, but it might be the case that the driver has suffered a nervous spasm and purely by accident has followed the rule. However, against the latter view, one could argue that it is unlikely that there will be a large number of cases where the rule is followed purely because of accident, habit, unconscious behaviour, etc. Therefore there will be not be a regular pattern of convergence behaviour due to equivocation. Consequently, the theorist who supports the 'social version of the acceptance thesis' will assert that the criticism is not well-grounded and that his interpretation of Hart's internal point of view is sound. However, we might object that the SVAT simply establishes *the conditions of existence of the acceptance of the rule.* In other words, the acceptance is *given* and the explanation provided only elucidates the existence condition of the *given*, the acceptance. The existence conditions are the ones established in the SVAT. It would become more perplexing had Hart adumbrated the acceptance of legal rules, ie the internal point of view towards the rules, as an explanation of the existence condition of a legal system. This might lead to an *infinite regress* as follows: do we need to analyse the existing conditions of our existing conditions of acceptance, ie the social pattern of behaviour and the recognition of the social pattern of behaviour as described in the SVAT?

Arguably, to avoid cases in which the recognition of the pattern of behaviour does not coincide with the intentional action, we need to rely on the description of the intentional action provided by the agent *himself or herself.* It is thus, in terms of the deliberative or agent's point of view that we can understand the intentional action and this is an element that the SVAT lacks. Furthermore, Hart emphasises the importance of the 'internal aspect' of the rule, where the agent is able to justify and criticise actions that aim to be

---

[52] The SVAT seems to be supported by Hart in the 'Postscript' to his *The Concept of Law*: 'Acceptance consists in the standing dispositions of individuals to take some patterns of conduct both as guides to their own future conduct and as standards of criticism which may legitimate demands and various forms of pressure for conformity'. See Hart (n 1) 255.

categorised under 'rule-following' and it can be argued that to justify and criticise these actions is somehow to describe them in terms of the point of view of the agent. Consequently, SVAT cannot be the view advocated by Hart to explain his notion of the internal point of view. The SVAT is rather *too close* to what Hart called the 'external point of view'.

I have defended the argument that the 'acceptance thesis*' better grasps the deliberative or first-person point of view. The 'acceptance thesis' is the view that comes closest to Hart's notion of the acceptance of legal rules. However, I do not wish to defend the view that the 'acceptance thesis' is false, rather I would like to defend the idea that *if the 'acceptance thesis' is sound, it is an explanation that depends on the deliberative point of view and on the 'acceptance thesis*'*. In other words, *qua* another legal participant who shares the internal point of view, if I am able to comprehend that you believe that reversing the vehicle and driving away from the Park is an instance of the type of action indicated by the legal rule, and I grasp your desire to follow the rule 'vehicles are not allowed to park in the Park', it is because I understand that you avoid parking in the Park *because* you see it as good to be a law-abiding citizen, or because, for you, the following of legal rules in general is good, or because it is good to have a peaceful Park.

5.3.4 Detached Point of View of the 'Acceptance Thesis*'

It has been argued that the 'acceptance thesis*' does not require a direct evaluation[53] of the good-making characteristics that are the ends of actions which are aimed at following legal rules. Raz adumbrates a 'detached viewpoint' or uncommitted viewpoint that provides practical advice and advances reasons for action without endorsing said reasons for action.[54] Thus, a barrister or a solicitor may explain *what* the reasons for actions are according to the legal system they live in. They do not explain the *beliefs* of the people, for instance of judges and legislators, but the reasons for actions; what, in other words, should be done according to the legal system. Yet the solicitor, advisor or barrister is only giving a *report* on or a *theoretical reason* for what ought to be done, *given* that the legal system is accepted.

Let us imagine the following extreme example. There is an island called 'Diablo's Island' where the legal officials and some citizens share the internal point of view towards the basic rule or rule of recognition and the legal rules of the legal system. There is, *inter alia*, a rule that imposes upon officials and citizens the obligation to kill disabled children and it is well known that this takes place through the poisoning of dairy products. A man has been asked by

---

[53] See Raz (n 6). For an interpretation of Raz's view see J Dickson, *Evaluation and Legal Theory* (Oxford, Hart Publishing, 2001).
[54] Raz (n 6) 170–77.

legal official Z to buy butter and milk and the man is conscious of the evil purposes of the command. He asks for advice from his lawyer who states 'from the legal point of view, Z has moral authority' and the lawyer may also add 'from the legal point of view, you ought to buy the milk and the butter'. If this proposition has any practical force on the man, it needs to be part of his practical reasoning. But how does a mere *theoretical reason* became part of his practical reasoning? Arguably, unlike the case of the man who is asked by his wife to buy butter but buys margarine because it is healthier, in this example the man neither has (a) a transparent reason nor (b) a reason in terms of good-making characteristics. The authoritative reasons of Z are presented to him as a theoretical reason. Let us think about the following analogy; when, as an A-level student of Physics, you were given reasons for believing in the truth of classical mechanics, the reasons were presented on the evidence given. Some classical laboratory experiments were performed during class and you came to have these reasons 'on observation'. Similarly, the lawyer provides reasons in terms of the evidence she has. She has read and carefully studied the basic norm of the island's legal system, and knows that the order that has been given to her client is compatible with all of the norms of the legal system. She merely reports the reasons that she has learned by evidence. But the man does not 'have' these reasons as *practical reasons* because he *simply* cannot acquire *reasons for actions* by observation.

For these reasons to make a change in his practical situation, he needs to 'have' them. Let us suppose that, after consultation with his lawyer, he declares: 'I intend to buy the butter and the milk as ordered by Z'. If it is an act that follows a practical authority for *reasons*, then the question *why* is applicable. We ask the man *why* and he responds, 'because it is the point of view of the law'. But he has (now) probably misunderstood the question. We are looking for a *reason for action* and he has not provided this. We can continue our inquiry and ask *why* he intends to buy the butter and the milk and follow the 'point of view of the law', and his answer might be 'because authority is good'. The man can continue: 'Though the authority *does not purport to do the good*, it is good'. We can now stop our inquiry. The reason provided is both (a) transparent and (b) presented by the agent as a good-making characteristic. But now we see that the only reason he can give is from the *deliberative viewpoint*. The phrase of the lawyer 'from the legal point of view' has no independent force in his deliberations. If I am asked whether 'X believes that p', I need to assess X's *beliefs* about p. However, if I am asked to do something because 'X believes that p', I do not assess X's beliefs and her mental states, I rather look outward and assess p (TC for reasons for actions, section 5.3.1). Similarly, if someone asks me whether a legal official *believes* that the law has moral legitimate authority, I need to examine the mental states of the legal official. However, if I am asked by the legal official to do p, I need to look outward and assess whether I should do p in terms of reasons for p. The phrase 'according to the law' simply indicates who has issued the allegedly authoritative command, but to understand any subsequent actions, we need to understand why the man takes the boat to the mainland, why he goes to the shop, why he buys the butter and milk, and the end of this series of actions. We also need to assess the man's response. Only the agent can justify and explain why he is following the legal rule. We need to understand and determine whether his reasons are 'good-making' characteristics. Like him, we need to look outward, at the reasons for action (TC for reasons for action, section 5.3.1), not *at what his beliefs or mental states are*. The agent can be mistaken about his reasons as good-making characteristics and to assess this we need to engage in thinking about the end of the action. The man could assert that '"to kill disable children" is good' as 'it will produce a better world'(!) But is this a reason for action as a good-making characteristic? Proponents of the acceptance thesis could avoid this result by arguing that 'it is his desire to produce a better world' and it is his belief that his action is an instance of 'producing a better world' that rationalises and explains his action, but this is not the position of the 'detached point of view'. The detached point of view aims to describe not *mental states*, but the reasons *why* a person ought to accept a legal rule, and purports to describe this from an uncommitted point of view. I have, however, argued that if this description is successful it has to be parasitic on the deliberative or first-person point of view and therefore on the acceptance of the rule from such a viewpoint, ie the acceptance thesis*.

5.4 OBJECTIONS TO THE ARGUMENT THAT THE DETACHED VIEWPOINT OF THE 'ACCEPTANCE THESIS*' IS MERELY THEORETICAL AND IS THEREFORE PARASITIC ON THE 'ACCEPTANCE THESIS*'

5.4.1 'Detached Point of View' is Neither Deliberative nor Theoretical, but Rather a 'Third Point of View'

However, this 'third point of view' is, like the deliberative one, a practical point of view; the difference lies in the fact that it is formulated from a third-person perspective.[55] The 'detached point of view', an objector might point out, is neither a deliberative viewpoint, ie from the first-person perspective, nor a theoretical viewpoint. Following Raz, an objector might say that I have presented a very narrow interpretation of the

---

[55] Following Aquinas, *Summa Theologica* (n 46) I, q.14, a.16, we could say that the 'detached viewpoint' is only partly deliberative (practical) and partly theoretical. But if it is deliberative, it is only in a 'secondary' sense. I argue in this section that the 'detached point of view' is *not deliberative* in the primary sense and therefore cannot lead us to action.

practical point of view and have reduced the 'detached point of view' to the deliberative point of view. According to Raz, the 'detached point of view' has two core features and should be characterised as follows:

> First, they are true or false according to whether there is, in the legal system referred to, a norm which requires the action which is stated to be one which ought to be done; secondly, if the statement is true and the norm in virtue of which it is true is valid, then one ought to perform the action which according to the statement ought legally to be performed. Such statements are widespread in legal contexts. It should be emphasised again that statements from a point of view or according to a set of values are used in all spheres of practical reason, including morality. Their use is particularly widespread when discussing reasons and norms which are widely believed in and followed by a community. There are always people who accept the point of view and want to know what ought to be done according to it in order to know what they ought to do.[56]

Let us first think about examples outside the law as suggested by Raz. When you give advice to a friend who, for example, is vegetarian you do not, according to Raz, consider *your* reasons for actions, but rather *her* reasons. You probably love meat, but you give advice to your friend within the framework of her normative system, ie her vegetarianism.

My reply to this objection is as follows. In the example used by Raz, being vegetarian is good and you tell your friend, when you go to a restaurant that she has to eat either the spinach or the cabbage (the only vegetables on the menu) because both are good things to eat *qua* being vegetarian and *qua* being human. In this example you can tell her 'you'd better have the cabbage as you are vegetarian'. There is no further question about *why* that advice has been given. The goodness of eating either cabbage or spinach is obvious in the context. Thus, it is given as a good-making characteristic and is transparent to both of you. It is, I argue, parasitic on the deliberative viewpoint. The reasoning might be as follows:

(I) Cabbage is good for vegetarians

You are vegetarian

Cabbage is on the menu

Let us order cabbage!

The dependence or parasitic relationship of the 'third point of view' on the deliberative viewpoint is also apparent in examples very different from premise I. Franz Stangl[57] was the commander of Treblinka. When he first was

---

[56] Raz (n 6) 177.

[57] Example given by Eleonore Stump to explain the interrelation between intellect and will in Aquinas (E Stump, *Aquinas* (London, Routledge, 2003) 355). See also Gita Sereny, *Into that Darkness: An Examination of Conscience* (New York, First Vintage Book Editions, 1983).

appointed as head of a euthanasia clinic, he was morally repelled by the actions of the Nazis. But then he was afraid that he would lose his job and career. He began to think that euthanasia was a necessary evil and it was a favour to those killed. Let us suppose that Stangl was my friend in 1943 and that before he began his process of self-deception, he asked me for advice on *what he should do*. According to Raz, I could have replied to Stangl 'according to the normative system of National Socialism, you ought to continue being head of the clinic'. But, according to Raz, like a vegetarian who has accepted the normative framework of being vegetarian, Stangl has already accepted the normative point of view of National Socialism. His question is like the question of a chess player: given the rules of chess, how ought I to play? He has *already* accepted the rule.

In response to my assertion 'according to Nazi law, you ought to remain head of the euthanasia clinic', Stangl might sensibly have asked '*why should I?*' The *why* is directed to the action that I have given as advice. He has asked for advice in terms of *a reason for action*, not just in terms of an action *simpliciter*, for example, a voluntary action that is done for *no* reasons, and my answer also needs to be in terms of *reasons for actions*. When people look for practical advice they are seeking for reasons. Children do this all the time. They ask parents, teachers, relatives and friends *how* to do this and this, and *why* should they do this and this. They learn that some ends are valuable and worth pursuing and others are not. To give advice to Frank Stangl in terms of *reasons for actions*, as in the case of the vegetarian friend, I need a premise like (*I*) *vegetables are good*. What kind of premise can play this role? My argument is that only a premise that is (a) transparent and (b) that describes the action as a good-making characteristic could play this role. In this case, the premise 'Legitimate authority is a good sort of thing' can play the role of premise I. The reasoning could be as follows:

> (*II*) *Legitimate authority is a good sort of thing*[58]
>
> Nazi law has legitimate authority
>
> A Nazi official has commanded that 'you ought to remain head of the euthanasia clinic'
>
> Let us obey the command(!)[59]

But here my advice is mistaken. I know that Nazi law has no legitimate authority because it is not an instance of 'legitimate authority as a good sort of thing'. The second premise is false. It is similar to the case of vitamins and oranges as follows:

---

[58] I use 'good' as an attributive adjective instead of an attribute predicate, following P Geach, 'Good and Evil' (1956) *Analysis* 32.

[59] For a discussion on the correct form of practical syllogism, see section 4.2.1.

Vitamin C is good for the immune system

This synthetic orange without vitamins is a good sort of thing

You have a cold, you ought to boost your immune system

Let us eat this synthetic orange(!)

As in the case of Nazi law, my advice is mistaken because my reasoning is defective as the second premise is false. Stangl has no reason to surrender his judgement. If my advice stops at the moment of expressing 'from the legal point of view, you ought to obey the law', my advice is incomplete. He can legitimately demand *reasons for actions*; namely, an answer to the question *why*. Then I need a premise like I or II.

5.4.2 We Do Not, and Cannot, Commit Ourselves to All the Different Normative Systems that Coexist in our Practical Experience

In other words, we act following different norms that we do not fully endorse. a citizen of a state does not commit a contradiction in saying: 'I ought to do what the legal official has commanded, but I do not believe they have legitimate authority'. The 'detached point of view' aims to explain the cogency of the latter statement. The objection raises a sound point. True, there is no logical contradiction in such a sentence, but it nevertheless has a paradoxical nature. There is a parallel between Moore's paradox types and the statement 'I ought to do what the legal officials have ordered, but I do not believe they have legitimate author-ity'. Moore's paradox[60] can be found in statements such as 'It is raining, but I do not believe it'. The oddness is caused by an assertoric sentence and its negation such as 'x, but I do not believe x' or 'I ought to x, but I do not believe "I ought to x"'. To believe or assert is to look outwards to the world and deter-mine whether the *object* of your belief or assertion is true or not. Presumably, when a person says 'I ought to do what the legal officials have ordered' she conveys the idea that she has surrendered her judgement on the basis of believing that the authority is legitimate, otherwise she will use sentences such as 'I am obliged', 'I am ordered', 'I am coerced', and so on. Then she adds,

---

[60] For discussions on Moore's paradox see R Sorensen, 'The All-Seeing Eye: A Blind Spot in the History of Ideas' in M Green and JN Williams (eds), *Moore's Paradox: New Essays on Beliefs, Rationality and the First Person* (Oxford, Oxford University Press, 2007) 37–52; J Adler and B Armour-Garb, 'Moore's Paradox and the Transparency of Belief' in M Green and JN Williams (eds), *Moore's Paradox: New Essays on Beliefs, Rationality and the First Person* (Oxford, Oxford University Press, 2007) 146–64; A Gallois, 'Consciousness, Reasons and Moore's Paradox' in M Green and JN Williams (eds), *Moore's Paradox: New Essays on Beliefs, Rationality and the First Person* (Oxford, Oxford University Press, 2007) 165–88 and J Heal, 'Moore's Paradox: A Wittgensteinian Approach' (1994) *Mind* 5.

'I do not believe they have legitimate authority'. This clause can be replaced by 'I do not believe "I ought to do what the legal officials have ordered"'. The paradox arises because propositional attitudes are outward looking and we are required to look at the *object* of our beliefs. The paradox, arguably, might be explained because the person takes a 'distanced' or 'detached' viewpoint on herself. It is as if there are two different people inside her:[61] the one who believes in the legitimacy of the 'ought' demanded by legal officials, and the one who denies that the 'ought' of legal officials has any legitimacy. This problem arises only from the first-person perspective, both deliberative and theoretical viewpoints. There is no paradox in asserting 'she ought to do what the legal officials have ordered, but she does not believe it'.

Arguably there is a kind of alienation when, from the deliberative viewpoint, the citizen engages in a thought such as 'I ought to obey the law', but then denies avowal or practical endorsement of his own thoughts by asserting 'I do not believe that I really *ought* to obey the law, because it does not have legitimate authority'.

5.5 CONCLUSIONS OF THIS CHAPTER

The argumentative strategy of this chapter can be summarised as follows:

(a)   Hart's internal point of view plays an important role in explaining the social normativity of law.

(b)   The internal aspect of rules is made explicit through the acceptance of the rule. To accept the rule is to use it as a justification for the behaviour or as a standard of criticism of conduct that deviates from the rule. The rule is used by the legal participant as *guiding*.

(c)   Hart argues that the Austinian explanation of habitual obedience is unsatisfactory in accounting for the guiding and duty-imposing character of legal rules.

(d)   Hart advocated non-cognitivism, but remained unclear on what kind of non-cognitivism he advocated and how this, and his rejection of the predictive theory of law, might be reconciled.

(e)   I argue that in order to fill this explanatory gap, we need to understand the notion of 'acceptance' of a legal rule. I propose beginning with the more sophisticated account of non-cognitivism offered by Gibbard. For Gibbard there is acceptance of norms as the result of a biological adaptation strategy to coordinate our activities with others. However, he argues

---

[61]   See S Shoemaker, 'Introspection and the Self', 'On Knowing One's Own Mind' and 'First-Person Access' in *The First-Person Perspective and Other Essays* (Cambridge, Cambridge University Press, 1996).

that this acceptance is *expressed* through our behaviour, including linguistic behaviour. He also argues that acceptance to a norm is a *psychological* state that involves *beliefs*.

(f) I ask what kind of explanation of action is required that will correctly show the role of beliefs and psychological states and actions. I use Davidson's approach and argue that an intentional action has two components: (a) a belief and (b) a pro-attitude. As a result we can formulate the acceptance thesis as follows: 'C accepts the legal rule if and only if (a) he believes that the type of action or pattern of behaviour that is indicated by the rule is one that he has a pro-attitude towards and (b) he has a pro-attitude (desires, motives) towards the pattern of behaviour indicated by the rule'.

(g) I argue that the 'acceptance thesis' is the strongest interpretation of Hart's internal point of view. However, I criticise the 'acceptance thesis' as it cannot provide a complete explanation of intentional action. I offer instead the Aristotle/Anscombe model of intentional action, and show that the notion of intentional action in terms of other actions and a reason that is presented to the first-person deliberator as transparent and having good-making characteristics is more basic or primary than any sophisticated explanation. Following the Aristotle/Anscombe model I formulate the 'acceptance thesis*' and argue that the 'acceptance thesis' is parasitic on the 'acceptance thesis*'. The 'acceptance thesis*' grounds a justified conception of legal normativity and consequently the social normativity of law is parasitic on the justified normativity of law. In other words, Hart's internal point of view can explain the acceptance of norms and their use in practical justifications because we can understand action in terms of other actions and in terms of good-making characteristics.

6

*A Defence of the Parasitic Thesis II: Does Kelsen's Notion of Legal Normativity Rest on a Mistake?**

6.1 KELSEN'S JURISPRUDENTIAL ANTINOMY

S TANLEY PAULSON FAMOUSLY has emphasised the need to understand Kelsen through the lens of Kant[1] and through, primarily, the idea of 'jurisprudential antinomy'. Like Kant, who conceived the idea that there is both a theoretical-empirical realm where knowledge of the sensible world is possible and a practical one where freedom is manifested,[2] Kelsen conceives that there is a realm of facts and a normative domain. The jurisprudential antinomy establishes that, on the one hand, if the content of the law is determined by morality, then the law-making process is redundant; if, on the other hand, law is merely the outcome of a law-making process, then the law is the result of power and arbitrary will. The antecedent of the second horn advances the view that law can be reduced to human will and power, and therefore does not need to resort to morality. From the empirical perspective, human will and power can be observed, and known and theorised as facts. By contrast, the antecedent of the first horn establishes that law can be reduced to morality. Kelsen rejects both views: the separability thesis and the reductive thesis. However, the problem that arises is how we should understand the notion of 'will'.

---

* This chapter was previously published as 'Does Kelsen's Notion of Legal Normativity Rest on a Mistake?' (2012) 31 *Law and Philosophy* 725. It is used with kind permission from Springer Science+Business Media.

[1] See S Paulson, 'The Neo-Kantian Dimension in Kelsen's Pure Theory of Law' (1992) *Oxford Journal of Legal Studies* 313. Other important works that emphasise the relationship between Kelsen and Kant are A Wilson, 'Is Kelsen Really a Kantian?' in R Tur and W Twinning (eds), *Essays on Kelsen* (Oxford, Clarendon Press, 1986) 37–64; I Stewart, 'Kelsen and the Exegetical Tradition' in ibid 123–48 and R Tur, 'The Kelsenian Enterprise' in ibid 149–86 and E Bulygin, 'An Antinomy in Kelsen's Pure Theory of Law' (1990) *Ratio Juris* 29.

[2] I Kant, *The Critique of Pure Reason* (P Guyer and A Wood (trans) from *Reine Vernunft*, 1st and 2nd edns, Cambridge, Cambridge University Press, 1998) A131/B169, A298/B355, A547/B575.

In this chapter I will argue that Kelsen's triumph in overcoming reductivist naturalism[3] is only possible (a) because he advanced a much more sophisticated account of intentional action than his predecessors; and (b) because he adumbrated a methodological turn to explain the normative and authoritative character of law without morality. I will argue that Kelsen advanced a sophisticated naturalist conception of intention and that he adumbrated a methodological strategy that would enable the transformation of the sophisticated naturalist conception of 'intention' into a cognizable object of legal science while simultaneously providing an explanation of the legal 'ought'. The methodological strategy is the 'inversion thesis' which establishes that legal norms enable us to objectively identify and determine the 'will' or the intention of legal authority. Contrary to nineteenth century psychologism, Kelsen argues that it is not the case that the will or the intention of the sovereign determines what the norm is, rather it is the legal ought that 'objectifies' the will.

However, it is argued that in spite of the fact that Kelsen advanced a sophisticated account of intentional action, he fails to understand the complexities of the notion of the 'will' and intentional action. Furthermore Kelsen does not take seriously Kant's two realms of the theoretical and the practical, and indeed rejects the latter.[4] Why does he not take seriously Kant's two realms?[5] It is, I will argue, because he fails to understand the complex nature of the practical and its relationship to intentional action. What does he miss in his understanding of the notion of the practical? I will advance the view that the notion of the practical or deliberative involves, both in Kant and Aristotle,[6] the transparency condition which establishes that the agent or deliberator intentionally acts for reasons that are self-evident or transparent to him or her (sections 5.3.1 and 3.3). It is a recalcitrant feature of the deliberative standpoint that cannot be theorised. For Aristotle,[7] Aquinas[8] and Anscombe,[9] the

---

[3] G Pavlakos has argued that Kelsen's legal theory does not overcome naturalism. See his 'Non-naturalism, Normativity and the Meaning of Ought' (ms with the author).

[4] For a discussion on Kelsen's interpretation of Kant's practical reason see Marcelo Porciuncula in 'Razón Práctica y Absolutismo Político: una relación probable – la perspectiva Kelseniana' (ms with the author).

[5] In his book *General Theory of Law and the State* (Anders Wedberg (trans), Cambridge, MA, Harvard University Press, 1945), Kelsen points out: 'the pure theory of law rests not on Kant's philosophy of law but on his theory of knowledge' (444).

[6] 'A voluntary act would seem to be an act of which the origin lies in the agent, who knows the particular circumstances in which he is acting' (Aristotle, *Nichomachean Ethics* (H Rackham (trans), Cambridge, MA, Harvard University Press, 1934) III.1111a 20–21).

[7] Aristotle (n 6) I.1094ai-2; III.1114b 18–21. See also D Charles, *Aristotle's Philosophy of Action* (London, Routledge, 1984).

[8] T Aquinas, *Summa Theologica* (Latin and English text, Thomas Gilby (trans), Cambridge, Cambridge University Press, 2006) Ia2æ.12, I. See also J Finnis, *Aquinas* (Oxford, Oxford University Press, 1998) 62–71 and 79–90 and A Kenny, *Aquinas on Mind* (London, Routledge, 1993).

[9] E Anscombe, *Intention, 2nd edn* (Cambridge, MA, Harvard University Press, 2000, originally published in 1957) para 32. For an analysis of Anscombe's work see R Teichman, *The Philosophy of Elizabeth Anscombe* (Oxford, Oxford University Press, 2009).

deliberative standpoint can be known through the end of the intentional action[10] as this provides the *form* of the action. The end is presented as a good-making characteristic.[11] As problematic as that might be, this means that the end needs to be presented as a good-making characteristic[12] and therefore it involves evaluation. The soundness of this conception is an insurmountable obstacle when trying to theorise the 'ought' and therefore the 'will'. Yet, surprisingly and contrary to Kelsen's own notions and beliefs, I will show that Kelsen's 'inversion thesis' is parasitic on Aristotle-Anscombe's 'ought'. If we can theorise about what 'a person ought to do according to the law' it is because we have an understanding of what that person 'ought to do' and therefore of what 'I ought to do'. Following Chapter 5, I will call this the 'parasitic thesis'. Paulson has argued that there can be two readings of the normative and authoritative character of law in Kelsen: first, a strong and robust notion of normativity that involves *guidance and bindingness*; secondly, a weak notion of normativity that aims to explain how law *regulates* human behaviour through empowerment. In the former case, the addressee of the legal statement is the citizen and the official whereas in the latter case the addressee is (only) the legal official. The weak reading sits well with a theoretical understanding of normativity whereas the strong reading seems to fit better with a practical understanding of normativity. Paulson asks: 'What can be said about the fact that Kelsen appears to be running off in two different directions at once?'.[13] These conflicting directions have their origins in two conflicting views advocated by Kelsen: he aims to give a scientific status to the

[10] For a summary of the debate on actions in the period post-*Intention*, see M Alvarez, 'Agents, Actions and Reasons' (2005) 46 *Philosophical Books* 45 and *Kinds of Reasons* (Oxford, Oxford University Press, 2010). For other important work see B O'Shaughnessy, *The Will* (Cambridge, Cambridge University Press, 1980); J Hornsby, *Actions* (London, Routledge, 1980); E Anscombe and S Morgenbesser, 'Two Kinds of Error in Action' (1963) *Journal of Philosophy, Symposium of Human Action* 393; K Donnelan, 'Knowing What I am Doing' (1963) *Journal of Philosophy 401*; J Hyman and H Steward (eds), *Agency and Action* (Cambridge, Cambridge University Press, 2004).

[11] For contemporary formulations of the Aristotelian theory of intentional action see J Raz, 'Agency, Reason and the Good' in *Engaging Reason* (Oxford, Oxford University Press, 1999) 22–45; W Quinn, 'Putting Rationality in Its Place' in *Morality and Action* (Cambridge, Cambridge University Press, 1993) 228–55; C Korsgaard, 'Acting for a Reason' in *The Constitution of Agency* (Oxford, Oxford University Press, 2008) 207–29; C Vogler, *Reasonably Vicious* (Cambridge, MA, Harvard University Press, 2002); R Stout, *Action* (Acumen, 2005); S Tenenbaum, *Appearances of the Good* (Cambridge, Cambridge University Press, 2007).

[12] For a criticism of the idea that a reason for action ought to be presented as a good-making characteristic, see R Hursthouse, 'Arational Actions' (1991) 57 *Journal of Philosophy* 57; M Stocker, 'Desiring the Bad: An Essay in Moral Psychology' *(1979) Journal of Philosophy* 738; K Setiya, *Reasons Without Rationalism* (Princeton, NJ, Princeton University Press, 2007) 62–67 and D Velleman, 'The Guise of the Good' in *The Possibility of Practical Reason* (Oxford, Clarendon Press, 2000). Cf J Raz, 'Agency, Reason and the Good' in *Engaging Reason* (Oxford, Oxford University Press, 1999) 22–45. For a helpful discussion of the idea of values as part of our actions see G Watson, 'Free Agency' (1975) *Journal of Philosophy* 205. For a discussion of these criticisms, see Chapter 3.

[13] S Paulson, 'The Weak Reading of Authority in Hans Kelsen's Pure Theory of Law' (2000) *Law and Philosophy* 131.

law while at the same time rejecting the fact-based conception of law.[14] The 'parasitic thesis' adumbrated in this chapter aims to provide an answer to the puzzle posed by Kelsen's conflicting views.

The chapter below is divided into four sections. Section 6.2 discusses Kelsen's notion of subjective meaning of intentional action and 'will'. Section 6.3 explains the deliberative viewpoint as opposed to the theoretical viewpoint in Aristotle, Aquinas and Anscombe. Section 6.4 advances arguments to show that Kelsen's 'ought' is parasitic on Aristotle-Aquinas-Anscombe's ought. The final section discusses some possible objections to the 'parasitic thesis'.

6.2 KELSEN'S NOTION OF THE 'SUBJECTIVE MEANING' OF AN INTENTIONAL ACTION

My general interpretive hypothesis is that Kelsen advocated a version of what I call the two-component model of intentional action[15] (section 1.2), namely, that intentional action is composed of two elements: first, a mental state such as desires, wants and intentions, and a second component which is the outcome of such mental states.[16] Thus, an act such as 'x is y-ing' is divided into the mental state of x and the outcome of this mental state. But this model of intentional action is problematic and unsatisfactory when it is applied to the law. The idea that the 'will of the Parliament' has caused the enactment of a statute neither explains (1) the idea that law *is not* a set of rules that aims to predict behaviour, nor (2) the special meaning of the 'legal ought'.

Kelsen advances an inversion of the relationship between the 'will' and the norm in a truly Kantian fashion.[17] For Kelsen, the will of the sovereign nei-

---

[14] ibid 170.

[15] In his 'criticial constructivist' and 'classical' period Kelsen advocated this model of intentional action which is more 'causalist'. In his later book *General Theory of Norms* (M Hartney (trans), Oxford, Oxford University Press, 1991), Kelsen is more explicit about the two elements of action: a mental state that is discovered by *introspection* or inward-looking and the action that can be observed. However, the argument that we can discover what we intend through looking inwards is used as an argument against the view that mental states 'cause' actions. Yet, Kelsen asserts that this is not important for his inquiry since he is considering the act of will that is directed not to the *movement of the muscles* but to a certain *behaviour* (Kelsen, *General Theory of Norms*, 31). Here we see the ambiguous use of the term 'action'. Sometimes he refers to 'movement of muscles' and sometimes to 'behaviour'. Kelsen explains his inward-looking approach as follows: '*If I can intend different things with the same expression – if this expression can have different meaning-contents – there must exist an inner process of intending which is different from the process of speaking*' (*General Theory of Norms*, 35).

[16] For an argument that supports the view that mental states cause the outcome of the action, but not the action itself, see J Hyman and M Alvarez, 'Agents and their Action' (1998) *Philosophy* 219.

[17] Kelsen's constructivism was influenced not only by the Baden Neo-Kantian School but also by Rudolf Von Jhering's legal constructivism which distinguished between the *concept* of law and the *practical form of a legal command*. See R von Jhering, *Geist des römisches Rechts*, 4th edn (Leipzig, Breitkopf and Härtel, 1978–88). Jhering's consructivism is expanded to public law in scholars such

ther determines nor makes intelligible the normative and authoritative character of the law; on the contrary, the issue is inverted, it is the norm that enables us to identify and determine the 'will' of the sovereign so to speak, and in this way makes intelligible for legal science the normative and authoritative character of the law.

Kelsen finds the two-component model limited in explaining intentional action and advances the 'inversion thesis', namely, the idea that we need to transform the subjective meaning of an intentional action into the objective legal meaning and in this way we succeed in avoiding a fact-based explanation of the legal ought. Kelsen described the 'inversion thesis' as follows:

> A transaction is willed in so far as or because it is valid, with the property of validity serving as the basis of cognition for the property of being willed. 'Will' in this relation is seen at a glance to be something other than a so-called psychical fact.[18]

But what if the two-component model is not a *complete* explanation of intentional action? What if a more *basic* or *naive* explanation of intentional action is required to make sense of the two-component view which is the material upon which the legal scientist performs his transformation? What if the two-component view does not help us to make intelligible the material to be transformed? I will argue that Kelsen's inversion thesis is not justified as the *primary* explanation of the legal ought because a more *basic* or *naive* explanation of intentional action is prior to and more fundamental than Kelsen's. Furthermore Kelsen's methodological turn cannot explain specific normative features of the 'legal ought' without the more *basic or naive* explanation of intentional action. In other words, Kelsen's legal ought can only explain the regulatory role of norms and not their guiding function.

---

as Gerber, Laband and Jellinek. See H Paulson, 'Hans Kelsen's Earliest Legal Theory: Critical Constructivism' (1996) 59 *Modern Law Review* 797, 800. However, as Paulson has pointed out, Kelsen criticises Gerber, Laband and Jellinek because of their psychologism and endeavours to radicalise their constructivist project. This radicalisation is possible due to his methodological dualism, namely, the view that the 'ought' and the 'is' belong to two unbridgeable realms. Contemporary scholars, inspired by the more robust reading of Kelsen's authoritative and normative character of law advocated by Joseph Raz in 'Kelsen's Theory of the Basic Norm' in *The Authority of Law* (Oxford, Clarendon Press, 1979) 122–45 and 'The Purity of the Pure Theory of Law' in S Paulson and B Litschenwski Paulson (eds), *Normativity and Norms: Critical Perspectives on Kelsenian Themes* (Oxford, Clarendon Press, 1998) 57–60, have also adhered to the idea of unbridgeable realms between 'the legal point' of view, the 'religious point of view' and the 'moral point of view'. See J Gardner, 'Law as a Leap of Faith' in P Oliver, S Douglas-Scott and V Tadros (eds), *Faith in Law* (Oxford, Hart Publishing, 2000) 1.

[18] H Kelsen, *Hauptprobleme der Staatrechtslehre*, 2nd edn (Tübingen, JCB Mohr, 1923) 133. For a discussion of this inversion thesis see S Paulson, 'Hans Kelsen's Earliest Legal Theory' (1996) *Modern Law Review* 797, 803.

6.2.1 Some Textual Analysis

In the following paragraphs, I will concentrate mainly on the two initial periods of Kelsen's works;[19] what scholars[20] have identified as the critical constructivist period dating from 1906 when Kelsen wrote the *Hauptprobleme* until 1920, and the classical period which lasted from 1920 to 1960, best represented by *Pure Theory of Law* (*Reine Rechtslehre*, 1934 and 1960)[21] and *General Theory of Law and State* (1945).[22]

In the first pages of *Pure Theory of Law*,[23] Kelsen attempts to isolate the autonomous meaning of legal norms, that is, the meaning of a norm independent of both natural events that obey causal laws and moral considerations that resort to eternal laws rooted in our nature as human beings or divine law. His main purpose here is to identify the object of legal cognition and thereby to guarantee an autonomous legal science. He begins with a series of important examples to illustrate the distinction between an action as both subjective meaning and material fact, on the one hand, and, on the other, the objective meaning attributed by the legal norm. In the first example, people assemble in a hall, give speeches, some rise and some remain seated.[24] According to Kelsen, these are mere external events, but their *meaning* is that a statute in Parliament has been enacted. In a second example, a man is dressed in robes and says certain words from a platform, addressing someone standing before him. Kelsen tells us that 'this external event has as its meaning a judicial decision'. In the third example, a merchant writes a letter to another merchant, who writes back in reply. In this case, according to Kelsen, the *meaning* is that they have entered into a contract. In all of these cases, Kelsen refers to the *objective meaning* of an act, namely, 'the specifically legal sense of the natural or material event in question'. This meaning is assigned or attributed by a norm 'whose content refers to the event and confers legal meaning to it'.[25] In this way, the natural event, the movements of muscles, the sounds of voices, etc

---

[19] For an analysis of the different periods of Kelsen's theoretical development see S Paulson, 'Four Phases in Kelsen's Legal Theory? Reflections on a Periodisation' (1998) *Oxford Journal of Legal Studies* 153, a review of Carsten Heidemann, *Die Norm als Tatsache. Zur Normentheorie Hans Kelsen* (Baden-Baden, Nomos, 1997); see also C Heidemann, 'Arriving at a Defensible Periodisation of Hans Kelsen's Legal Theory' (1999) *Oxford Journal of Legal Studies* 351; C Heidemann, 'Norms, Facts and Judgements: A Reply to SL Paulson' (1999) *Oxford Journal of Legal Studies* 345.

[20] See S Paulson, 'Hans Kelsen's Earliest Legal Theory: Critical Constructivism' (1996) 59 *Modern Law Review* 797.

[21] H Kelsen, *Reine Rechtslehre*, 1st edn (1934). All the citations are from *Introduction to the Problems of Legal Theory* (B Litschewski Paulson and S Paulson (trans), Oxford, Clarendon Press, 2002) (hereafter 'PTL1'); *Reine Rechtslehre*, 2nd edn (hereafter 'PTL2').

[22] Kelsen, *General Theory of Law and the State* (n 5).

[23] Kelsen, PTL1 (n 21).

[24] ibid 8.

[25] ibid 10.

become meaningful due to the scheme of interpretation provided by the legal norm.[26] An event becomes a theft, a death penalty, a murder, a contract. According to Kelsen, only through the help of the notion of a norm and its correlated 'ought' can we grasp the meaning of legal rules.[27] Kelsen goes on to assert that the meanings of these different acts are not observational; their meaning cannot be inferred from empirical facts such as colour, weight, for example, and we could add that we cannot determine what the action is merely by looking at the movement of muscles and the sounds agents produce. These phenomena are given, what I believe to be, the ambiguous term of 'material facts'. Kelsen tells us that apart from the material facts of actions, acts and especially social acts have a self-attributed meaning. Thus, the agent himself attributes meaning to an act. For Kelsen, however, this subjective meaning of an act cannot be the object of legal science, but, disappointingly, he does not tell us much of the nature of such subjective meanings.[28] There are two possible interpretative views that will fill Kelsen's gap and which, consequently, might enable us to understand his early notion of 'subjective meaning'.[29] First, we could assert that his idea of the subjective meaning of an act collapses into a reductive naturalistic view of mere events. We implicitly talk in this way when we assert that material facts or events acquire objective meaning due to the norm as a scheme of interpretation. Thus, self-interpreted acts can be reduced to movements of muscles, sounds of voices, and so on, and can be explained in terms of causality. In my view, even though there are some passages in Kelsen's work that could be taken to support this view, it would be an uninteresting and unfruitful interpretation. If this is all that Kelsen had in mind, why would he give examples of self-interpreted acts and try to show that on some occasions the objective and subjective meanings may not coincide? Alternatively, we could attempt a more coherent interpretation to understand his early notion of subjective meaning and to this end we could examine the passages where Kelsen discusses his understanding of what a mental state is, and what his understanding of an intentional action is in order to grasp what he means by the subjective meaning of an act. I will proceed according to the latter strategy.

In a number of passages in *Pure Theory of Law*, Kelsen distinguishes between two differing elements of acts (including social acts): mere natural facts or events that can be perceived by our senses, and the 'immanent' or 'subjective'

---

[26] For ease of exposition, I will use the terms 'rule' and 'norm' interchangeably, although Kelsen explicitly rejected the view that they are interchangeable.

[27] Kelsen (n 5) 37.

[28] Kelsen explains the character of the subjective meaning of acts in a very incomplete fashion in *General Theory of Norms* (n 15) ch 9 paras III and IV.

[29] For a criticism of the distinction between 'subjective and objective meaning' in Kelsen, see L Vinx, *Hans Kelsen's Pure Theory of Law* (Oxford, Oxford University Press, 2007) 32–37.

meaning of an act.[30] The latter, 'if it can express itself verbally, can declare its own sense'.[31] By contrast, a plant cannot say anything and cannot declare any sense about its processes and activities.[32] Legal science, whose task is to understand the legal act and the way that legal norms function as a scheme of interpretation[33] ought to be separated from the natural sciences but also from the cognitive sciences. For Kelsen, subjective meaning belongs to the latter domain as it can be explained in causal terms, and legal sociology is one of these cognitive sciences.[34] Legal sociology does not examine the connection between the subjective act and the legal norm, it rather relates the act to mental states such as motivation. For Kelsen of the classical period, the relationship or connection between acts and mental states is causal.[35] The aim of the legal sociologist is to understand what prompts the behaviour of the citizen, what motivates him or her to act, and what wishes, motive or desires he or she has when following legal rules.[36] For the legal sociologist, law is the object of inquiry as it is presented in the consciousness or mind of those human beings who issue legal norms, comply with them or violate them.[37] However, Kelsen tells us, the Pure Theory of Law does not examine the mind or the conscious-

---

[30]   My interest here is in the subjective meaning of an act and not in the idea of law in the subjective sense. For Kelsen, law in the subjective sense, which is manifested as legal right, legal obligation and legal subject, can be reduced to mere individual interests. Kelsen points out: 'In understanding so-called law in the subjective sense simply as a particular shaping or a personification of the objective law the Pure Theory renders ineffectual a subjectivistic attitude toward the law, the attitude served by the concept of so-called law in the subjective sense. It is the advocate's view, which considers the law only from the standpoint of the individual's interests, only in terms of what the law means for the individual, to what extent it is of use to him by serving his interests, or to what extent it is detrimental to him by threatening him with something untoward. This subjectivistic attitude toward the law is the characteristic posture of Roman jurisprudence, a posture that has emerged largely from the expert practice of lawyers representing individuals with just such interests at stake, a posture that was part of the reception of the Roman law generally. The posture of the Pure Theory of Law, on the other hand, is thoroughly objectivistic and universalistic' (PTL1 (n 21) 53, para 26).

[31]   Kelsen, PTL1 (n 21) 8–9.

[32]   ibid 9.

[33]   On this point, Kelsen in PTL1 (n 21) 10, para 4, tells us: 'The norm functions as a scheme of interpretation. The norm is itself created by way of a legal act whose own meaning comes, in turn, from another norm. That a material fact is not murder but a carrying-out of a death penalty is a quality, imperceptible to the senses, that first emerges by way of an act of intellect, namely, confrontation with the criminal code and with criminal procedure'.

[34]   Kelsen, PTL1 (n 21) 13, para 7. In *Hauptprobleme der Staatrechtslehre* (n 18), Kelsen defends the view that the key feature of laws' heteronomy entails the view that there *must be* a separation between law and morality, on the one hand, and, on the other hand, the historical or sociological explanations of law and the normative explanation of law (33–53).

[35]   Kelsen, PTL1 (n 21 above) 14, para 7: 'Legal sociology does not relate the material facts in question to valid norms; rather it relates these material acts to still other material facts as causes and effects. It asks, say, what prompts a legislator to decide on exactly these norms and to issue no others, and it asks what effects his regulations have had'.

[36]   Kelsen, PTL1 (n 21) 29, para 14.

[37]   ibid 14, para 7.

ness of those human beings who issue, comply with or violate a norm. The subject matter of the Pure Theory of Law is legal norms *qua* objective meaning. However, these subjective meanings or materials are the content of the legal norms.[38] Kelsen establishes a parallel between an analysis of the mind from the chemical and biological points of view and the psychological perspective. The latter, he tells us, cannot be reduced to the former. Similarly, the investigation of the the Pure Theory of Law cannot be reduced to the kind of investigation carried out by legal sociology.[39] However, for Kelsen, the subjective meaning can be understood if one understands the motives of actions as represented by states of the mind, ie desires, passions, intentions. These are the causes of certain effects, namely, other material facts such as a signed paper, a man's speech, the killing of a man. If the man desires to sign a contract, then his *mental state* or inner processes *cause*[40] the signing of the paper, but only when this material fact or subjective meaning is transformed into the objective meaning is it intelligible to the legal theorist. The legal theorist can now say that a contract has been signed and he uses the norm as a scheme of interpretation. The theorist does not connect the material facts through causality, but rather through imputation.[41] Nor does he establish an imperative 'you ought to comply with the contract' as this will merely reflect a conflict of interests in the garment of morality,[42] for Kelsen a type of ideology. Rather the legal theorist establishes from the material facts a legal condition and a legal antecedent, and transforms the material facts into the reconstructed legal norms (*rechtssätze*) which reflect the particularly normative and autonomous character of law. The legal scientist can now say 'if you breach the contract, you ought to be punished'. A causal explanation cannot explain the normative character of law; it can only predict it. In our example, the desire to sign a contract will enable us to say that because of his intense desire to buy a house, a man *will* sign the contract. By contrast, imputation establishes a

---

[38] ibid 14, para 7, 48, para 25(a). For an illuminating discussion on the tension between law as an intentional object and law as authority see B Celano, 'Kelsen's Concept of the Authority of Law' (2000) 19 *Law and Philosophy* 173.

[39] Kelsen, PTL1 (n 21) 14, para 7.

[40] In later work it seems as if Kelsen rejects the causalist interpretation that mental states cause actions. See his criticism of Wittgenstein in *General Theory of Norms* (n 15) 299.

[41] Kelsen distinguishes between peripheral imputation (PTL1 (n 21) 23–34, para 11(b)) and central imputation (para 25(a) and (d)). The former is the link between the antecedent and the consequent in reconstructed legal norms. The latter is where material facts (human behaviours) are connected to the unity of the system. Kelsen explains the distinction as follows: 'This human being is an organ of the legal community only because and in so far as his act, by virtue of being established by the legal subsystem constituting the legal community, can be connected to the unity of a legal subsystem or comprehensive legal system to be. This central imputation, however, is an entirely different operation from the peripheral imputation mentioned earlier, where a material fact is connected to the unity of the system, that is, where two material facts are linked together in the reconstructed legal norm' (PTL1 (n 21) 50–51, para 25(d)).

[42] Kelsen, PTL1 (n 21) 17, para 8.

link between the subjective act of the man transformed into the objective meaning of a legal act, ie signing a contract and the legal consequences. The result is the reconstructed legal norm: 'if you breach the contract, then you *ought* to be punished'. In order to understand the main criticism of Kelsen's conception of the subjective meaning of an act of will it is necessary to make some fundamental distinctions and it is to this task that I now turn.

6.3 A DEFENCE OF THE PARASITIC THESIS

The reflection on the distinction between the theoretical and the practical standpoint (section 5.3) sheds light not only on Hart's notion of acceptance of a rule, but also on Kelsen's 'inversion thesis'. How does this distinction enable us to formulate our main criticism of Kelsen's 'inversion thesis', namely, the 'parasitic thesis'? Let us begin with an example similar to that provided in section section 5.3. Let us suppose that there is a country called 'Kelsen Island'. The authority of the island asks a man to go to the nearest town by boat and buy some products, including butter. He buys butter as commanded, though he believes that margarine is healthier. What are the conditions that make this action an action according to reasons? The reasons for actions are not his. What does it mean that the reasons for actions are not his reasons? He can still describe his own actions, but not in terms of his own reasons; he could say that he bought some products in the supermarket, including butter, because the authorities have asked him to do so. However, he thinks that he has better reasons to buy margarine, and therefore in buying butter he acted contrary to his reasons. Any account of legitimate authority needs to justify the 'surrendering of my own judgement'. How can we assert that the man acted for reasons? From the deliberative viewpoint, the reasons for buying butter are not transparent for him. Nor can he answer the question 'why did you buy butter' by providing reasons in terms of good-making characteristics. He could, however, provide a justification in terms of the 'special status' of authority. He might intelligibly say that the authorities purport to do good for the community and therefore such authority is good. This is why he bought butter instead of margarine. This is why he has surrendered his judgement to the authority. The fundamental premise in his reasoning is 'this authority is a good sort of thing' and it can be formulated as follows:

> *(I) This authority is a good sort of thing*
>
> The authority has asked me to buy butter
>
> I will buy butter(!)

This answer is both transparent to the agent and in terms of good-making characteristics. This is the answer that Raz provides. In normal cases, ie central cases, authority is good and purports to do good because if the agent obeys the law, she will be complying with the reasons that apply to her. However, if she decides to act following her own reasons, she will probably not succeed in complying with the reasons that apply to her (Raz's normal justification thesis).[43]

Notice that the previous reasoning is not different from the following:

(II) Vitamin C is good for your immune system

I have a cold, therefore I need to boost my immune system

This orange contains Vitamin C

I will eat this orange(!)

There is no difference between premises (I) and (II). If we follow Raz, legal authorities present a similar structure. In the normal case, authority is good and Raz explains what it means to say that 'authority is a good and purports to do good'.

Kelsen advances a methodological turn, ie the 'inversion thesis', to explain the normative and authoritative character of the law. Norms determine and identify the intention and will of the legal authorities and therefore the norm itself makes intelligible the normative and authoritative character of the law. In other words, norms provide the form of the intention or will of the legal authority.

Let us illustrate the 'inversion thesis' by returning to our example of the man who lives on 'Kelsen Island'. Everyone on the island knows that the authorities are corrupt and that they do not purport to do good. This is evidenced by their claims and their actions. They have designed a kind of constitution that is the basic norm of the island. The legal norms of Kelsen Island require the elderly and children to carry out hard labour, these norms also authorise the rape of women and men, and the execution of people without fair trial. The legal norms also authorise the authorities to kill babies who have been born with physical or mental disabilities. It is customary that the authorities do this with poisoned dairy products. A man is asked to go to the nearest town by boat and buy many kilograms of butter and milk. Is it intelligible to say that the authorities have legitimate authority and that, therefore, the man ought to buy the butter and surrender his judgement? Kelsen would say that the norm confers a sanction upon the man, if he does not buy the milk and the butter. 'If the man does not buy the milk and the butter, he ought to be punished'. In other words, if the man does not follow the norm, then he 'ought legally' to be sanctioned. The norm itself determines the objective meaning of the authority's act, namely, that in case the man does not follow the norm, then he ought to be punished. But this is not an answer to

---

[43] J Raz, *The Morality of Freedom* (Oxford, Oxford University Press, 1986) 53–57.

the moral puzzle of why the man ought to surrender his judgement. The moral puzzle of legal authority shows the normative and authoritative character of law in its guiding as opposed to his regulative function. Legal rules not only regulate the behaviour of the citizens, but also guide their behaviour, that is to say that the citizens find an answer to their question of what they ought to do legally when they consider, examine and look at legal rules. My argument is that the 'inversion thesis' under-estimates the parasitic relationship between the idea that 'norms determine the objective meaning of the authority's acts or will', and the moral puzzle of legal authority contained in the question 'why should I surrender my judgement to the will of the legal authorities?'.

Let us go back to our previous example of Kelsen Island. The man has been asked by legal official Z to buy butter and milk and the man is conscious of the evil purposes of this request. He asks his lawyer for advice and she states: 'if you do not buy the milk and the butter, then you will be sanctioned' and may possibly add to this: 'you ought legally to buy the milk and the butter'. Notice that Kelsen emphasises that imputation should not be confused with a 'psychological compulsion', namely, that the agent acts because he is motivated to act. In the case of threats he is motivated by the fear of punishment. Kelsen's aim is to show that the notion of imputation, namely, the attribution of a sanction to an agent who does not follow the norm, describes theoretically the legal ought. Imputation has no practical force on the man. It regulates his behaviour if the hypothetical condition is met. However, if the law also plays a guiding role, how can a mere theoretical reason or report guide the conduct of the citizen? Arguably, unlike the case of the man who is asked to buy butter but buys margarine because it is healthier, the second man living on Kelsen Island neither has (a) a transparent reason nor (b) a reason in terms of good-making characteristics. The authoritative reasons of Z are presented to him as a theoretical reason. The lawyer therefore merely reports the reasons that she has learned by evidence. But the man does not 'have' these reasons as practical reasons because he simply cannot acquire reasons for actions by mere observation (sections 3.3 and 5.3.1). For these reasons to make a change in his practical situation, he needs to 'be engaged' with them and it is only when the reason for action is presented as a good-making characteristic that the agent can engage with the reason. Let us suppose that, after consulting with his lawyer, he declares 'I intend to buy the butter and the milk as ordered by Z'. If it is an act that follows a practical authority for reasons, then the question why is applicable. We ask the man why and he responds, 'because if I do not follow the law, then I will be sanctioned'. We can now stop our inquiry. The reason provided is both (a) transparent and (b) presented by the agent as a good-making characteristic. Notice that it is not primarily because he is in a mental state of fear, rather he believes that he follows the norm because he aims at avoiding the sanction. He looks outward to the world, he perceives what is fearful, namely, the sanction, and intends to avoid it; he does not look at his internal states. But now we see that the only reason he can give is from the deliberative point of view. The phrase of the lawyer 'if you do not follow the law, you will be sanctioned' has no independent force in the deliberation. If I am asked whether 'X believes that p', I need to assess X's beliefs about p. However, if I am asked to do something because 'X believes that p', I do not assess X's beliefs and her mental states, I rather look outward and assess p. Similarly, if someone asks me whether a legal official believes that the law has moral legitimate authority, I need to examine the legal official's mental state. However, if I am asked by the legal official to do p, I need to look outward and assess whether I should do p in terms of reasons for p. To solve the moral puzzle, the only authority is the agential authority. This means that only the agent can justify the command and surrender his judgement. The legal legitimacy of authority is primarily from the deliberative point of view.

But one might object that this analysis is not sound as Kelsen's inversion thesis is meant to apply to authorities rather than citizens. However, a similar criticism can also be adumbrated for the case of authorities. In our example the 'inversion thesis' establishes that 'if the man does not buy the milk and the butter, the man ought to be punished' and the addressee of this reconstructed legal norm is the authority. The moral puzzle for the authority is, why should the legal official surrender his judgement and apply the norm? Why does the legal official have to punish the man if the antecedent condition is met? If the law serves to guide a man's actions, including the actions of legal officials, and he is to follow legal rules because of reasons for actions, he needs to 'have' these reasons, ie it is necessary to make the reasons for action transparent to him or her, and the reason needs to be presented as a good-making characteristic. The 'inversion thesis' as a theoretical standpoint on action is parasitic on the naive or basic explanation of action. The theoretical standpoint depends on the deliberative point of view.

An adequate explanation of the normative and authoritative character of legal norms needs to explain both the regulative and guiding function of the law. In this section we have shown that the 'inversion thesis' and the notion of imputation in Kelsen conceive of the normative and authoritative character of the law from a merely theoretical point of view and consequently cannot explain the guiding function of the 'legal ought', namely, the idea that legal rules guide our actions and might give answers to the two questions (a) what ought I to do *qua* legal authority? and (b) why should I do what the legal authority says?

Arguably, an objector might point out that my criticism is not a difficulty for Kelsen as he only aimed to explain the regulative function of the norm.

However, I would argue that if the proposition 'if X does not obey the norm, then X ought to be punished' is intelligible at all, it is because it is parasitic on the citizen's deliberative viewpoint that says 'I ought to obey the norm, because I have a reason to act'. If the proposition 'if X does not obey the norm, then X ought to be punished' is intelligible to the legal official, it is because it is parasitic on the legal official's deliberative point of view that says 'I ought to apply the norm, because I have a reason for action "y" that is a good-making characteristic'. This good-making characteristic can be 'authority is good'. Consequently, the regulative role is parasitic on the guiding role. We can explain how norms regulate human behaviour because we can explain how norms guide our behaviour. Otherwise, a purely causal explanation would suffice. Thus, norms regulate the behaviour of human beings through reasons, in a meaningful way rather than through causes, but to show how reasons regulate human behaviour, we need first to understand how reasons enter into the deliberation of human beings *qua* agents; in other words, we need to understand the deliberative point of view. The latter is a naive explanation of action. My argument is not that a theoretical explanation of action is false; on the contrary, my argument is that the naive explanation of action is prior to and more basic than the theoretical explanation. In a nutshell, the naive explanation of action cannot be ignored or reduced to the theoretical standpoint.

I have shown that the transparency condition is a recalcitrant feature of the deliberative point of view. When an agent acts for reasons following legal norms these reasons are transparent to the agent and, if we can explain the way that norms regulate the actions of the agent, then we can understand what the agent's reasons are. In the language of Kelsen, the subjective meaning is manifest in the reasons that the agent has to follow the norms, whereas the objective meaning is the attribution of the 'legal ought' to the action by the norm.

Let us imagine the following example. A man steals a gun and threatens the Mayor of Sheffingham with it. We would like to elucidate the reasons for his actions and ask the man why he took the gun; the man tells us that he took the gun in order to force entry into the Mayor's office and he did this in order to threaten him. In response we ask the man why he wanted to threaten the Mayor with a gun, the man tells us that the Mayor is not a legitimate authority but that he himself is. He adds that only legitimate authorities can rule. We now understand his action. We can grasp the meaning of his act and understand that he is confused and mistaken in his reasons for action, ie the Mayor is not a legitimate authority. This is possible because we understand, in Kelsen's terminology, the subjective meaning of the intentional action, ie the reasons that explain why he took the gun and threatened the Mayor. We can now say that the norm attributes an objective meaning to his action and we can intelligibly say: 'If a man threatens a legitimate authority, exercising power in an illegitimate way, then he ought to be punished'. In Kelsenian terminology but contra Kelsen, my point is that the objective meaning can only be attributed because we understand the subjective meaning. In other words, Kelsen's 'inversion thesis' works as an explanation of the normative and authoritative character of the law because we can understand the naive explanation of action, namely, the explanation of action from the deliberative point of view. The naive explanation of action is prior to and more basic than any other explanation. In our example the actions of the man, taking the gun and threatening the Mayor, were guided by the general rule that establishes that only legitimate authorities can exercise power. The rule was presented as a reason that (a) has a good-making characteristic and (b) is transparent to the agent.

Imagine a modification of the example provided by Kelsen. Men are assembled in a hall, some give speeches, some stand up, others remain seated. They have the intention to enact a statute to kill rats, but because of a typing mistake they actually enact a statute that authorises the killing of domestic cats. The process of a valid enactment has not been breached and therefore we have a valid statute. Therefore, the subjective meaning of the act is the enactment of a statute that obligates the killing of rats in specific circumstances by the general population; however the objective meaning of the act is the enactment of a statute that obligates the killing of domestic cats in specific circumstances by the general population. In this case, the objective meaning and the subjective meaning will not coincide. The legal scientist will get wrong the basic subjective act. Let us suppose that a legal official has been giving the job of applying the statute. The reconstructed legal norm will say 'if a man in the specified circumstances does not kill the domestic cat, then he ought to be punished'. To the question why he ought to apply such norm, the legal scientist will refer to the antecedent and respond that this is the objective meaning of the act after transforming the subjective meaning of the act of the men in parliament. But in the example the subjective meaning was not soundly grasped. Consequently, transforming the objective meaning of the act is also mistaken. In answer to the question 'what is the subjective meaning of an act to be transformed?', Kelsen would be forced to reply that it is what the legislators intend to do and then he would need to provide a sound understanding of the subjective meaning of an act of will and this can only be obtained when we understand the deliberative point of view.

The problem that emerges is that the legal scientist cannot ignore the subjective meaning of intentional actions as his task is to transform the meaning. In other words, the subjective meaning is the basic material upon which the legal scientist will reconstruct the objective meaning of a legal act. Furthermore, the legal scientist needs to get the subjective meaning correct in order to transform it into the objective meaning. These are all imaginary examples that work as thought-experiments, but the purpose is to show that there is something intuitively wrong in the assertion that a satisfactory and complete explanation of legal normativity is provided by the 'inversion thesis', and that the 'inversion thesis' can explain legal normativity without a sound understanding of what intentional action is.

6.4 TWO POSSIBLE OBJECTIONS TO THE PARASITIC THESIS OF KELSEN'S NOTION OF SUBJECTIVE INTENTION

6.4.1 The Parasitic Thesis is Sound, but Kelsen's Inversion Thesis does not Need to be Parasitic on Aristotle-Anscombe's Explanation of Intentional Action

Kelsen could argue that the inversion thesis is rather parasitic on the notion of intentional action as a two-component view. There is some textual evidence[44] that shows that Kelsen recognises that the idea of action as subjective meaning is prior to the attribution of objective meaning to a subjective meaning by the norm. Kelsen could argue that the subjective meaning of an act can be satisfactorily explained in terms of the two-component view. However, if this is correct, then we envisage that the two-component view faces difficulties in providing an intelligible explanation of intentional action and therefore making intelligible the subjective meaning. We therefore look to Donald Davidson to further our understanding of the two-component view. For Davidson, if someone does something for a reason he can be characterised as (a) having some sort of pro-attitude towards actions of a certain kind, ie desires, and (b) believing (or knowing, remembering, and so on) that this action is of that kind.[45] Thus, let us suppose that a man drives his vehicle, stops it at a parking space and get out of his vehicle because he wants to go to the supermarket. On the way to the supermarket he meets a friend. What he has done for a reason and intentionally is only to park his vehicle and go to the supermarket; he did not intentionally meet his friend. His desire to go to the supermarket and his belief that driving his vehicle will get him to the supermarket constitute the reasons for his actions. The pairing belief-desire is a mental state. The presupposition that is operating here is that to understand the mental state of desiring and the mental state of believing is the same as to understand the content of the belief and the content of the

---

[44] In PTL1 (n 21) 9, Kelsen asserts: 'Cognition encompassing the law usually discovers a self-interpretation of data that anticipates the interpretation to be provided by the legal science'.

[45] D Davidson, 'Actions, Reasons and Events' in *Essays on Actions and Events* (Oxford, Clarendon Press, 1980) 3–19. This analysis is modified in his essay 'Intending' which is published in the same collection. However, he still maintains the causal account of intentions.

desire. In other words, to establish whether I believe that I am intentionally driving, I need to look introspectively[46] at my mental state of believing.[47] Let us suppose that this sophisticated account is the only one that Kelsen needs to defend in order to show that his 'inversion thesis', ie a theoretical explanation of the normative character of law, is parasitic on another theoretical perspective such as the 'sophisticated two-component model'. The objector will argue that it does not need to rely on the Aristotelian-Anscombe notion of intention because the 'sophisticated two-component model' is a sound explanation of intentional action. However, let us suppose that the man who is driving to the supermarket intends to kill his enemy later on that day. Whilst he is driving his car, and by mere coincidence, he sees his enemy walking on the pavement and the man suffers a nervous spasm that causes him to turn the wheel of the vehicle and run over his enemy. Obviously, he did not kill his enemy intentionally. However, according to the sophisticated two-component view, in order to have an intentional action we need two conditions: (a) a pro-attitude or a desire for the action, and (b) the belief that the action is of that kind. In our example, the man has the desire to kill his enemy and has the belief that driving his vehicle will result in the death of his enemy. Nevertheless, although in this case the conditions of intentional action as advanced by the sophisticated two-component view are met, the man did not act intentionally.

There is clearly something wrong with the sophisticated two-component view of intentional action as it cannot explain cases where there is deviance from the causal chain. The objective meaning will say: 'if the man commits a murder, then he ought to be punished'. Following the objection, Kelsen only needs to say that to understand the subjective meaning of the intentional action that is the basis of the objective meaning, the legal scientist simply needs to resort to the two-component model. But the example shows that the legal scientist will not understand the basic material that should be transformed, namely, the subjective meaning of the action. My argument is that we can only understand the subjective meaning of an intentional action if we examine the description of the action as advanced by the agent, not in terms of his own mental states, but in terms of the ends of the action.[48] In this case,

---

[46] Kelsen talks about subjective meaning as mental states or internal processes that are known by introspection.

[47] In this book, we have criticised this idea and argued that to know whether I have reasons for belief or action I do not need to look at the mental states since reasons for belief or reasons for actions are transparent from the first-person perspective.

[48] In *Hauptprobleme der Staatrechtslehre* (n 18) 57–94, Kelsen advocates a very narrow and mistaken conception of teleological actions. Kelsen reduces the teleological conception of action to the two-component view. According to Kelsen, the will is a mental state that aims or desires an end. The end is the outcome of the action and belongs to what *it is* as opposed to what *it ought to be*. He argues that the creation of a norm according to an end is a historical-sociological process. Therefore, the legal theorist cannot rely on teleological conceptions of actions in order to explain the normative character of law.

we will ask the man, why he drove his vehicle, why he turned the wheel and why he ran over his enemy. The answers respectively will be 'to go to the supermarket', 'because I had a nervous spasm', and 'I did not intentionally run over my enemy'. These reasons are transparent, ie self-evident to him, and he does not need any evidence of his own mental state to understand *why* he accidently killed his enemy. Because of his own description of the action we understand that it is not an intentional action and we can grasp the subjective meaning of the action which is the primary material upon which the legal scientist will make his reconstruction.

6.4.2 Kelsen Can Prescind from the 'Subjective' Meaning

Furthermore, the subjective meaning can be either inaccurate or an invention. the legal scientist only needs to recognise that the action is a human action. The objector might point out that for Kelsen the 'subjective' meaning might not coincide with the objective meaning and that, therefore, the subjective meaning could be completely inaccurate. Furthermore, it could even be an invention or a fiction. There is no need to have a 'subjective meaning'. In most cases, the objector will continue, the legal theorist will need to identify an act as a human act and this will suffice. Let us imagine that there is a statute that establishes that 'the killing of animals for religious reasons is forbidden'. A group of men and women are intentionally following a religious ritual and killing chickens. The subjective meaning of their actions is that they intend to perform a religious rit- ual. According to the objection, the legal authority can prescind from such a meaning or, even further, it might have an inaccurate understanding of such subjective meanings. Accordingly, the legal theorist mistakenly believes that the group is preparing a feast and killing the chickens to prepare a soup. There is something anomalous about the proposal that the subjective meaning is dispen- sable. How will the legal scientist transform his inaccurate subjective meaning into the reconstructed objective meaning of the act, which will be 'if a group of men kill animals for religious beliefs, then they ought to be punished'? Because of his misinterpretation of the subjective meaning, he cannot accurately recon- struct it and therefore there is no normative statement to address to the legal official. In other words, he cannot identify the antecedent and cannot determine whether or not the group of men is breaching the norm.

6.5 CONCLUSIONS OF THIS CHAPTER

Legal norms play two fundamental roles. First, they *regulate* human behaviour. Secondly, they *guide* the actions of the addressees. Kelsen's 'inversion thesis' can only provide a satisfactory explanation of the regulative role of norms and not of their guiding function. Consequently he only gives a partial explanation of the 'legal ought'. The guiding function of a norm can be better explained by the outward-looking approach to intentional action. However, Kelsen defends the two-component view of intentional action which is an inward-looking approach, namely, it examines the mental states of the agents and their internal processes. Thus, the subjective meaning of an act, which is the primary material which legal science transforms into the objective meaning of an act, is conceived in terms of the inward-looking approach. The inward-looking approach cannot explain a key feature of the deliberative point of view which is the transparency condition. We have explained the distinction between the theoretical and the deliberative standpoints in understanding intentional action. The agent is guided by the legal norm only when he takes the deliberative viewpoint and this entails that reasons for actions are self-intimating or self-evident, but since the 'inversion thesis' is simply a theoretical stance where reasons for actions are *opaque*, it cannot explain the guiding role of legal norms. We have also shown the way in which the 'inversion thesis' is parasitic on the deliberative viewpoint.

Kelsen is not insensitive to these difficulties and it seems that in his later work he recognised, though not in an obvious way, the importance of understanding correctly the 'subjective meaning' and he *explicitly* acknowledged the need to understand the subjective meaning of an act in order to correctly describe the objective meaning of a norm, including legal norms. A long passage from his *General Theory of Norms* conspicuously makes this point:

> It is only when the addressee of a command *understands* the meaning of the expression addressed to him that he can – subjectively – comply with the command. The willing, the intending on the part of the commander or norm-positor and the understanding on the part of the addressee of the command or norm are essentially inner processes which occur when a command is issued or a norm posited and a command or norm is obeyed. When I order another person to behave in a certain way, I can discover by introspection an inner process which is a willing directed to the behaviour of someone else; similarly, when I receive a command, I can discover by introspection that I perceive inwardly the utterance of another person addressed to me, that is, that I hear certain spoken words, that I see a gesture or written or printed characters, and *furthermore* there occurs in me something different from this hearing or seeing, namely, I understand the utterance I hear or see, and I understand it as a *command* and not as a *statement*, ie I grasp the *meaning* expressed in it, the meaning that I *am* to behave in a certain way.[49]

Then he continues:

> Thus, if in the case of a command issued or received by oneself, the inner process of willing, and understanding can be discovered by introspection and are essential

---

[49] Kelsen, *General Theory of Norms* (n 15) 35, para IV.

for a correct description of what occurred – relying on the arguments which support the possibility of an objective psychology – we can, indeed we *must*, make use of them in the description of a command given by one person and received and obeyed by another.[50]

Kelsen's approach on the subjective meaning of an act and intentional action is an inward-looking one,[51] but he offers no explanation as to the way in which the objective meaning of legal norms is parasitic on the inward-looking approach that considers and examines the internal processes of the mind. Does it mean that the explanation of the legal scientist depends on the explanation provided by the cognitive psychologist? How does the inward-looking approach explain the guiding role of legal norms? In my view, Kelsen has ingeniously mapped out all of the elements required to understand legal normativity; however, he under-estimated the power of the outward-looking approach of intentional action as a sound explanation of the subjective meaning of intentional action, and this limited his approach to a full understanding of legal normativity.

The core arguments of the chapter can be summarised as follows:

(a)   Kelsen's investigation is motivated by two different directions. On the one hand, he aims to provide a scientific explanation of law and, on the other, he aims to negate a fact-based explanation.

(b)   Kelsen advocates an explanation of intentional action that overcomes nineteenth century psychologism. This is called the 'subjective meaning' of an act. However, in the early classical period his explanation of the 'subjective meaning' of an act lacks depth and sophistication.

(c)   The 'subjective meaning' of an act is, according to Kelsen, still fact-based and therefore unable to explain the legal 'ought'.

(d)   The 'inversion thesis' aims to transform the 'subjective meaning of an act' into the objective legal meaning. This transformation will ensure the avoidance of an explanation of the legal ought in terms of a a fact-based explanation.

(e)   I offer a reconstruction of Kelsen's explanation of intentional action and therefore of what he called the 'subjective meaning of an act' in its stronger form, namely, as a sophisticated explanation of the two-component model of intentional action, and show that this explanation is parasitic on a more *naive or basic* explanation, which is called the Aristotle-Anscombe explanation of intentional action.

---

[50]   ibid 36, para IV.

[51]   In my view, he misunderstands Wittgenstein and attributes to him the view that Wittgenstein establishes a causal connection between the external events of uttering linguistic expressions and the respective reaction, without reference to 'internal processes'. See Kelsen, *General Theory of Norms* (n 15) 299.

(f)   I show that since (1) the 'inversion thesis' needs to transform the 'subjective meaning of acts' into objective legal meanings, and (2) the Aristotle-Anscombe explanation of intentional action is the primary explanation, then the 'inversion thesis' needs to rely on the Aristotle-Anscombe model of intentional action.

7

Authorities' Claims as Expressions of Intentions*

I N THIS CHAPTER I will focus on the claims of legal authorities. Legal authoritative directives and legal rules should be interpreted as expressions of intentions on the part of the authority; an intention aimed at ensuring that citizens perform specified actions. This is not controversial.[1] It is implicit in the notion of command. Thus, I command or order you to φ entails that it is my intention that you φ. This view is not far from the idea expressed by Aquinas in the analogy of a builder or architect who knows what the building will look like. [2] Let us say that an architect orders the plumber, the mason and the electrician to perform different tasks, and his orders are expressions of his intention that they perform the actions as he dictates. These are *his* intentions, namely, he has an idea of what the building will look like and *why*. Similarly, legal authorities know, so to speak, what the successive steps of a directive or rule might look like and *why* the directive or rule should be followed.

Let us illustrate this point with the following example. In English tort law, an employee can recover damages for psychiatric injury that he has suffered during the course of his employment if the psychiatric illness that he has suffered was reasonably foreseeable.[3] Through his decision the judge expresses his intention that employers should compensate employees for any psychiatric

---

* This chapter was first published as 'Claims of Legal Authority: the Limits of the Philosophy of Language' in M Freeman and F Smith (eds), *Law and Language*, Current Legal Issues vol 16 (Oxford, Oxford University Press, 2013). By permission of Oxford University Press.

[1] For example, Raz points out: 'How can actions communicating intentions to create reasons or obligations (for ourselves or others) do so just because they communicate these intentions?', J Raz, 'The Problem of Authority: Revisiting the Service Conception' (2006) *Minnesota Law Review* 1013; 'Authorities tell us what to intend, with the aim of achieving whatever goals they pursue through commanding our will' (ibid 1003). Reprinted in *Between Authority and Interpretation* (Oxford, Oxford University Press, 2009) 1012; see also L Green, *The Authority of the State* (Oxford, Oxford University Press, 1998) 60.

[2] T Aquinas, *Summa Theologica* (Latin and English text, Thomas Gilby (trans), Cambridge, Cambridge University Press, 2006) II–II q 57 a.1 ad 2. See also J Finnis, 'Foundations of Practical Reason Revisited' (2005) *American Journal of Jurisprudence* 109 and E Anscombe, *Intention* (Cambridge, MA, Harvard University Press, 2000, originally published in 1957).

[3] *Hatton v Sutherland* [2002] 2 All ER 1.

injury that they suffer during the course of employment if certain conditions are fulfilled. Like an architect building a house, the judges *know* what their decision entails and how employers should follow their decision. But the judges also know *why* the decision should be followed. It is found in the justification of the decision, namely, that an employer owes a duty of care to an employee who suffers reasonably foreseeable psychiatric illness during the course of employment; the judge avows the view that it is a good sort of thing for the individual victim and for our society in general that employers assume responsibility for psychiatric injury caused by negligence. In the case of legal rules, the justification is not always explicit as in the case of court decisions. I have argued, however, that, in paradigmatic cases, if citizens follow legal rules or authoritative directives *intentionally,* the citizens need to follow such rules because they have *reasons for actions as good-making characteristics.*

The hypothesis of this chapter is that authorities' claims of legitimate authority and moral correctness are expressions of intentions as to *how* a legal action will be performed. If the hypothesis is sound and authorities' claims are expressions of intention[4] about *how* an action will be performed, then the analysis of authorities' claims cannot be reduced to their true propositional content. However, authorities' claims as expressions of intention entail practical knowledge (section 3.3 and Chapter 4). They do not involve actual facts *(facta)* but, rather, *something will be brought about (facienda).*[5] It expresses a direction of fit from mind to world and the legal authority is the *cause of what it understands.*

The assertion that intentions cannot be known by observation tends to be exaggerated. The key issue is whether we can *primarily* rely on observation only and this is the point that Anscombe was trying to advance. You know *primarily* the position of your own body not by observation, but it is somehow transparent to you (sections 3.3 and 5.3.1). More controversially, in this chapter, I argue that when legal authorities *claim* legitimate authority and correctness, they express an intention to perform their actions and commands (intentions) *in a specific way,* ie through norms, rules, decisions. If the expressions are genuine, they will, most of the time, succeed in their intentions.[6] The steps of my argument are as follows:

---

[4] The analysis of 'expressions of intentions' as involving performance and commitment to act does not mean that expressions of intentions are performative speech-acts dependent on conventional means. The analysis follows rather Anscombe's use of 'expressions of intentions'.

[5] See D Velleman, 'The Guise of the Good' in *The Possibility of Practical Reason* (Oxford, Oxford University Press, 2000) 99, 109–18.

[6] Anscombe points out: 'Surprising as it may seem, the failure to execute intentions is necessarily the rare exception. This seems surprising because the failure to achieve what one would finally like to achieve is common; and in particular the attainment of something falling under the desirability characterisation in the first premise. It often happens for people to do things for pleasure and perhaps get none or little, or for health without success, or for virtue or freedom with complete failure; and these failures interest us' (*Intention* (n 2) paras 47–48).

(a) the directives, rules and norms of legal authorities are *partly* expressions of intentions that citizens or specific groups should perform an action;
(b) the claims of legal authorities involve practical knowledge;
(c) legal authorities have intentions and most of the time, if the claims are genuine, they succeed in performing them;
(d) legal authorities also express their intentions about *how* their actions will be performed and this takes the form of claims of moral correctness and moral authority. It might also include expressions of intentions about following most, or all, of the eight desiderata of the Rule of Law.[7] Again, most of the time and if authorities are genuine about their claims, they succeed in performing their actions *in the way* conceived by their intentions. These claims involve practical knowledge.

Prior to analysing these arguments, I will discuss the thesis on 'claims of correctness and legitimate authority' as found in the literature and will explain why they should be understood as expressions of intentions that involve practical knowledge.

7.1 CHARACTER OF AUTHORITIES' CLAIMS

Raz develops his theory of legal authority on the premise of a 'conceptual claim'. In his view, the notion of authority and the claims of legitimate authority by officials play an important role in the understanding of our concept of law and in shaping our attitude towards law. In *The Morality of Freedom*,[8] Raz imagines a society where the authorities do not claim legitimate authority, namely, authorities do not claim that the population has a duty to obey nor do the authorities claim that they have a right to rule:

> We are to imagine courts imprisoning people without finding them guilty of any offence; damages are ordered, but no one has a duty to pay them. The legislature never claims to impose duties of care or of contribution to common services. It merely pronounces that people who behave in certain ways will be made to suffer. And it is not merely ordinary people who are not subjected to duties by the legislature: courts, policemen, civil servants and other public officials are not subjected by it to any duties in the exercise of their official functions either.

The claims of authorities are always present in the context of commands, rules or norms. They are also present in judicial decisions, statutes and in the parliamentary discussions of legislation. But there is something puzzling and absurd about this imaginary scenario.

---

[7] L Fuller, *The Morality of Law*, 2nd edn (New Haven, CT, Yale University Press, 1969).
[8] J Raz, *The Morality of Freedom* (Oxford, Clarendon Press, 1986) 27.

We find two puzzling features. First, the authorities do not need to communicate to their citizens what they ought to do and punishment follows from breach of the rules. Consequently, the population is arbitrarily punished. Secondly, authorities do not express the intention to perform their actions and decisions in a way that will or *try* to create a right to rule and a duty to obey. Expressions of intention about *what* to do and expressions of intentions that officials will perform their roles in a correct and legitimate way involve the idea that orders are guided by *reasons*. Let us recall that we have argued that expressions of intentions, intentional action and intentions with which we perform actions should be understood in a unified manner (section 4.2). Expressions of intentions do not merely play a linguistic function, but show that the authority is exercising its faculty of practical reasoning. Of course, this faculty might be exercised defectively (Chapter 4 and Chapter 9).

Raz connects authorities' claims on moral legitimacy to two key concepts: capacity and action.[9] Concerning the connection between authorities' claims and capacities, Raz points out that trees cannot have authority over people[10] and if I say that trees do have authority over people, then you can infer that I do not understand *our* concept of authority. Raz adds '*since the law claims to have authority it is capable of having it*'. Furthermore, the possibility of a mistake or insincere claim is not the paradigmatic case.

How should we interpret this connection between authorities' claims and capacities? For example, we know that birds have the capacity to fly because they have wings, human beings have the capacity to walk because they have feet. *Can* we infer that authorities have a capacity to exercise legitimate authority because they *communicate* and give orders to others and, furthermore, because they *can* claim to do so? Can legitimate authorities act legitimately because they express their intention to do so? The difference between officials and trees is that the former are agents who can act intentionally and express their intentions whereas the latter cannot communicate their intentional actions and what they intend to do. There is a strong conceptual connection between our communicative capacities when we use terms such as 'I intend', 'I will', and our capacity to act.

According to Raz, there are two kinds of reasons for the failure to exercise legitimate authority. First, the moral conditions of the authorities' directives are not present. Secondly, the non-moral conditions, such as the ability of the authority to communicate its orders, are not present. Raz argues that in order to identify authorities' claims, the population will only need to heed the non-moral conditions of the claim.[11] In other words, the population needs only to

---

[9] See also Green (n 1) 60, who establishes the connection between the agent who performs the action and authorities' claims.

[10] J Raz, *Ethics in the Public Domain* (Oxford, Oxford University Press, 1995) 217.

[11] ibid 218.

understand the linguistic utterance of the authority.[12] We will discuss in Chapter 8 the problematic nature of this argument, but in this chapter I intend to focus on showing that the claims of legal authorities are expressions of intentions as to *how* they will perform their legal actions.

As already noted, Raz also connects authorities' claims to the concept of action. Raz considers that the 'courts very utterance of its opinion is claimed by it to be a reason for following it, whereas my utterance of my opinion is not claimed to be a reason for following it. At best it amounts to informing the persons concerned of the existence of reasons which are themselves quite independent of my utterance'.[13] In other passages, Raz asserts that authorities' claims on legitimate authority are exclusionary reasons for action[14] and that we judge them by their claims. 'We look to see whether their actions are such as to justify their own claims to general authority.'[15] Other authors who discuss authorities' claims, such as Green, establish the connection between authorities' claims and actions: 'authority is to be identified from the point of view of those who participate in it and for whom the relation has a special meaning. Someone claims authority when he makes requirements of another which he intends to be taken as binding, content-independent reasons for action'.[16] Gardner also points out: 'the official claims as she acts'.[17]

Authorities' claims communicate the *character* of their acts, ie the legitimacy or the moral correctness of their acts, to the addressee and the effect is that the addressee takes the act as *partly* binding because of the authorities' claims.

Can we reduce authorities' claims to their true propositional content (actual facts)? Can they be assertions about the future that can be verified or falsified? I will raise three arguments in favour of the view that they should not be reduced to mere true propositions or actual facts. First, authorities' claims involve the idea that the performance will take place in the future and involve endurance and continuity of action. By contrast, if the analysis of authorities' claims is reduced to its true propositional content, the idea of an action and a capacity that will unfold and persist in the future is lost. When an official claims legitimate authority or a judge claims moral correctness in deciding a legal case, he or she claims legitimate authority or moral correctness in relation to his or her actions in the future and in relation to all the successive steps taken to achieve the application of a rule, the decision or other legal outcome (sections 2.1 and 2.2). The claims of legitimate authority and moral correctness

---

[12] For a criticism of Raz's conditions, see R Dworkin, 'Thirty Years On' (2002) *Harvard Law Review* 1655.

[13] Raz (n 10) 205.

[14] J Raz, *The Authority of Law* (Oxford, Clarendon Press, 1979) 30.

[15] Raz (n 8) 4–5.

[16] Green (n 1) 60.

[17] J Gardner, 'How Law Claims, What Law Claims' in *Institutional Reason: the Jurisprudence of Robert Alexy* (Oxford, Oxford University Press, 2012) 29.

concern facts about things that will *be done* in the future, ie *the fact* that the judge will decide according to moral correctness or t*he fact* that the official will exercise authority in a legitimate way. However, this is not a *prediction*. Authorities' claims are about something that will be brought about (*facienda*) as opposed to actual facts (*facta*). This point is clearly shown when we look closely at authorities' claims from the first-person point of view. These claims are the salient ones in the context of practical authorities and entail consequences in terms of actions that authorities' claims from the third-person perspective do not possess. Let me illustrate this. You wish to get married in a boat on the high sea and the captain of the boat claims '*I* have legitimate authority to marry you'. This situation is different if a passenger in the boat claims, with no purpose of giving advice, but merely describing actual facts 'The captain of the boat has legitimate authority to marry you'. In the latter case, the proposition can be true or false, but it does not say much about the legal action to be performed by the captain, whereas in the former case, the captain's claim from the first-person perspective aims to convey his intention to perform a legal act and to have the legitimate power to perform it. These two sentences are not interchangeable and they remain asymmetrical.

Secondly, the contexts in which authorities make claims become unintelligible if claims are reduced to their propositional content. Officials claim legal authority or moral correctness in the context of giving rules and directives with the intention that the addressees perform actions according to the rules or directives. Officials aim at a goal, ie that the addressees perform the action. If claims are reduced to their true propositional content, then the directiveness towards the addressees' actions is lost. Authorities' claims have a practical stance, they cannot be reduced to a property that the authority possesses that can be verified as true or false, nor are they about a theoretical stance that the authority takes towards its own actions, ie decisions, enactments of statutes, application of rules, and so on. The authority does not state 'Look at me, observe that I have legitimate authority' or 'Observe and verify that I decide according to moral correctness'. Authorities' claims entail practical[18] knowledge. In our ordinary life we use similar expressions to convey our intentions about how we perform actions. Let us think about the following examples: to friends who are having a barbecue, I say 'I will cook the lamb to perfection' and to the mother and child who I will give a lift to, I say 'I intend to drive well'. I should emphasise that I am not referring to the linguistic

[18] For an analysis of the practical character of authorities' claims along Kantian lines see S Bertea, *Normative Claim of Law* (Oxford, Hart Publishing, 2009). For an examination of the importance of social and historical practices of law's normative claims, see S Delacroix, *The Genealogy of Legal Normativity* (Oxford, Hart Publishing, 2006). For a discussion on pathological cases of theoretical stances of ourselves see R Moran, *Authority and Estrangement* (Princeton, NJ, Princeton University Press, 2001) 170–82.

phenomenon, but rather to the deliberative or practical character of intentional statements, to the special 'direction of fit' of expressions of intentions.

Thirdly, a textual analysis of some passages in Raz's work shows that when he discusses authorities' claims he does not have in mind the consideration of their propositional content. Raz tells us that the population acknowledges authorities' claims, but that they can be mistaken about this acknowledgement. But if authorities' claims can be reduced to their propositional content, why does Raz refer to *acknowledgement* rather than to the possibility of establishing whether they are true or false? Raz tells us: *'since the law claims authority should its claims be acknowledged? Is it justified?'*.[19] It is clear that for Raz orders and commands are expressions of intentions, but he also thinks that only those who claim authority can command.[20] If authorities' claims were reducible to their true propositional content, then this latter feature would be unintelligible. Suppose that as an authority I claim: 'I am the captain of this boat and therefore have legitimate authority over you at sea'. If the proposition is true, I can command you but if the proposition is false I cannot command you. If the propositional interpretation is sound, then Raz's statement should say 'only those who claim authority and whose claim is true can command'. Raz, however, does not make the point in this way. On the contrary, Raz tells us that authorities' claims are evident from the language they adopt.[21] Finally, Raz points out that authorities' claims can be *sincere* or *insincere*.[22] If they were reducible to propositions, he should say 'authorities' claims can be true or false'.

Alexy also argues that authorities make claims and, more specifically, claims of moral correctness.[23] He begins with the example of a senseless order of individuals where the purposes of the ruler or rules are not discernible. It is a rapacious and predatory order. But the predatory order proves not to be

---

[19] Raz (n 14) 33.
[20] Raz (n 8) 37.
[21] Raz (n 10) 217.
[22] Ibid 217.
[23] For a comparative analysis of Alexy's and Raz's views on authoritative claims, see Gardner (n 17). Gardner argues that judges do not claim moral correctness and he illustrates his point with the example of an extract from Lord Goff's speech in *Elliott v C* [1983] *2* All ER 1005, 1010, 1012. Here Lord Goff tells us about his struggle to find an interpretation that will enable him to reach a decision that will depart from the principles established in precedent cases, which he does not find satisfactory. However, to his displeasure, he is obliged to follow the precedent as any other interpretation will be an *illegitimate departure* from the principles established in previous cases. Gardner is right in pointing out that Lord Goff is not saying that the law is morally correct, but on the other hand, Lord Goff is expressing *his intention* to decide *according* to moral correctness. It will be *illegitimate and not morally correct* to depart from the precedent. Lord Goff recognises that Lord Diplock's solution is not the *best* one; however, he does not think that Diplock's rule is morally incorrect. Lord Goff considers that under the circumstances of the case, he cannot change the precedent. It is morally correct, he argues, to follow the precedent, in spite of it not being the *best* law.

expedient and the bandits strive for legitimacy. They transform the predatory order into a governor system. They have a rules-driven practice that serves a higher purpose, the development of the people, for instance. The system is still unjust, but the governors claim correctness. This *claim to correctness* changes the order into a legal system.[24] Two examples illustrate Alexy's point on correctness: (a) 'X is a sovereign, federal and unjust republic' and (b) 'The accused is sentenced to life imprisonment, which is an incorrect interpretation of prevailing law'. In the latter case, Alexy tells us, '*the judge gives rise to a performative contradiction*'.[25] Why is this a performative contradiction? It is *practically* contradictory to make the following statements from the first-person perspective: (1) 'I will decide according to what is morally correct'; (2) 'I will not interpret correctly the law'; and (3) 'In my view, not to interpret correctly the law is morally incorrect'. It is also practically contradictory to say: (1´) 'I will draft a Constitution for the State in a morally correct way' and (2´) 'X is a sovereign, federal and unjust republic'. An exemplary analogy might illustrate the point. It is paradoxical to say from the first-person perspective: 'I intend to make coffee' and 'I will stop myself from making coffee'. The 'direction of fit' in cases of practical knowledge is to bring something about *(facienda)* and the contradictory is to stop the action. The 'direction of fit' in cases of theoretical knowledge is to establish whether the proposition is true or false. The contradictory statement of 'it is raining' is 'it is not raining'. If authorities' claims of correctness are interpreted as expressions of intentions about how they will perform their actions, then the *practically* contradictory character of the previous statements (1, 2 and 3; 1´ and 2´) becomes apparent. This is the point that we will now show in the next section, where I will argue that authorities' claims should be interpreted as expressions of intentions about *how* they will perform their actions.

I should emphasise that I am not claiming that Raz's and Alexy's arguments purport to show that authorities' claims are expressions of such intentions. My interpretive point is that Raz's and Alexys' arguments about authorities' claims *should* be reconstructed as expressions of such intentions. This interpretation enables us to have a better grasp of the core features and roles of authorities' claims in both our actions and understanding of the concept of law.

---

[24] R Alexy, *The Argument from Injustice* (S Paulson and B Litschewski Paulson (trans), Oxford, Oxford University Press, 2002) 33–35.
[25] ibid 39.

7.2 EXPRESSIONS OF INTENTIONS ABOUT HOW ACTIONS WILL BE PERFORMED

In the previous section I argued that (a) the directives, rules and norms of legal authorities are *partly* expressions of intentions that citizens or specific groups should perform an action; and (b) the claims of legal authorities involve practical knowledge (see section 4). I will now concentrate on the following two premises: (c) legal authorities have intentions and, if the claims are genuine, they will succeed most of the time in performing them; (d) legal authorities also express their intentions about *how* their actions will be performed and this takes the form of claims of moral correctness and moral authority. It might also include expressions of intentions about following most or all the eight desiderata of the Rule of Law. Again, most of the time and if authorities are genuine about their claims, they succeed in performing their actions *in the way* conceived by their intentions. These claims involve practical knowledge.

It is common to distinguish between (i) knowledge about the future known by evidence or known empirically and justified by some rule of inference, and (ii) knowledge about the future that is non-observational. In the former case, the knowledge is mainly propositional and I can verify or falsify its propositional content. In this way, I exercise my theoretical reasoning. For example, if I ask whether David Cameron will win the general election and you reply 'yes, he will as he is winning in the polls', then, I can now say that I have evidence, ie your testimony about the polls, that David Cameron will win the general election. It is a mere prediction, one might say, of what will happen in the future. By contrast, let us suppose that John asks me whether I will come to the party tomorrow and I deliberate as to whether I should go or not. I evaluate my options. I then reach a decision and express my intention to John: 'Yes, I will come to the party tomorrow'. I have expressed my intention to come to the party and there is certainty about my action. Hampshire and Hart calls this certainty a certainty based on reasons as opposed to certainty based on evidence and induction.[26] In this case, I exercise my practical reasoning rather than my theoretical reasoning. If someone asks me how I know that I will come to the party tomorrow, I will reply 'because I intend to'. My

---

[26] S Hampshire and HLA Hart, 'Decision, Intention and Certainty' (1958) *Mind* 1. They explain this practical certainty as follows: 'The characteristic termination of the practical inquiry is the settled frame of mind when we are no longer undecided what to do. We have made up our mind and are both certain what to do and certain what we will try to do. In describing this termination of deliberation, we cannot separate the temporal reference to the future from the solution of the practical question. We have decided what to do, and that we shall at least try to do it. We cannot have this form of confident belief about our future voluntary action without this form of practical certainty about what to do' (12).

knowledge is practical and non-observational.[27] But is this a proposition that can be verified? The response is negative. We can say about propositions that they are true or false whilst we say about intentions that they are 'satisfied' or 'non-satisfied'. If I do not come to the party and if the expression of my intention was genuine, we will *not* say that the proposition 'I intend to come to the party' is false. You would rather say that I have failed to come to the party as I did not act according to the expression of my intention. There was a failure in performance and you will think that some happening has taken place which has impacted on my attendance, for example, that I had an accident on my way to the party, or that a policemen fined me for speeding on the motorway and that this put me in a bad mood and made me change my mind about the party. We are in the world as agents and planners. We structure our lives around our expressions of intentions which, most of the time, are carried out successfully.

Let us imagine a person whose name is Sham and who, most of the time, fails to perform the actions that she expresses as intentions. Thus, Sham intends to wake up at 6 am in the morning to read a chapter of a book before taking her daughter to school; she then intends to meet a friend at 9 am for breakfast and to work in the library until 4 pm in the afternoon; and then she will leave the library to collect her daughter from school at 4.30 pm. Sham then intends to take her daughter to a music lesson and to have dinner with her husband at 7 pm in the evening. However, Sham fails to wake up at 6 am and wakes up at 8 am instead, consequently it is too late to take her daughter to school and she now has to stay at home. She has to change her initial intentions. Sham intends to ask the babysitter to look after her daughter whilst she goes to the library, but she fails to make the phone call to the babysitter. Her friend is waiting for her to have breakfast, but Sham also fails to answer her mobile phone. She now needs to make up her mind about another plan: she intends to make lunch for her daughter, but she also fails to make lunch. They both are starving and her daughter is crying in despair and hunger. This happens almost every day of her life. Sham's life is a sham. She has no control over her actions and we doubt whether she is truly an agent in the full sense. This is, however, not the normal case of agency. Most of the time we succeed in performing the expressions of our intentions.

When I talk about deliberation, I do not mean that for every decision or intention to act there is a prior process of deliberation. The idea, rather, is that we can reconstruct the reasons for the decision and this is the objective of the why-question methodology (section 3.2).

---

[27] For further discussion on the distinction between theoretical and practical knowledge, see S Hampshire and S Morgenbesser, 'Reply to Walsh on Thought and Action' (1963) *Journal of Philosophy* 410.

I have presupposed that expressions of intentions are genuine and non-self-deceptive. Of course, many expressions of intentions are not genuine and this becomes obvious, in most occasions, through the agent's performance of other actions and, sometimes, the disingenuity of such intentions is clear by their trivial formulation,[28] together with the context and the knowledge of the character or role of the agent.[29] For example, you might say 'I will give up smoking', but I know that you 'gave it up' just three months ago and that you took it up again last week.

I will argue that we not only succeed in performing our intentions, which I think is not a controversial point, but also that we have intentions about *how to perform* our intentions and that we succeed in this most of the time. Let us go back to our previous example. Sham has a twin sister whose name is Exito. Let us suppose that Exito also intends to do exactly the same actions as Sham, ie to wake up at 6 am in the morning to read a book before taking her daughter to school, and so on. Exito, however, is always successful in performing her intentions; she has, in addition, intentions about *how* she will perform her actions. She intends to wake up at 6 am in the morning but *with a fresh mind*. This means that the night before she intends not to drink alcohol and not to go to bed too late. She intends to read a book, but she also intends *to read it thoroughly and thoughtfully*. She intends to have breakfast with her friend at 9 am, but she also *intends to have a delicious breakfast and be kind, entertaining and polite to her friend*. Exito intends to go to the library and do research, but also *to concentrate on a specific question and focus on material relating only to that question*, and so on. In other words, we have intentions about *how* we will perform our actions and, most of the time, if we do not act *under incontinence (akrasia) or depression*, dominated by some pathological condition, we somehow succeed in performing them.

Intentions as conceived within the model of practical reasoning enable us not only to plan our lives, but also to coordinate our activities with others. If you express your intention to come to my house for supper tonight, I know that most of the time you will succeed in your intention. I can then rely on your action and invite other friends, go to the market and buy vegetables and meat, clean the house and prepare supper. If intentions play this function, then intentions cannot only be a matter of reasons for actions in terms of the two-component model.[30] According to this latter model, intentions are just mental states that cause our actions. If intentions are only mental states that cause my actions, then the causal chain can be broken and I cannot rely on

---

[28] S Hampshire, *Thought and Action* (London, Chatton and Windus, 1960).

[29] Anscombe (n 2) para 25.

[30] Thomas Pink argues, in my view correctly, that the function of intentions as coordinators shows that intentions cannot be mental states. See T Pink, 'Purpose Intending' (1991) *Mind* 343. I will rather say that they are not *primarily* mental states (see Chapters 2, 5 and 6).

the performance of intentions by agents. Let us suppose that you say 'I plan to come to your house for supper tonight with my car'. This is your mental state that will cause the action. If your car breaks down you will need to formulate another intention and put yourself in another mental state to be able to come for supper at my house. Then you say to yourself: 'I will go for supper to Veronica's house by bus'. Let us suppose that you miss the bus to my house. You need now another intention to be able to come to my house. Of course, all this can be avoided if you say to me from the beginning 'I plan to come to your house for supper tonight using whatever transportation is available'. But still, it might happen that there is no way to get to my house either by car or by bus, and that you might need to walk. How can this account help us to understand intentions as coordinators? How many intentions do you need to perform an action when you need to continually control and adjust your conduct to the contingencies (see sections 2.6 and 2.7)? If intentions belong to the domain of practical reasoning and are better explained by the 'guise of the good' model then you can say to me: 'I intend to come to your house for supper tonight by car because it is good to be with good friends like you'. Let us suppose that your car breaks down and that you need to re-adjust your conduct to the contingencies as you still intend to come for supper at my house. You will not come by car, but you will come; you do not need to form another intention. Thus, you will take the bus, arrange a taxi or walk, since your *will* is *directed* to the goal of coming to my house *because* you have a reason as a good-making characteristic, ie it is good to be with friends. If intentions are understood as *merely* mental states it is unclear how your *earlier* mental states can control your *later* mental states and actions. In other words, we might say, your intention is not playing any controlling role.[31]

We need to distinguish between the purpose of an action, on the one hand, and the intention with which I perform the intentional action and the expression of an intention (section 3.2), on the other. The purpose of the action can be assessed observationally whereas my knowledge of the intentions with which I perform the action and the expression of the action, we have learned from Anscombe, are practical and non-observational. Let us suppose that you express the intention to disconnect a bomb and say 'I will disconnect this bomb'. You take out all your tools from the toolbox, you find the manual *How to Disconnect a Bomb*, and you begin to cut the red wire as instructed by your manual. You say 'I intend to disconnect this bomb' and if you were pushed to

---

[31] A number of authors have criticised the belief/desire model because it fails to account for the idea that full intentional agency, in its paradigmatic form, is something that the agent *does* rather than something that just *happens* to him or her. The agent is at the centre of the action and this is the reason why we want to learn *why* the agent has done so and so. See J Hornsby, 'Agency and Action' in H Steward and J Hyman (eds), *Agency and Action* (Cambridge, Cambridge University Press, 2004) 1.

reflect in response to the question '*why?*', your answer might be 'because it is good to disconnect bombs to save my life and the life of others'. Mistakenly, however, you cut the black wire and the bomb explodes. We know by observation that you have failed in your *purpose*. There is propositional knowledge concerning the purpose of an action and thus it is either true or false. We will say 'it is not true that you disconnected the bomb'. Our knowledge of the *purpose* of the action might be known empirically. However, the knowledge of your intentions is non-observational. If your expression of intention and the intention with which you act are genuine, you cannot *systematically* be mistaken about your intention. It is, one might say, groundless, though not incorrigible (section 3.3).

7.3 AUTHORITIES' CLAIMS AS EXPRESSIONS OF INTENTIONS

We have explained that intentions are non-observational and entail practical knowledge. However, we might be aided by observation in terms of the results or purposes of our intentions. Let us think again about the example of a person making an espresso and realising that he was about to pour in some milk, but stops in his actions because he is committed to carrying out his intentions of making an espresso. He does not change his mind, rather he changes his bodily movements and transforms the world to fit his intentions. But to carry out our intentions, we need to be sensitive to the world and some observation might enable us to carry out our intentions. We can be aided by perception, but we do not *base* our practical knowledge on the observation of our actions. Practical knowledge involves instead practical and conceptual capacities (Chapter 4 and section 9.2).

Thus, a judge who claims to have legitimate authority to decide according to moral correctness needs to master concepts such as 'legitimacy', 'authority', 'justice', 'correctness', and so on (section 9.2). However, these conceptual capacities alone will not suffice, he would also need the *know-how* to make a legitimate and valid command, rule or order following the precepts of the Rule of Law (section 8.6.2): the *know-how* to correct and revise legal and moral principles; the *know-how* to apply precedents and interpret statutes, and so on. As in the case of the man making the espresso, he can identify mistakes and make self-corrections to adjust the state of affairs to his intentions. He needs to be sensitive to differences and discriminations made by past legal decisions, he needs also to be able to envisage new ways of doing things using his practical imagination and following the grounding reasons as (hypothetical) good-making characteristics of legal rules. Of course, he *can fail* in his performance or he might be mistaken about either his beliefs or evaluations about the state of affairs, objects or events, and this is what the idea of authorities' claims as expressions of intentions enables us to explain. We will examine the judge's decisions in the light of his intentions and the results he has obtained. We find, subsequently, the main following possibilities, which should not be considered exhaustively:

(a) The legal authority successfully performs the intention to act and might have sound intentions as to how the act should be performed, but the legal authority has mistaken beliefs about the grounding reasons as good-making characteristics of the legal rule. Suppose that a legal authority makes permissible the murder of disabled children because these children are believed to debase the national race. The authorities claim legitimate authority and moral correctness and, as I have argued, their claims, if they are genuine, should be understood as expressions of intentions about how legal actions will be performed. However, the authorities' beliefs about the grounding reasons as the good-making characteristics of rules are mistaken. They believe, for example, that moral correctness is about the maximisation of overall well-being even at the cost of the violation of fundamental human rights, such as the right to life. The authorities will engage in moral and political arguments to show that their solution is the morally correct and legitimate one.[32] They will perform their intentions successfully, but their beliefs about the grounding reasons as the good-making characteristics of a rule that makes permissible the murder of disabled children are false. Nor are there reasons to create a presumption of the authoritative moral force of the authorities' legal decisions (see section 8.6.1). A caveat should be put forward. We have said that the legal authority might have a sound understanding about how to perform the action but that this is, however, unlikely. Arguably, their mistaken beliefs about the grounding reasons as the good-making characteristics of the legal rule will most likely affect their beliefs about how to perform the action. If my beliefs about the grounding reasons of legal rules are mistaken, how can my procedural views on how to make law be sound? Correct law-making procedures involve a commitment to fairness, reciprocity, right expectations, and so on. In other words, if a legal authority cannot acquire sound substantive reasons in the legal decision-making process, how can they acquire sound procedures for the legal decision-making process? This is an alternative reading of Simmonds' point[33] about the impossibility of having an unjust regime that fully complies with the eight desiderata of the Rule of Law (section 8.6.2). In the above example, the authority's intentions to perform the legal action in an excellent way, ie following the desiderata of the Rule of Law, is undermined by its sub-

---

[32] In this kind of system, we can say that there is an inversion of values, see H Pauer-Studert and D Velleman, 'Distortions of Normativity' (2011) 14 *Ethical Theory and Moral Practice* 329.

[33] N Simmonds, *Law as a Moral Idea* (Oxford, Oxford University Press, 2007); J Finnis, *Natural Law and Natural Rights* (Oxford, Clarendon Press, 1980); Fuller (n 7). Cf M Kramer, 'Big Bad Wolf: Legal Positivism and its Detractors' (2004) *American Journal of Jurisprudence* 1.

stantively wrong beliefs about the good-making characteristics of legal rules. There is a clear conflict between 'having morally wrong beliefs about the grounding reasons of rules' and 'knowing how to make rules with (procedural) good-making characteristics'.

(b) The legal authority has correct beliefs about the grounding reasons as good-making characteristics of the legal rule, but mistaken beliefs about how the legal act should be carried out. However, there is successful performance of the mistaken intention on how to perform the legal act. Authorities can also have mistaken beliefs about how to perform their actions, namely, how to apply and create legal rules. They might believe, for example, that legal rules should not be made public and should apply retroactively. In spite of this, their beliefs about the grounding reasons as good-making characteristics of the legal rule in question might be sound. For example, they think that the value of life is the grounding reason for the road traffic rules, but they apply and create them privately and retroactively. What has failed is their understanding about how rules should be applied and be created. In other words, they have failed on the issue of how to perform their intentions. Let us put the following example. My aim is to spend more time talking to you because you are my friend and, in my view, to spend time with friends is a good sort of thing. My belief about the good-making characteristics of the reason for the action, ie friendship, is sound. However, I have mistaken beliefs about what good quality time with friends means. I become nosey and treat you very impolitely. I did carry out my intention and there was performance, but the purpose or outcome was a failure. You are now able to evaluate the purpose or outcome of my action. Similarly, in the case of legal authorities, we can evaluate the purpose or outcome of the authorities' expressions of intentions about how they have performed their actions and see whether the action is a failure or not. For example, retroactive and private road traffic legal rules create complete chaos. Legal authorities claim legitimate authority and moral correctness but because they have mistaken beliefs about how to create and apply rules, the outcome of the performance is a failure. To succeed in a claim of legitimate authority and moral correctness, to succeed in an expression of an intention of performing actions, such as the creation or application of a rule in a legitimate and morally correct way, the officials, judges and legislators need not only to engage with the grounding reasons as good-making characteristics of legal rules, and with the differences and discriminations of the particulars and the general principles that are part of the precedent cases and statutes, but also they need to engage with how one should create and apply legal rules, and this know-how is provided, in part, by complying with the eight desiderata of the Rule of Law (section 8.6.2).

(c) The legal authority has correct beliefs about the grounding reasons as good-making characteristics of the legal rules and sound intentions about how to perform their legal acts, but they fail in performing the latter. In this scenario, authorities fail in their intentions on how to perform the legal act, in spite of having the correct beliefs about how to perform the act. For example, a judge believes that a good rule should be public, coherent and non-retroactive but nevertheless the judge fails to apply or create a legal rule that is coherent and non-retroactive because she lacks the adequate skills to do so. Her failure is in terms of her intentions about how to perform the legal act. As regards the previous example, I have sounds beliefs about how to be entertaining and polite, but I fail in my performance that afternoon, contrary to my intentions, because, for example I lack the required social skills. In the case of the law, judges and legal authorities might lack the required legal and intellectual skills to bring about their good intentions.

In general terms, there cannot be a complete and general disconnection between authorities' expressions of intention of legitimate authority and moral correctness and their performance. There cannot be a total failure of practical knowledge. Evil and less-than-perfect legal systems are possible precisely because any or some of the previous alternatives are possible.

This chapter has aimed to show the importance of authorities' claims in shaping and creating the law according to the 'guise of the good' model. The story that emerges is a complex one where expressions of intentions, intentional actions, failure and success in performance, and the concept of the good as good-making characteristics are intertwined.

The idea of authoritative claims, including claims on compliance with the eight desiderata of the Rule of Law, as expressions of intentions enables us to create this complex picture where practical knowledge and its possible failure is involved.

8

Authority and Normativity: A Defence of the 'Ethical-Political' Account of Legal Authority*

8.1 RAZ'S EXCLUSIONARY REASONS AND THE GUISE OF THE GOOD MODEL

IS OUR UNDERSTANDING of legal rules under the 'guise of the good' model compatible with the solution provided by Raz concerning the character of legal rules? An inquiry into the nature of legal normativity aims to elucidate the reason-giving character of law whereas an investigation into the nature of legitimate legal authority aims to show how legal authorities have a right to rule and the citizens a duty to obey them.[1] Raz advances a model of legal legitimate authority that connects legal rules and reasons and at the same time adumbrates the view that there is no need to evaluate the grounding reasons of legal rules to determine how they bind us.[2] He indirectly provides an answer to the problem of legal normativity, ie the reason-giving character of rules, and shows that the agent does not need to resort to moral or evaluative reasons to determine the reasons that legal rules or norms provide. Raz tells us that you can conform to the norm without evaluating the content of the norms or legal rules. This is the way that authoritative legal rules operate and influence our practical reasoning.[3]

* This chapter has been written on the basis of material that was published in 'Legal Authority and the Paradox of Intention in Action' in *Reasons and Intentions in Law and Practical Agency* (Cambridge, Cambridge University Press, forthcoming 2015).

[1] P Soper, *The Ethics of Deference* (Cambridge, Cambridge University Press, 2002) 54; J Raz, *The Morality of Freedom* (Oxford, Clarendon Press, 1986) 24–27; RP Wolff, *In Defense of Anarchism* (New York, Harper Torch Books, 1970) 4. Cf W Edmundson, *Three Anarchical Fallacies* (Cambridge, Cambridge University Press, 1998) 7–70.

[2] In its paradigmatic case, legal rules are binding because they fulfil the 'dependence' and the 'normal justification theses'. See Raz (n 1) 47–57.

[3] For interesting interpretations and criticisms of Raz's notion of authority see DS Clarke, 'Exclusionary Reasons' (1975) *Mind* 252; C Gans, 'Mandatory Rules and Exclusionary Reasons' (1986) *Philosophia* 373; H Hurd, *Moral Combat* (Cambridge, Cambridge University Press, 1999) 73–94; M Moore, 'Authority, Law and Razian Reasons' (1988–89) *Southern California Law Review* 827; S Perry, 'Judicial Obligation, Precedent and the Common Law' (1987) 7 *Oxford Journal of Legal Studies* 215; D Regan, 'Authority and Value: Reflections on Raz's *Morality of Freedom*' (1988–92) *Southern California Law Review* 995.

In previous chapters, I defended the 'guise of the good' model for legal rules. It was argued there that when we follow legal rules the rule itself is not the primary reason for action, instead the grounding reasons as good-making characteristics of the rule are the primary explanation, and these grounding reasons need to be *transparent* to the agent. If it is the case that the guise of the good model as applicable to the legal rule-following phenomenon holds true, this contradicts the exclusionary reasons view on legal rules. Raz has defended the guise of the good model of reasons for actions in general, but thinks that it does not apply to authoritative legal rules.[4] Raz advances hence two different conceptions of reasons for actions. In law, legal rules are exclusionary reasons for action[5] whereas actions in general follow the 'guise of the good' model.[6] In the latter case intentional action plays a key role in showing what our reasons for action are (see Chapter 4).

Contra Raz, I have proposed a unified account of reasons for action for both ethics and law. I have thus attempted to show that the 'guise of the good' model applies also to legal rules. Raz advocates the idea that when we follow legal rules, we follow them *unintentionally*; the action is a voluntary one, however, the will of the agent as pursuing reasons as good-making characteristics *is not* engaged. Consequently, says Raz, the 'guise of the good' model *does not apply* to authoritative legal directives and rules. From these considerations, a paradox arises which I shall call 'the paradox of intentionality'. If it is truly the case that we follow legal rules unintentionally then, for example, when I sign a mortgage contract, stop at the traffic lights, follow the fire and safety regulations of my office building, pay my taxes, and so on, all these actions are done *unintentionally*. Are these voluntary but *unintended* actions? Since they are unintended, are they also irrational or arational actions? Raz tell us that they are not irrational or arational because, in the normal case, if we follow legal rules, then we *can conform* to the reasons that apply to us and we have a better chance of succeeding in *conforming* to the reasons that apply to us than if we try to follow independently such reasons. Consequently, legal directives as exclusionary reasons *help us to comply* with the reasons that apply to us. For example, stopping at the traffic lights means that I can avoid collisions; following health and safety regulations means that I can avoid injury in the event that my

---

[4] Arguably, there are traces of the 'guise of the good' model in his early work. Thus, the idea of a complete reason (*Practical Reason and Norms* (Oxford, Oxford University Press, 1999, originally published Hutchinson & Co, 1975) 23) and the idea of the normal justification thesis can be seen as seeds of the 'guise of the good' model. However, this view is combined with other elements that are not compatible with the 'guise of the good' model such as the *opacity* of the reasons for action for the deliberator who follows legal rules.

[5] Raz, *Practical Reason and Norms* (n 4) 73–84.

[6] Raz, 'Agency, Reason and the Good' in *Engaging Reason* (Oxford, Oxford University Press, 1999) 22–45 and 'Guise of the Good' in S Tenenbaum (ed), *Desire, Practical Reason and the Good* (Oxford, Oxford University Press, 2010).

office catches fire. However, the idea that we follow legal rules *unintentionally* is certainly counter-intuitive. Furthermore, it does not provide a solution to the problem of 'surrendering our will'. Thus, Raz's philosophical account of legal authority aims to give a justificatory response to the question *why* we ought to surrender our will to that of another.[7] It will be paradoxical if the answer is that 'you do not need to surrender your will, you merely *suspend* your will as you can act unintentionally and still act rationally'.

In search of a unified account of reasons for actions, a reconstruction of Raz's view on legal rules in the light of the 'guise of the good' model might be as follows. I follow legal rules *because* authority is a good sort of thing (section 8.6). This interpretation is in line with the teleological justification provided by Raz (section 8.4.2) and *the normal justification thesis*.[8] But the question that arises is how can the goodness of legal rules exclude the goodness of my other intentional actions? The answer is this. Authoritative legal rules express an intention: they *intend you*, for example, to stop at the traffic light, and follow health and safety regulations and, in order that you do this, you need to have as the end of your action a central description of a good-making characteristic, ie avoiding collisions with other vehicles, staying healthy and alive. In the ideal or paradigmatic case, the authorities and law-abiding citizens are able to avow good-making characteristics and they constitute the *logos* or grounding reasons of legal rules. These can be found through applying the why-question methodology (section 3.2 and Chapter 4). Suppose an imaginary dialogue with a road traffic officer:

Citizen: Why do you intend that I press the brake pedal?

Road traffic officer: Because there is a red light.

Citizen: Why do you intend that I stop at the red light?

Road traffic officer: Because doing so will protect your life and the lives of others.

---

[7] Raz points out: 'The problem I have in mind is the problem of the possible justification of subjecting one's will to that of another, and of the normative standing of demands to do so. The account of authority that I offered, many years ago, under the title of the service conception of authority, addressed this issue, and assumed that all other problems regarding authority are subsumed under it' (J Raz, 'The Problem of Authority: Revisiting the Service Conception' (2006) *Minnesota Law Review* 1003, reprinted in *Between Authority and Interpretation* (Oxford, Oxford University Press, 2009). He also formulates the problem as 'surrendering one's judgement' (J Raz, 'The Problem of Authority: Revisiting the Service Conception' 1019). However, I do not think that this latter formulation is entirely satisfactory as the surrendering of one's judgement does not necessarily entail action. Raz also formulates the problem as both a submission of one's will and one's judgement (1012).

[8] The normal justification thesis is advanced by Raz in the following terms: 'the normal way to establish that a person has authority over another person involves showing that the alleged subject is likely better to comply with reasons which apply to him (other than the alleged authoritative directives) if he accepts the directives of the alleged authority as authoritatively binding and tries to follow them, rather than trying to follow reasons that apply to him directly' (*The Morality of Freedom* (n 1) 53).

Citizen: Why do we have to protect my life and the lives of others?

Road traffic officer: Because life is valuable.

Does this mean that, according to the 'guise of the good' model, I need to have *transparent* grounding reasons for following rules? The answer is positive. However, Raz would argue, this reconstruction contradicts the idea that rules are authoritative and hence undermines their function, ie they perform a mediating role between reasons and persons. In other words, we act not because of the rule, but because of the grounding reasons as good-making characteristics of the legal rules which we can decide not to avow. Consequently, rules will be redundant since they will play no role in our practical reasoning. Raz would strengthen his position that in order for rules be part of our practical reasoning, they *cannot* be transparent to us.

Contra Raz, I will defend the view that the guise of the good model is compatible with the authoritative character of the law. I will adumbrate the view that we *can* act according to a presumption of the goodness of the rules and therefore a *presumption* of the authoritative force of legal rules. In this way, legal rules will play a service for us, but only because either one of the following:

(a) One recognises the goodness of the authority, due to the authority' claims and the compliance with most of the eight desiderata of the Rule of Law (section 8.6.2), and from this recognition a presumption about the goodness of authority and its legitimacy arises (section 8.6.1). Furthermore, one avows the grounding reasons as good-making characteristics of the legal rules. In these cases, there is full agency, ie full intentional action, in the context of the law.

(b) One recognises the goodness of the authority and the compliance with most of the eight desiderata of the Rule of Law (section 8.6.2), and from this recognition a presumption about the goodness of authority and its legitimacy arises (section 8.6.1). However, one does not avow the grounding reasons as good-making characteristics of the legal rules. In these cases, there is full agency in the context of the law.

(c) One follows the authority's directives and legal rules by avowing the grounding reasons as good-making characteristics of the legal rules. In these cases, there is also full agency in the context of the law.

(d) One follows the authority's directives and legal rules by merely *theoretically* understanding the grounding reasons as good-making characteristics or *logos* of the legal rules. However, one does not avow the grounding reasons as good-making characteristics of the legal rules. In this case, one is alienated from the law and if this alienation is systematic and continuous, there is no full agency in the context of the law. However, one might argue that in these cases it is a mystery how one can follow legal rules that involve complex actions (see Chapter 1).

In this way, the service that legal rules provide to us will be delivered in an 'ethical-political' way, which means that law tries either to create a presumption of legitimacy or to engage our will and for this we need the grounding reasons as good-making characteristics of legal rules to be transparent. Prior to developing these substantive views, I will try to explain and advance a criticism of Raz's notion of exclusionary reasons. This is the task I now turn to.

8.2 REASONS FOR ACTIONS IN RAZ'S LEGAL AND MORAL PHILOSOPHIES

In the early work *Practical Reason and Norms,* Raz established that only reasons understood as facts are normatively relevant. Beliefs can help us to determine reasons for actions because they make us aware of the facts in the world.[9] The premise for this conclusion is the idea that reasons *guide* us in our actions and, consequently, in order to decide what we should do we need to look at what the world looks like.[10] Reasons as mental states, ie beliefs and desires, are merely *explanatory.* They do not help us to understand *why* the agent has acted as he or she did; they play a secondary role in understanding action.[11]

8.2.1 Some Key Distinctions for Understanding Exclusionary Reasons

Raz distinguishes between (a) complete and operative reasons, and (b) first-order and second-order reasons. A complete reason is, Raz tells us, not always explicitly stated and has different parts which are also reasons. For example, let us suppose that I tell you that I am going to the train station, however I do not tell you *why* I am going to the train station. If I am asked *why,* I might reply:

Enquirer: Why are you going to the train station?

(a) 'Because James will be arriving at the train station'; (b) 'James will be pleased if I meet him at the station'; and (c) 'I would like to please James'

Enquirer: But why would you like to please James?

---

[9] Raz, *Practical Reason and Norms* (n 4) 18–20.

[10] ibid 18.

[11] Raz: 'A person's action can be judged as being well grounded in reason or not according to whether there actually are reasons for performing the action. It can also be assessed as reasonable or rational according to whether the person had reason to believe that there were reasons for his actions. It is the world which guides our action, but since it inevitably does so through our awareness of it, our beliefs are important for the explanation and assessment of our behaviour', *Practical Reason and Norms* (n 4) 22.

'Because (d) I have promised that I will meet James at the train station; (e) One ought to please one's friends'.

For Raz, a complete reason is a set of complex reasons; something similar to what one obtains as a result of the *why*-question methodology (section 3.2 and Chapter 4). However, in *Practical Reason and Norms*, Raz does not endorse the view that the chain of successive steps of action can be unified in an intelligible form by a reason as a good-making characteristic. On the contrary, in his early work, Raz asserts that (d) and (e) are not reasons for going to the station, but rather *reasons for reasons* for going to the station. He states: *'They are not parts of reasons which John has for going to the station. They are reasons for the reasons for going to the station'.*[12] The idea of reasons for reasons and that reasons have a relative strength as some reasons can override other reasons[13] entails the view that there are second-order reasons in addition to first-order reasons. According to Raz, every complete reason includes an operative reason.[14] Operative reasons are either values or desires or interests.[15] One should not interpret operative reasons as subjective motivational reasons since operative reasons might include values.[16]

8.3 A CRITICISM OF SECOND-ORDER REASONS

Raz argues that exclusionary reasons are a sub-species of second-order reasons. However, when we look closely at the examples provided by Raz, we see that there is truly only one action that is explained by successive steps of action, or so I will argue.

I have explained the structure of agency that is obtained when one engages in the *why-question* methodology (Chapter 2, section 3.2, Chapter 4). Thus, reasons for actions can be elucidated when one is asking the agent *why* such and such an action was performed. Actions are explained in terms of other actions and the inquiry stops when a reason as a good-making characteristic is provided. This reason is the end of the action that unifies all the successive actions. Applying the 'guise of the good' model of intentional action to the example of collecting James from the train station, the series of actions, ie taking the vehicle, driving to the train station, parking at the train station, getting out of the vehicle, entering the train station and meeting James, is explained in virtue of the two reasons, namely, the promise that I have made

---

[12] ibid 23.
[13] ibid 25–28.
[14] ibid 33.
[15] ibid 33–34.
[16] Raz points out: 'Every value is a reason for action. It is an open question whether all operative reasons are either subjective or objective values', *Practical Reasons and Norms* (n 4) 34.

to James and the fact that to please friends is a reason as a good-making characteristic for the action. If I am asked why I have fulfilled my promise to James, the answer might be 'because fulfilling promises to friends shows our respect for them'. Thus (d) and (e) are not second-order reasons or another layer of reasons, but they are the reasons for action for going to the train station. Following the structure of the Aristotelian practical syllogism,[17] a reformulation of (d) or (e) as the premises of the good-making characteristics of the action are as follows:

(e') It is good to please one's friends and (d') It is a good to fulfil one's promises

(c) James is my friend and I would like to please James and (c') I have promised that I will meet James at the train station

(b) James will be pleased if I meet him at the train station

(a) James will be arriving at the train station

I will go to the train station(!)

Raz denies this explanation. He asserts 'there are *reasons for the reasons* for going to the station'. However, if I am going to the station because James will be arriving there, this does not necessarily make intelligible the action. It might be that James will arrive there, he is my enemy and wishes to kill me. Obviously, I have no intelligible reason for going to the station. The answers 'I have promised that I will be there' or 'One ought to please one's friends' are *the reasons as good-making* characteristics that illuminate the other parts of the intentional action. The explanation that there is another layer of reasons contradicts the way we think about reasons for actions within the classical tradition also advocated by Raz in his later work.[18] Does this argument show that there is no such thing as second-order reasons and that, therefore, the status of exclusionary reasons as second-order reasons can at the very least be put in doubt? The argument only shows that we need a better characterisation of second-order reasons.

---

[17] Kenny points out that the practical syllogism does not really look like a syllogism of the Aristotelian logic. He points out: 'First, talk of the "major premise" and the "minor premise" suggests that practical reasoning, like the traditional Aristotelian syllogism, involves exactly two premises, whereas Aristotle is very flexible in the number of premises he allows. Secondly, Aristotle himself never uses the expressions "major" and "minor" of practical premises'. A Kenny, *Aristotle's Theory of the Will* (London, Duckworth, 1979) 122. For a criticism of this conception of practical syllogism, see section 4.2.1.

[18] Raz, *Engaging Reason* (n 6) 22–23.

8.4 THE GUISE OF THE GOOD MODEL AS COMPETING WITH THE EXCLUSIONARY REASONS MODEL

There are three independent arguments advanced by Raz that aim to show that there is another layer of reasons, as opposed to first-order reasons or a continuum of reasons and successive steps towards an action. These arguments are: a phenomenological argument, the teleological argument, and the analogy argument. I will argue that the 'guise of the good model' can satisfactorily explain the phenomenological and teleological arguments and I will offer some criticisms of the analogical argument.

8.4.1 Phenomenological Argument

Raz gives three different examples to show the plausibility of exclusionary reasons.[19] In the first example, Ann wishes to make a good financial investment. Late in the evening, a friend tells her about a possible investment opportunity. The drawback of the offer is that Anne needs to decide that evening about the investment otherwise the offer will be withdrawn. Due to her fatigue she decides not to accept the offer. She rejects the offer not because she has considered the merits of the case and takes it that there are good reasons to reject the offer, rather she rejects the offer because she cannot trust her own judgement due to her fatigue. Anne, consequently, has not acted on the balance of reasons, but her first-order reasons are excluded by an undefeated exclusionary reason, ie the fact that she cannot trust her own judgement. In the second example, Jeremy, a soldier, is ordered by his commanding officer to appropriate a van. His friend urges him to disobey the order; however, Jeremy believes that he should obey and that it is not up to him to decide whether or not to obey an order. The order of the commanding officer excludes Jeremy's first-order reasons for action. In the third example, Colin promises his wife that in all decisions affecting the education of his son he will act only according to the best interests of his son. He now needs to consider whether to send his son to a private school; doing so will mean that he will be unable to quit his job to write his book. Colin's promise does not affect his first-order reason, ie the fact that he has reasons to pursue a career as a writer, rather it excludes his first-order reason.

We can criticise the examples and question whether they are cases of acting according to reasons for *actions*. In the case of Anne, following the 'guise of the good' model, we can say that there is only one action: she goes to bed because she is tired and she needs to sleep. On the other hand, before this action she

---

[19] Raz, *Practical Reasons and Norms* (n 4) 35–39.

takes a decision '*not to act* and *not to* invest her money' and as there is no action involved, there is no execution of any action. Alternatively, we can say that she intends an inaction, ie not to invest her money and her reason for such inaction is that she does not intend to lose money because avoiding ill-considered investments has, in her view, good-making characteristics. In the case of Jeremy, we could say that he obeys the authority because authority is a good sort of thing (see section 8.6.1 for a detailed explanation of cases in which citizens follow legal authorities because authorities are a good sort of thing, without avowing the grounding reasons as good-making characteristics of an action). In the case of Colin, we have seen from the example of 'I am going to the train station to collect James' that a promise can be a reason for action as a good-making characteristic. The action is 'Colin takes his son to a private school' and the reason for action as a good-making characteristic is that 'he has promised his wife that he will act only according to the best interests of his son' and Colin believes[20] that 'one should fulfil one's promises'. These two reasons are the reasons for actions as good-making characteristics that unify all of Collin's actions, ie completing the application form for the school, accepting the offer of a place on behalf of his son and paying the school fees.

Let us for the sake of argument accept that Anne, Jeremy and Colin are acting for exclusionary reasons. Raz tells us that when we disregard exclusionary reasons and act following our first-order reasons, we feel torn and uneasy[21] in a way that we do *not* feel when we decide not to act for overriding reasons and act according to weaker reasons. The phenomenological argument aims to show that the strength of exclusionary reasons is different from the strength of overriding first-order reasons. Let us suppose that Jeremy decides to disobey and not to follow the order of his commanding officer. He has good reasons not to obey the authority's reasons and knows that he has done the right thing by disobeying. Nevertheless, he still feels torn and uneasy in a way that is different from occasions when he acts according to weaker reasons. To account for this phenomenological experience, Raz tells us, we need to postulate that there are different layers of reasons. Exclusionary reasons, consequently, explain the phenomenon in a satisfactory manner.

However, the guise of the good model can explain the phenomenon of uneasiness as follows. If we consider that authority is a good sort of thing (this is compatible with Raz's teleological argument analysed in section 8.4.2), then we feel that we have sacrificed one good, most likely a good that is impartial and that affects many people in the community, for another good which is

---

[20] When we talk about belief we refer to the *content* of the belief and not to the mental state. For a clarification on this see M Alvarez, *Kinds of Reasons* (Oxford, Oxford University Press, 2010) 44–50.

[21] See B Williams, 'Ethical Consistency' (1966) *Proceedings of the Aristotelian Society* 103 for a similar argument on moral conflicts.

more personal, and this might produce feelings of a loss, ie the loss of the good that the authority could have delivered not just to me, but to many people if I had followed the authority's rule or directive. It seems natural to feel that the goodness that the authority could have delivered is more important than the goodness of my act and that, therefore, the feelings of being torn are stronger than when I decide between two different personal goods. In Jeremy's case, he might feel that by disobeying the order of the commanding officer he had risked or lost the goodness of the coordinating actions that the authority provides. However, he knows that he has acted well in not appropriating the van. He feels torn because the authority of the commanding officer seems to him key to succeeding in the military operation that they are involved in.

8.4.2 Teleological Argument

Like many other legal philosophers Raz has argued that authoritative legal rules are a good sort of thing.[22] They help us to avoid personal errors and reduce the risk of such errors. They are labour-saving devices and we can rely on the fact that others will follow them, and consequently they provide certainty in our interactions with others. Authoritative legal rules provide a service for us and they cannot serve their purpose unless they are treated as exclusionary reasons for actions.[23] Authorities can secure coordination only if legal norms are considered exclusionary reasons. Citizens must defer to the authority and put their first-order reasons to one side.

I will show in section 8.6 that the teleological argument can equally be explained by the 'guise of the good' model.[24] However, there is some ambiguity in the notion of 'service' and I use this ambiguity to make apparent the idea that authoritative legal rules serve us in a 'ethical-political' manner.

It should be emphasised that Raz's phenomenological and teleological arguments are not used to support the idea of rules under the guise of the good model. Rather, Raz's arguments are used to show that they favour rules as exclusionary reasons, but also rules as construed by the guise of the good model. What so far has been shown, at least, is that the idea of rules conceived under the guise of the good model compete with the idea of rules as exclusionary reasons.

There is a third argument against Raz's view on legal rules as exclusionary reasons that will be advanced. It is, in my view, the most compelling argument and to its examination I now turn.

---

[22] Raz, *Practical Reasons and Norms* (n 4) 58–59, 195.

[23] ibid 72.

[24] Green asserts: 'law has ends, and law should serve good ends; but what marks law off from other social institutions are the means by which it serves ends'. See L Green, 'Law as Means' in *The Hart-Fuller Debate in the 21st Century* (Oxford, Hart Publishing, 2010) 169–88.

8.4.3 Analogical Argument

Raz argues that there is an analogy between decisions and legal rules;[25] in both cases, once they have been formed, you do not submit them to revision.[26] Arguably, however, decisions are acts of the will, they do not merely involve a mental state because if they are merely mental states the question that arises is how they can cause our actions in the *right sort* of way (sections 5.3.2 and 10.3). Furthermore, the mentalist or inward interpretation of the notion of decisions is not compatible with Raz's views on beliefs and reasons. For Raz, neither beliefs nor reasons are merely mental states. Beliefs are relevant for actions to the extent that they make us aware of facts in the world and enable us to act according to such facts. No obvious arguments support the mentalist interpretation of decisions in conjunction with the rejection of the mentalist interpretation of beliefs and reasons. If no such distinction is made, then decisions are more than merely mental states. Decisions, in the classical tradition, are acts of will. Aquinas points out:

> The term 'electio' implies a quality of reason or intellect and a quality of will; Aristotle refers to it being both understanding as desirous and desire as understanding. Accordingly then, that will-act which turns towards an object proposed to it as being good, that is, as being reasonably subordinate to the end, is 'materially' one of will, but 'formally' one of reason. To appetite belongs the texture of the act, to knowledge its shape. In this sense choice is substantially an act of will, not of reason, wrought in a certain going out of the soul to a good which is preferred, clearly an act of appetite power.[27]

Raz argues that rules are like decisions or 'electio'. He makes a distinction between a deliberative and an executive stage of decision-making. In the former stage, we make choices and in the latter stage, we just follow rules and neither make choices nor deliberate. In other words, at the deliberative stage, we form our decisions, but once they are formed we enter into the executive stage. Rules, like decisions, always seem to work, Raz tells us, at the executive stage.[28] This view seems to contradict the perspective advocated by the classical tradition on the matter.[29] In Aristotle, for example, not all deliberation is

---

[25] The analogy argument aims to show the role that rules and decisions play in our practical reasoning (Raz, *Practical Reasons and Norms* (n 4) 74).

[26] ibid 67.

[27] T Aquinas, *Summa Theologica* (Latin and English text, Thomas Gilby (trans), Cambridge, Cambridge University Press, 2006) Ia2æ q13, I.

[28] For Raz, decisions and intentions belong only to the deliberative stage, *Ethics in the Public Domain* (Oxford, Oxford University Press, 1995) 205–6.

[29] For a discussion of this point see E Anscombe, 'Thought and Action in Aristotle: What is "Practical Truth"?' in *From Parmenides to Wittgenstein* (Oxford, Basil Blackwell, 1981) 66–77; and Kenny (n 17) 69–80. See also J Finnis, *Aquinas* (Oxford, Oxford University Press, 1998) 62–71.

with the view to making a choice, there is also deliberation when one *executes a choice*. Choices or decisions (*prohairesis*) require not only virtue in selecting the end, but also 'cleverness' in executing the choice (*Nichomachean Ethics*, 1144a20). We can only deliberate on the things that are within our powers. True, we do not deliberate on the *blind* following of rules or science. Let me quote in full the following passage of *Nichomachean Ethics* that makes this point apparent:

> We deliberate about things that are in our control and are attainable by action.[30] Also there is no room for deliberation about matters fully ascertained and completely formulated as sciences, such for instance as orthography, for we have no uncertainty as to how a word ought to be spelt. We deliberate about things in which our agency operates but not always produce the same results; for instance about questions of medicine and of business; and we deliberate about navigation more than about athletic training, because it has been less completely reduced to a science; and similarly with other pursuits also. And we deliberate more about the arts than about the sciences, because we are more uncertain about them. Deliberation then is employed in matters which, though subject to rules that generally hold good, are uncertain in their issue; or where the issue is indeterminate, and where, when the matter is important, we take others into our deliberations, distrusting our own capacity to decide.[31]

Thus, the doctor needs to deliberate about the best treatment and other means to cure his patient in just the same way that the legislator, judge and citizen need to deliberate about the way to proceed according to the grounding reasons as good-making characteristics of legal rules. Legal rules are not determined and specified as are the rules of orthography.[32] Nevertheless, knowledge of the rules of orthography is not sufficient to write an essay. Analogically, nor it is sufficient to know the meaning of words and legal concepts to create and follow legal rules. Thus, to create and follow legal rules, because law is a purposive activity, one needs to deliberate on how to achieve the grounding reasons as good-making characteristics of rules. They might be presented in a complex way or unfold as we follow and create them. 'Good' is a complex thing (Chapter 9). The phenomenology of following legal rules

---

[30] Aristotle, *Nichomachean Ethics* (H Rackham (trans), Cambridge, MA, Harvard University Press, 1934) 1112a37.

[31] ibid 1112b3–12.

[32] For analyses on the vagueness and indeterminacy of the law, see T Endicott, *The Vagueness of Law* (Oxford, Oxford University Press, 2000), and A Halpin, *Reasoning with Law* (Oxford, Hart Publishing, 2001) 83–102. Interestingly, L Fuller, *The Morality of Law* (New Haven, CT, Yale University Press, 1969) 6, quoting Adam Smith's *Theory of Moral Sentiments*, gives the following example to illustrate the connection between the morality of duty and the morality of aspiration: to know how to write well, you need the basic rules of grammar, but they will not guarantee an elegant and sublime composition. Arguably, we can say that to follow legal rules and to create legal rules, citizens, judges and legislators need to know the formal features of law, but also need to engage with more substantive aspects of legal activity.

shows that we do not follow legal rules blindly, we engage with legal rules and believe that we do so as autonomous and active agents, controlling the steps or successive actions necessary to follow and create rules, and thus we conceive ourselves as exercising deliberation and practical reasoning. When the law makes requirements and demands on us, such as stopping at traffic lights, paying the correct amount for a train ticket, parking our vehicle where it is legally permissible to do so, smoking only in designated areas, paying council tax, signing a mortgage contract, and so on, we do not think that we carry out these activities blindly, we feel and think that our active self is engaged.

Let us think about my decision to go to the train station to collect James. I go to the train station because he will be there, I wish to please him and in my view it is good to please one's friends. According to Raz, you do not need to deliberate any further on your reasons for going to the station. I execute the decision which cannot be submitted to revision. True, it might be that the decided act, ie going to the train station, is not submitted to revision; however, according to the classical tradition, in executing my choice or decision I need to engage in deliberation. This engagement is necessary in order to deliberate about *how to execute the choice* or decision. Consequently I need to understand the end of my decided act in order to assess the means to achieve it. I know that I am going to the train station to collect James in order to please him. I need to deliberate on whether I should take the car, the bus or two bikes, one for me and one for James. I know that James does not like to cycle, and because my grounding reason is to please James, it then seems obvious that I chose between the bus or the car. I also know that he has just completed a very long journey and therefore may be unwilling to walk to the bus station and sit on a crowded bus. It seems then better to bring the car. Let us suppose that you order me to collect James at the train station, but the grounding reasons of your order are not transparent to me, ie the good-making characteristics that you are pursuing. I collect James but I bring a bike for him to cycle, not knowing that he hates to cycle. You will obviously not achieve the end of your action, ie pleasing James.

Let us imagine the following legal example. In 'Treeland' there is a rule that establishes that trees above a certain height must be cut in order to avoid casting shadows on the neighbouring property. If you know the rule 'Tall trees planted in private gardens need to be cut', without knowing the grounding reason as a good-making characteristic of the rule, you might find it difficult to be able to follow the rule. Furthermore, the pure execution of the rule without deliberating about the means to achieve the grounding reason of the rule might, in many cases, be an impediment to following the rule. Knowledge of the grounding reason as a good-making characteristic of the rule will enable you to decide how much of the tree needs to be cut and what is the most appropriate tool for doing so, etc. Let us suppose that you do not know the grounding reason of the rule and simply cut too little of the tree, then one might say that you have failed to follow the rule.

The argument so far has attempted to undermine the idea that there is always a clear line between the decision/deliberative stage and the executive stage in both decisions and legal rules. In many cases there is instead a continuous spectrum between the two stages. Consequently, the argument, indirectly, aims to undermine the idea of rules as exclusionary reasons where engagement with deliberation is absent and mere execution is required. True, there will be legal rules where engagement with deliberation at the executive stage is not necessary due to the fact that in some cases they involve a single or non-complex action (see Chapter 1). But if there are cases in which the continuity of the stages is shown, then this will suffice to throw doubt on the soundness of the analogy argument as construed by Raz. If it is true that decisions are like legal rules, then due to the fact that the execution of decisions requires deliberation, we might say that execution of legal rules also requires engagement with deliberation. The argument also shows that in the normal cases the grounding reasons as good-making characteristics need to be somehow *transparent* to the agent. By contrast, exclusionary reasons are *opaque* to the agent.

8.5 EXCLUSIONARY REASONS AND THE PARADOX OF INTENTION IN ACTION

Let me summarise the core arguments that support the idea of legal rules as presented in the guise of the good model: (a) the guise of the good model is the *primary* explanation of how we act intentionally (Chapters 2, 3, 4); (b) the claims of authorities should be interpreted as expressions of an intention about *how* authorities *will perform* their legal actions (Chapter 7); (c) when we follow or comply with legal rules, paradigmatically, we follow or comply with them intentionally (Chapter 2), therefore following from (a), we can say that *the guise of the good model is the primary explanation of following or complying with legal rules.*

Raz points out:

> Authority can secure co-ordination only if the individuals concerned defer to its judgement and do not act on the balance of reasons, but on the authority's instructions. This guarantees that all will participate in one plan of action, that action will be co-ordinated. But it requires that people should regard authoritative utterances as exclusionary reasons, as reasons for not acting on the balance of reasons as they see it even when they are right. To accept an authority on these grounds is not to act irrationally or arbitrarily. The need for an authority may be well founded in reason. But the reasons are of a special kind. They establish the need to regard authoritative utterances as exclusionary reasons. We have briefly examined two methods of justifying authority. There are others. But we may perhaps generalise on the basis of the cases examined and conclude that to regard somebody as an

authority is to regard some of his utterances as authoritative even if wrong on the balance of reasons. It means, in other words, that an authoritative utterance is regarded as an exclusionary reason.[33]

This paragraph summarises the core arguments of Raz's *Practical Reason and Norms*. The premises of the argument are the following:

(a) Authority can serve us, ie it can coordinate our activities, but only if individuals defer their judgements to it.
(b) Therefore, in the circumstances of authority, individuals cannot act according to their reasons for action, even if they are right.
(c) We, however, act rationally when we follow legal authorities in spite of the fact that we do not act according to our own reasons.
(d) Consequently, legal rules issued by legitimate legal authorities ought to be exclusionary reasons.[34] This means that the idea that legal rules provide exclusionary reasons is the best possible explanation of (a), (b) and (c).

In the following section, I will qualify (a), (b) and (c) and reject (d).

What is the conception of reasons in Raz's later work[35] and how is it compatible with the idea of exclusionary reasons as a sub-class of first-order reasons?

I have explained that to act for reasons is to act intentionally (Chapter 4). This notion of intentional action is characterised by Raz as 'the intention with which I perform an action'. He expresses this as follows: 'It *could be that I am drinking the water, but it could be otherwise. I may just distractedly pick up the glass of water and sip from it, while thinking about the implications of a flaw in my argument. My action is intentional, but there is no intention with which I perform it*'.[36] Raz's later conception of reasons for actions, except for the cases of legal authoritative directives, does not differ much from the one defended in this book. He asserts: '*Actions performed with an independent intention are actions performed for reasons, as those are seen by the agents*'.[37] Intentional action is taken as the paradigmatic case of action.

---

[33] Raz, *Practical Reasons and Norms* (n 4) 64–65.

[34] A later formulation by Raz of his own notion of authority in terms of protected reasons is as follows: 'Sometimes a person may have a reason for performing an action and also a reason for not acting for certain reasons against that very action. The son, in our example, may know that his coat is ugly. This is a reason against wearing it. It conflicts with his mother's instruction to wear a coat when he goes out at night. But the reason against wearing the coat is reinforced indirectly by the father's order to disregard the mother's instruction. In this and many other cases the fact that is a reason (the father's order) for disregarding certain reasons (the mother's instruction) for ϕ-ing (wearing the coat) is different from any fact that is a reason (the coat's ugliness) for not ϕ-ing. But sometimes the same fact is both a reason for an action and an (exclusionary) reason for disregarding reasons against it. I shall call such facts protected reasons for action' (*The Authority of Law* (Oxford, Oxford University Press, 1979) 17–18). According to Raz, all mandatory rules are protected reasons (*The Authority of Law* (n 19) 18).

[35] Raz, *Engaging Reason* (n 6).

[36] Raz, 'Guise of the Good'(n 6) 117.

[37] ibid 16.

In his early work,[38] however, Raz did not examine the legal agents' explanations of their own actions which reveal the reasons for their actions as good-making characteristics. Raz's focus was on reasons for actions as related to persons but there was no emphasis on the descriptions of the actions as provided by the agent.[39] In other words, Raz did not connect reasons for actions and intentional actions. If we follow legal rules *intentionally*, should not the 'guise of the good' model be the best possible explanation of the legal rule-following phenomenon? By contrast, if we follow legal rules according to the exclusionary reasons model, then we do not follow legal rules *intentionally*. Consequently, it seems that to follow legal rules under the model of exclusionary reasons is a case of peripheral agency and not of full agency.[40] However, what would justify conceiving reasons for actions under the guise of the good model, whilst conceiving exclusionary reasons as a different kind of reasons? In the latter case, contrary to the predominant view,[41] we would have reasons for actions, but not an *intentional* action. We might find some answers to this puzzle in Raz's texts. Raz, for example, asserts that intentional action should be considered as a matter of degree:

> The examples under discussion bring out that being intentional can be a matter of degree. Actions are characterised as intentional by a variety of criteria, several of which can be realised to various degrees, making it appropriate to speak of degrees of intentionality. There are cases of which one should say 'Yes, up to a point, or in certain respects it was intentional, but in others less so'.[42]

Anscombe's work on intentions also seems to support this interpretation.[43] There are cases, she tells us, in which the answer to the question 'why did you do so and so' is clearly a reason as a good-making characteristics as perceived by the agent. There are, however, other occasions when we answer as if we have only discovered that we are doing x because it has been *observed* that we are doing it. For example, you ask me why I have put a hot pan on your hand, and I reply, 'Oops, sorry, I didn't realise!'. I was obviously not aware of my action and my action is *unintentional*. There are other occasions when I act *involuntarily* and *unintentionally*, for example, I jump when I hear a loud bang. On other occasions I act voluntarily but for no reasons. '*The question (why) is not refused application because the answer to it says that there is no reason, any more than the*

---

[38] Raz, *Practical Reason and Norms* (n 4); *The Authority of Law* (n 34); and *The Morality of Freedom* (n 1).

[39] Raz, *Practical Reason and Norms* (n 4) 20–22.

[40] Raz supports the classical approach of reasons exemplified by Aristotle, Plato and Aquinas and according to him this view 'takes acting for a reason to be the distinctive and central case of human agency' (Raz, *Engaging Reason* (n 6) 22).

[41] E Anscombe, *Intention*, 2nd edn (Cambridge, MA, Harvard University Press, 2000, originally published in 1957) and M Alvarez, 'Acting Intentionally and Acting for a Reason' (2009) *Inquiry* 293 and *Kinds of Reasons* (n 20).

[42] Raz, 'Guise of the Good' (n 6) 123.

[43] Anscombe (n 41) para 17.

question how much money I have in my pocket is refused application by the answer "None".[44]
Anscombe concludes at para 18 with the following assertion:

> The answers to the question 'Why?' which give it an application are, then, more extensive in range that the answers which give reasons for acting. This question 'Why?' can now be defined as the question expecting an answer in this range. And with this we have roughly outlined the area of intentional actions.[45]

Can we say that when we follow exclusionary reasons we act within this wide range of intentional actions? We have learned that if there are reasons for action, then there is an intentional action. The application of the question 'Why?' enables us to distinguish actions that are intentional from the ones that are non-intentional or unintentional, but we have learned that because of the wide application of the question 'Why?' there is an equally wide spectrum between intentional and unintentional actions, and possibly a wide spectrum *within* the category of intentional actions; arguably, if we characterised intentional action in terms of reasons for actions, it is a matter of degrees, but the action is identified as *intentional*. If we follow legal rules as exclusionary reasons, then we follow them *intentionally* and the question that arises is how exclusionary reasons can be reasons as good-making characteristics for the agent who follows legal rules *without* assessing the content of the reasons. In other words, how do such reasons become *transparent* to the agent? The problem that arises, Raz would tell us, is that if such reasons become transparent to the agent, then the rule cannot perform its function of serving us. The pre-emptive thesis explains how rules provide a service for us. According to the pre-emptive thesis, the requirement of performance by an authority is a reason for its performance. This reason should not be added to all the relevant reasons (for actions) when assessing what to do. On the contrary, they exclude and replace all the relevant reasons (for actions). Therefore, because rules or authoritative directives reflect the reasons which apply to the subjects, then they replace *people's own judgements on the merits of the case*.[46] If the rules remain opaque, then they can preserve their function of serving us in our decisions, but then our actions are not because of the rule as a *reason*. We cannot characterise our actions as *intentional* and therefore say that we are *acting* for reasons. We can only characterise them using the terminology introduced by Raz; the agent merely *conforms with reasons for actions*.[47]

---

[44] ibid para 25; cf S Tenenbaum, *Appearances of the Good* (Cambridge, Cambridge University Press, 2007) 90–99.

[45] Anscombe (n 41) para 18.

[46] Raz, *The Morality of Freedom* (n 1) 59.

[47] Raz, *Practical Reason and Norms* (n 4) 178–82, 190, 194; *The Morality of Freedom* (n 1) 41; 'The Problem of Authority: Revisiting the Service Conception' (n 7) 1014, 1017–19, 1022; *The Authority of Law* (n 34) 29.

When we say that a man or a woman is not aware of what she or he is doing, we say that they are under the influence of drugs, or are somnambular or are under such a state of emotions, and urges that after the experience they cannot explain *why* they acted as they did; these are 'limit or borderline experiences' (at the edge of consciousness). We can also act at the edge of consciousness when we are fearful of all imaginary or real pressures (personal, social, legal, etc). Actions at the edge of consciousness are voluntary but unintentional. But these are not the paradigmatic cases of actions 'following legal rules'. When we follow legal rules, we know how to continue with the action despite the fact that something might have gone wrong during the action and this is the case because we are able to grasp the grounding reasons as good-making characteristics of the legal rules (see the 'guidance problem' in section 2.7). Therefore, *contra* Raz, I argue that, in the normal cases, we follow legal rules *intentionally*. For example, let us suppose that the traffic lights at a certain junction in my town have stopped working; I stop carefully and wait until there are no vehicles, cyclists or pedestrians continuing to drive, cycle or walk. I am able to follow the legal rules of road traffic, even though something has gone wrong, ie the traffic lights are faulty, because I understand that the grounding reasons of the rules of road traffic are the safety and protection of the lives of pedestrians, drivers and road users.

An objector might reply that we are able to continue with the rules of the road traffic because we follow what others are doing and we have learned this by convention. My response is that this is a mistake. If, while I am driving, I look at what others are doing and see that they are stopping at the red traffic lights and I also observe that they stopped at the traffic lights even when it was not working, I could conclude, in line with the objector, that they have learned about these contingencies through mere conventions. Following the convention, I will also stop. However, it is a mystery how I am supposed to continue driving. Should I stop when I see pedestrians or cyclists, or only pedestrians? Should I stop when I see someone on a scooter? What about a tricycle or a carriage? How can I learn all these contingencies just by convention *now* at the moment of acting? How can I learn all these contingencies on the rule and apply them at the *same* time as I am acting? How can I look and interpret the behaviour of others when in order to act I need to look at the road, the pedestrians, my own vehicle and the broken traffic lights? Furthermore, how can I do all these things whilst 'remembering' my mental state of 'acceptance'? (section 5.3.3).

These reflections enforce the view that in the normal cases when we follow legal rules we do so *intentionally*. The majority of contemporary scholars agree that law guides us.[48] We are now able to understand the paradox of intentionality that emerges from the notion of exclusionary reasons:

[48] J Finnis, 'Foundations of Practical Reason Revisited' (2005) *American Journal of Jurisprudence* 109; S Shapiro, 'What is the Internal Point of View' (2006) 75 *Fordham Law Review* 1157; HLA Hart, *The Concept of Law*, 2nd edn (Oxford, Clarendon Press, 1994). Raz points out: 'Reasons can

The paradox of intentionality: if we follow legal rules intentionally, then legal rules cannot be exclusionary reasons. If we do not follow legal rules intentionally, then legal rules do not have a reason-giving character. Therefore, either legal rules cannot be exclusionary reasons or legal rules do not have a reason-giving character.

From a textual analysis of Raz's works we can infer that he accepts the antecedent of the second horn of the paradox, ie we do not follow legal rules intentionally, and that he rejects the consequent, namely, he argues that we have exclusionary reasons for action. Let us analyse Raz's position. For Raz, compliance with reasons for actions is relevant only to the extent that it is a secure route to conformity with reasons for actions.[49] Paradoxically, however, conformity with reasons does not require the exercise of our practical capacities as we can act unintentionally.[50] Raz argues that in cases of non-feasance, over-determination and unintended action, conformity with reasons does not require being aware of the reasons which apply to one and reacting directly to them. He asserts that *there is good reason to think that we cannot reliably conform to reason unless much of the time we do so automatically and unthinkingly*.[51] We act, therefore, without deliberation and in the absence of our practical capacities. Raz also points out that in cases of authoritative directives there ought to be some reliable beliefs that the *conditions* for legitimate authority are met.[52]

---

be used for guiding and evaluating only because they can also be used in explanation, and their unique feature as a type of explanation is that they explain behaviour by reference to considerations which guided the agent's behaviour' (*Practical Reason and Norms* (n 4) 15); G Postema, 'Implicit Law' (1994) *Law and Philosophy* 361, 369; G Postema, 'Positivism, I Presume? . . . Comments on Schauer's Rules and the Rule of Law' (1991) *Harvard Journal of Law and Public Policy* 797, 799–800.

[49] Raz, *Practical Reason and Norms* (n 4) 190. In later work, Raz asserts: 'Part of the answer to the moral challenge to all authority is in the first condition, which says that authority can be legitimate if conformity with it improves one's conformity with reason. It provides the key to the justification of authority: authority helps our rational capacity whose function is to secure conformity with reason'. Raz, 'The Problem of Authority: Revisiting the Service Conception' (n 7) 1017.

[50] Raz puts this as follows: 'As it is possible perfectly to conform with reason without always acting for the reasons one conforms with, it follows that it is possible to conform with reasons to do what one has reason to do without wanting to do that act for that reason. It follows that it is possible to conform with reason without always wanting what one has reason to want' (*Engaging Reason* (n 6) 95).

[51] ibid 94. Raz also points out: 'There is a sense in which if one accepts the legitimacy of an authority one is committed to follow it blindly. One can be very watchful that it shall not overstep its authority and be sensitive to the presence of non-excluded considerations. But barring these possibilities, one is to follow the authority regardless of one's view of the merits of the case (that is, blindly). One may form a view on the merits but so long as one follows the authority this is an academic exercise of no practical importance. We can go further than that and say that sometimes the very reasons that justify the setting up of an authority also justify follow it blindly in a stronger sense – that is, following without even attempting to form a judgement on the merits' (Raz, *The Authority of Law* (n 34) 24–25).

[52] Raz, 'The Problem of Authority: Revisiting the Service Conception' (n 7) 1025–26.

The problem with this view is that if one can conform to reasons without assessing the merits or grounding reasons of authoritative directives or legal rules merely because one has reliable beliefs about the legitimacy of the authority, then the grounding or underlying reasons (in Raz's terminology) play no role in guiding our behaviour. But, Raz tells us, the authoritative directive or the rules are themselves reasons for actions (exclusionary ones). We have raised doubts about the possibility of layers of reasons and therefore the plausibility of second-order or exclusionary reasons for actions. Furthermore, in later work Raz asserts that we can respond to reasons because we have a will and *are capable of having intentions, and engaging in intentional actions.*[53] We need an explanation of why the same characterisation does not apply to secondary reasons and exclusionary reasons to the extent that they are also reasons.[54]

My arguments in Chapters 2, 3 and 4 show that one cannot follow rules unless one either avows the grounding reasons of rules or the goodness of the authority (section 8.6). This means that one can avow or understand the grounding reasons of rules if one follows legal rules *intentionally*. Let us analyse the example provided by Raz. He tells us that at the scene of an accident, coordination is required to recognise that one particular person is in charge of the rescue, and this is essential if lives are to be saved.[55] Let us call the coordinating authority at the scene of the accident 'Beatus'. According to the model of exclusionary reasons, I followed Beatus's instructions regardless of my reasons for actions (Beatus's reasons are exclusionary reasons). I do not need to be aware of or know the merits of the grounding reasons of the directives and rules issued by Beatus. However, my argument is that the grounding reason of the rule unifies the required series of actions, such as phoning for an ambulance, providing reassurance to the injured parties, helping to make them comfortable, and so on. The grounding reason as a good-making characteristic of all the different directives issued by Beatus at the scene of the accident is 'to save as many lives as possible'. Without engaging with the grounding reasons, the addressee will not be able to follow the instructions of the coordinating authority, Beatus, and adjust his or her conduct accordingly (Chapters 1 to 4). Let us suppose that at the scene of the accident, Beatus orders to move carefully wounded persons if there are exceptional circumstances only. Imagine that I find myself in the position of needing to move the first wounded person in order to make room for another wounded victim as there are no

---

[53] Raz, *Engaging Reason* (n 6) 115.

[54] Raz provides a partial explanation: norms are ontologically different from reasons. Norms are entities that are independent of their justified reasons. For example, if you give me advice and tell me 'there is a valid rule instructing you to do x', then I follow your advice. There is a reason to perform the action and to exclude the conflicting reasons (*Practical Reason and Norms* (n 4) 79–80). But this explanation does not tell us how the will is engaged with an exclusionary reason.

[55] Raz, 'The Problem of Authority: Revisiting the Service Conception' (n 7) 1016.

other suitable safe places. I must understand that the aim is to preserve life and that if I must move any injured person it must be with extreme care avoiding bending any limbs. I cannot carry out these actions unless I do so *intentionally* bearing in mind the grounding reason as a good-making characteristic of the authoritative directive, ie to preserve as many lives as possible. To merely follow the authority's order *unintentionally*, though conforming to reason, is not to exercise our practical reasoning.

Acccording to Raz, legal rules and directives mediate between the addressees and the reasons for actions that apply to them. Authoritative legal directives and legal rules facilitate compliance with reasons for action as objectively good or right and make a difference in the practical reasoning of the addressees.[56] There is, however, some ambiguity in the notion of 'service'. A strong reading advocates the view that the authority provides the service of mediating between reasons and the addressees. Thus, the addressees of a legal directive or legal rule accept they should obey it even if they believe there is no merit in performing the required actions.[57]

This is the view advocated by Raz. However, there is a weaker reading of the service conception. According to this reading, the authority provides the service of *showing* through the rules and authoritative directives the good-making characteristics that apply to the case. These reasons for actions as good-making characteristics are the grounding reasons of the rules and unify the successive series of actions that are required in order to follow the legal rules (Chapter 2). They provide this service in a 'ethical-political' manner, making legal rules and authoritative directives grounded on the reasons as good-making characteristics so that the will is able to engage with or 'tap into', so to speak, the grounding reasons or *logos* of the legal rules.

So far I have argued in favour of the weak reading of the service conception. However, it is not true that we always need to avow the grounding reasons of legal rules as good-making characteristics in order to follow legal rules. Authorities' claims and compliance with the Rule of Law can create a

---

[56] Raz, *The Morality of Freedom* (n 1) 58–62. Raz provides a solution to the dilemma regarding the relationship between reasons and rules in the following terms: 'The puzzle has always been, how can one avoid the following dilemma? If a rule is justified by certain reasons, then either the action it requires is invariably the action required by the underlying reasons, in which case one might just as well rely on the reason rather than the rule, or else the action the rule requires deviates from that justified by the underlying reasons, in which case following the rule is unjustified. Hence rules are either redundant or unjustified. One escapes from the dilemma in those cases where conformity with the underlying reasons is improved if one does not attempt to comply with them. In such cases conformity with the underlying reasons is secured by complying with the rule, or rather a better degree of conformity than can otherwise be achieved is so obtained. This can justify complying with the rule even when it requires actions which the underlying reasons do not. Such compliance may still be the best strategy to maximise conformity with the underlying reasons. The reason not to comply with another reason is an exclusionary reason' (*Practical Reason and Norms* (n 4) 194).

[57] Raz, *The Morality of Freedom* (n 1) 40.

presumption of the goodness of authority and its legitimacy. In the next section, I will show how we act under this presumption of the goodness of authority and its legitimacy without avowing the grounding reasons of the legal rules.

Why does the strong reading of the service conception have such argumentative force? The moral puzzle of legal authority[58] is formulated from the deliberative viewpoint, but the answer that Raz gives, ie rules are exclusionary reasons for actions, is from the theoretical perspective.[59] Thus, the answer seems unsatisfactory from the deliberative viewpoint. One view is that there is an asymmetry between the authority's perspective which is theoretical and the deliberative point of view.[60] Raz's view on the strong service conception seems appealing if we only consider the theoretical perspective or the third-person point of view, ie the point of view of the person who describes what following an authoritative directive means. However, from the deliberative point of view the agent, due to his own self-understanding as a full agent in the following of legal rules, needs to be engaged with the merits, in Raz's terminology, or the grounding reasons of rules.

8.6 PRESUMPTION OF LEGITIMATE AUTHORITY THESIS

When we act according to a presumption, we act as if something were correct or as if we have a justified belief. Reasons or pieces of insufficient evidence can create a presumption. What is the insufficient evidence or reasons that we have to create a presumption that legal authorities are legitimate? I will argue that there are two reasons or insufficient evidences that enable us to create a presumption of the goodness of legal authority and therefore a presumption of the legitimacy of legal authority. First, authorities make claims about their legitimate authority and moral correctness. In Chapter 7, I argued that authorities' claims should be interpreted as expressions of intentions that the authority will perform the legal action in a legitimate and morally correct

---

[58] Raz, 'The Problem of Authority: Revisiting the Service Conception' (n 7) 1003.

[59] S Smith, 'Cracks in the Coordination Account?' (2005) *American Journal of Jurisprudence* 249 and L Alexander, '"With Me, it's All or Nuthin": Formalism in Law and Morality' (1999) *University of Chicago Law Review* 551, mention the asymmetry between authoritative rules from the point of view of the deliberator and the third point of view, but do not develop the implications of such asymmetry. See also F Schauer, *Playing by the Rules* (New York, Oxford University Press, 1991) n 25.

[60] Schauer recognises this feature and provides a solution. See eg F Schauer, 'Rules and the Rule of Law' (1991) *Harvard Journal of Law and Public Policy* 635, 692–93. However, Schauer argues that because the authority aims that the rule-follower relinquish her best judgement, the rule-applier will be focused on punishment or reward. He does not consider the possibility that the rule-applier could focus on the 'objective' grounding reasons as good-making characteristics of the rule so that the rule-follower can understand them and surrender her judgement.

manner. Secondly, authorities make claims about complying with the eight desiderata of the Rule of Law.

In my discussion of Sham and Exito (section 7.2), I have said that most of the time we succeed in carrying out our intentions, therefore intentions helps us to coordinate our activities. I have also argued that intentions, in order to fulfil their coordinating function, need to be understood according to the 'guise of the good' model. Let us suppose that Sham is a legal authority and claims to have legitimate authority. Why should we defer our judgement to her authority since we know that her intentions are never carried out? We have explained that the claims of legitimate authority (Chapter 7) are expressions of intentions to perform actions in a specific way, and since we know that Sham does not carry out her intentions, we know also that we cannot rely on her to coordinate our activities if we intend our activities to be coordinated in a legitimate way. In other words, we know that she will fail to perform her actions in a legitimate way. By contrast, let us imagine that Exito is also a legal authority and claims to be a legitimate one. We know that Exito carries out most of her intentions and we can rely on the fact that her expression of intentions of legitimate authority, if the view that authorities' claims are expressions of intentions is true, will be carried out.

When an authority issues an order or a command, its command carries an expression of an intention that might contradict your intention. Let us suppose that you intend to park your vehicle in the Park but at the moment of reversing your car into a space, you read the sign 'Vehicles are not allowed to park in the Park'. The rule is an expression of an intention that contradicts your intention to park your vehicle in the Park. On other occasions, a legal rule does not contradict your intention to act. Let us suppose that as an industrialist you intend to provide your employees with excellent working conditions and there are a number of legal rules concerning the health and safety of workers. In this case, your intentions are not different from the authority's intentions. But the question as to why you ought to surrender your will to the authority can sensibly arise in both the cases of parking your car and following health and safety rules. In the latter case, you think that you know better than the authority about how to provide the best conditions for your workers. Let us go back to four possible responses to authority mentioned in section 8.1:

(a)   One recognises the goodness of the authority, due to the authority's claims and its compliance with most of the eight desiderata of the Rule of Law (section 8.6.2), and from this recognition a presumption about the goodness of authority and its legitimacy arises (section 8.6.1). Furthermore, one avows the grounding reasons as good-making characteristics of the legal rules. In these cases, there is full agency in the context of the law.

(b)   One recognises the goodness of the authority and its compliance with most of the eight desiderata of the Rule of Law (section 8.6.2), and from this recognition a presumption about the goodness of authority and its legitimacy arises (section 8.6.1). However, one does not avow the grounding reasons as good-making characteristics of the legal rules. In these cases, there is full agency in the context of the law.

(c)   One follows the authority's directives and legal rules by directly avowing the grounding reasons as good-making characteristics of the legal rules. In these cases, there is also full agency in the context of the law.

(d)   One follows the authority's directives and legal rules by merely theoretically understanding the grounding reasons as good-making characteristics or *logos* of the legal rules. However, one does not avow the grounding reasons as good-making characteristics of the legal rules. In this case, one is alienated from the law and if this alienation is systematic and continuous, there is no full agency in the context of the law. Arguably, in this case, it is a mystery how one follows legal rules that involve complex actions (Chapters 1 and 4).

In the following section these four possible responses will be scrutinised.

8.6.1 Equivalence Thesis: Presumption of the Goodness of Authority as Equivalent to the Presumption of Legitimate Authority

There is wide agreement among legal scholars that law is a good sort of thing despite controversy over the implications of this appraisal of the law in terms of a general moral obligation to obey the law. Thus, Finnis puts the example of a farmer or manufacturer who benefits from the national policy of eliminating river pollution. He cannot pick and choose which norms and rules to comply with as he obtains a wide range of benefits from the norms and rules. This is the difference, Finnis tells us, between the law and a spontaneous social practice. The subject derives a *wide range* of benefits from complying with the law:

> This particular law, just because it is the law, lays on him the burden of avoiding river-polluting methods of farming or manufacturing. But the law (not this particular law, but the same 'law of the land'), just as law, enforces against his neighbours the obligation not to burn down his buildings, and not to build new premises in defiance of zoning regulation, and the obligation to pay the purchase price of goods brought from him. The law presents itself as a seamless web. Its subjects are not permitted to pick and choose among the law's prescriptions and stipulations.[61]

---

[61]   J Finnis, 'The Authority of Law in the Predicament of Contemporary Social Theory' (1984–1985) *Notre Dame Journal of Law and Ethics and Public Policy* 115, 119–20 and J Finnis, 'What I Truly Should Decide' (2003) *American Journal of Jurisprudence* 107, 111.

Raz advances, as already noted, a teleological argument in favour of the law.[62] Like Raz, Aquinas,[63] Hurd[64] and other authors[65] agree that authority is a good sort of thing.

We give authority to the law and we act under the presumption of authority because although we disagree about the good-making characteristics of a specific coordination solution and therefore the grounding reasons of legal rules, we acknowledge the goodness of legal authority. Let us go back to the example provided by Finnis.[66] He considers a number of solutions concerning the national policy of eliminating river pollution:

(1) a river of pure running water; the benefits are beauty, enjoyment and conservation of marine flora and fauna;

(2) a river that is freely available as a sewer; producers can dispose of their waste in an efficient economic way and the community does not have to pay for the costs of policing the river;

(3) a river that is available for unlimited waste disposal by those willing to pay a waste-disposal fee; fees generated will be used for alternative drinking water supplies, the improvement of health services and other public services;

(4) a river that has limited waste disposal balanced with the conservation of marine fauna and flora.

The good-making characteristics of things, states of affairs, events and actions are plural, and legislators and judges can disagree on what constitutes the grounding reasons as good-making characteristics of legal rules. They can disagree over whether a river should be pure and clean in order to preserve fauna and flora. To coordinate our different activities and pursue the good, we act on the presumption of the goodness of legal authority. What are the grounding reasons for actions as good-making characteristics that the farmer or manufacturer needs to avow in order to follow the scheme of coordination in the form of a legal rule enacted by Parliament? Let us suppose that a statute is enacted according to the first solution, ie a river with clean running water. We observe that the farmer is loading his lorry with waste, and we ask him why he is doing this. In section 8.1, we have given four different possible responses to the law in terms of the 'guise of the good' model. According to

---

[62] Raz, *Practical Reason and Norms* (n 4) 59 and 195.

[63] Finnis (n 29) 269–74.

[64] H Hurd, 'Why You Should be a Law-abiding Anarchist (Except When You Shouldn't)?' (2005) *San Diego Law Review* 75 enumerates the following good features and roles that law plays in our life and which give us reasons to follow legal rules: correction of our moral errors in acting, respect for democracy, values of coordination and reliance.

[65] Alexander (n 59) 534–36.

[66] Finnis (n 29) 134. Cf L Green, 'Law, Coordination and the Common Good' (1983) *Oxford Journal of Legal Studies* 299.

alternative (a) the farmer recognises the goodness of the legal authority and avows the good-making characteristics of the legal rules. The dialogue between an enquirer and the farmer might be as follows:

Enquirer: Why are you loading your lorry with waste?

Farmer: In order to unload the waste at a specially designated area which is 10 miles from here.

Enquirer: Why are you driving to the designated area which is 10 miles from here to unload your waste?

Farmer: Because of the legal rule.

Enquirer: Why are you following the legal rule?

Farmer: Because legal authorities are a good sort of thing, ie they correctly and legitimately organise these affairs and the grounding reason of the rule, which is to have a river with pure running water, is also a good sort of thing.

Let us analyse alternative (b) in which there is recognition of the goodness of the authority that creates a presumption of its legitimacy, but *there is no avowing the grounding reasons as good-making characteristics of the rule*. In this case, the dialogue between the farmer and the enquirer will be as follows:

Enquirer: Why are loading your lorry with waste?

Farmer: In order to unload the waste at a specially designated area which is 10 miles from here.

Enquirer: Why are you driving to the designated area which is 10 miles from here to unload your waste?

Farmer: Because of the legal rule.

Enquirer: Why are you following the legal rule?

Farmer: Because legal authorities are a good sort of thing and they correctly and legitimately organise these affairs.

Enquirer: Do you know that the rule's grounding reason is to have a river with pure running water?

Farmer: I do not think that it is good to have a river with pure running water, but I follow the law because it is good that we have an organised and coordinated society.

The dialogue for alternative (c) in which *there is a direct avowing of the grounding reasons* of the rules might look as follows:

Enquirer: Why are loading your lorry with waste?

Farmer: In order to unload the waste at a specially designated area which is 10 miles from here.

Enquirer: Why are you driving to a designated area which is 10 miles from here?

Farmer: Because of the legal rule.

Enquirer: Why are you following the legal rule?

Farmer: In order to have a river with pure running water. It is a good sort of thing to have a river with pure running water.

Finally, alternative (d) might well be portrayed by the following dialogue:

Enquirer: Why are loading your lorry with waste?

Farmer: In order to unload the waste at a specially designated area which is 10 miles from here.

Enquirer: Why are you driving to a designated area which is 10 miles from here?

Farmer: Because of the legal rule.

Enquirer: Why are you following the legal rule?

Farmer: In order to have a river with pure running water, but I do not believe that this is a good sort of thing.

Of course, in (d), the farmer could also reply that he does so because he intends to avoid the sanctions that will follow if he violates the legal rule. But can he systematically obey legal rules simply in order to avoid sanctions? If this is the case, it is not the paradigmatic case of agency. The farmer is at the margins of agency when he follows the law *systematically* because he fears the legal sanctions. Imagine the life of an individual who systematically obeys the law in order to avoid sanctions. He puts on his seat belt, drives on the right side of the road, stops at the zebra-crossing so that children can cross the road, and begins and finishes his lectures on time as established by university regulations purely to avoid being sanctioned by either legal authorities or university authorities. He is not guided by the rules as he does not avow the grounding reasons of rules, he is merely following rules guided by the avoidance of sanctions (section 10.1).

The following objection might arise. Imagine an individual who avows the grounding reasons of legal rules, but knows better how to achieve the ends or grounding reasons of the rules. Let us suppose that a wise electrician understands the grounding reasons for the code on electric wiring of domestic dwellings;[67] the code has been establishing to preserve life and buildings and he knows that a 4 inch wire is as effective as a 5 inch wire. However, the latter is the one that is prescribed. Does the wise electrician have to follow *every single*

---

[67] The example is inspired by T Endicott's article 'The Subsidiarity of Law and the Obligation to Obey' (2005) 50 *American Journal of Jurisprudence* 233 and GV Bradley, 'Comment on Endicott: the Case of the Wise Electrician' (2005) 50 *American Journal of Jurisprudence* 257.

successive step advised by the code? We see that he follows the rule *because* of the grounding reasons, ie to preserve life and buildings; however, arguably, one step of the series of actions that are unified by the grounding reason, ie to use a 5 inch wire, might not be necessary in order to say that the wise electrician is following the code. It is not that he has no *reasons* to follow the rule,[68] because according to the 'guise of the good' model reasons for actions are the ends characterised as good which give unity to the successive steps of an intentional action (Chapter 4). In the case of actions aimed at following legal rules, the reasons for actions are the grounding reasons as good-making characteristics that give unity to the successive steps that are the content of an authoritative legal rule (Chapter 2). We have said that the rules of legal authority reflect a *know-how* (Chapters 3, 4) or a kind of practical knowledge that should be followed to achieve the grounding reasons as good-making characteristics. But in the example of the electrician, the electrician believes that he *knows better* than the rule *how* to achieve the desired end. We can say that either he can act according to the goodness of the legal authority or he can decide not to follow all the successive steps prescribed by the rule. However, in some sense, he is still guided by the rule as he is acting for the grounding reasons of the rule, ie to preserve life and homes. He chooses a wire which he thinks is safer, ie a 5 inch wire instead of 4 inch wire and not a wire that will risk the lives of those who inhabit the house.

The example of the wise electrician shows that there are two kinds of legal rules: (a) legal rules in the wide sense where deliberation is needed and the guise of the good model applies; and (b) legal rules in the narrow sense where *every single step* in the series of actions is prescribed by the rule. We have advanced the view that even in the latter cases the guise of the good model might also be applicable.

8.6.2 The Rule of Law

I have argued that compliance with most of the eight desiderata of the Rule of Law can create a presumption of the goodness of legal authority and its legitimacy. How is this possible? I will argue that the adequate form of something can constitute an insufficient evidence that something is a good sort of thing and that, therefore, we are entitled to create a *presumption* of the goodness of that thing.

Let us think about the example of making coffee. There are many ways of making coffee but only certain ways will result in tasty coffee; furthermore, if

---

[68] Smith argues that in these cases there is a fissure between authoritative rules and reasons for actions. Smith (n 59).

we follow certain 'tips' we can improve it. There are a number of successive steps to making coffee, ie boiling the water, putting the right amount of coffee in the cafetière and so on, and our intention to make coffee in the best possible way makes us aware of the possibility of discriminating and being attentive to the 'tips' on making coffee. We might, however, fail in our intentions. We follow the tips and right procedures but a mistake in, for example, the quantity and quality of the coffee can change the outcome of our actions. Let us suppose that I am invited to your house and you say to me 'I intend to make you an excellent cup of coffee'. I can see that you have the right equipment and, when you open the cupboard, I see that you have the best kind of coffee; I can now rely on the fact that you will be able to carry out your intention of making an excellent coffee. This is what I will call the *form* that reassures me that you intend to make an excellent coffee. Of course, you might fail in your performance. It might happen that you receive a phone call and get distracted and ruin the coffee. But most of the time under normal circumstances I can rely on the fact that you will succeed in carrying out your intention.

Similarly, arguably, the form of good-making law, ie the set of processes and steps necessary for good-making law, requires attentiveness and a discriminatory capacity. We can say that the *form* of good-making law is the Rule of Law. Fuller advanced the eight desiderata that will make law a good sort of thing:

> Rex's bungling career as legislator and judge illustrates that the attempt to maintain and create a system of legal rules may miscarry in at least eight ways; there are in this enterprise, if you will, eight distinct routes to disaster. The first and the most obvious lies in a failure to achieve rules at all, so that every issue must be decided on an ad hoc basis. The other routes are: (2) a failure to publicize, or at least to make available to the affected party, the rules he is expected to observe; (3) the abuse of a retroactive legislation, which not only cannot itself guide action, but undercuts the integrity of rules prospective in effect, since it puts them under threat of retrospective change; (4) a failure to make rules understandable; (5) the enactment of contradictory rules or (6) rules that require conduct beyond the powers of the affected party; (7) introducing such frequent changes in the rules that the subject cannot orient his action by them; and, finally, (8) a failure of congruence between the rules as announced and their actual administration.[69]

My argument is that when the authorities comply with the eight desiderata of the Rule of Law, they show to the law-abiding citizen the *form* which intentions to make a good law have been relying on and will be relying on in the future. My argument is not based on claims that tyrants do not rely on the Rule of Law.[70] My argument is that authorities who follow the Rule of Law

---

[69] Fuller (n 32) 38–39.
[70] N Simmonds, *Law as a Moral Idea* (Oxford, Oxford University Press, 2007); cf M Kramer, 'Big Bad Wolf: Legal Positivism and its Detractors' (2004) *American Journal of Jurisprudence* 1.

have an intention to perform a certain action, ie to judge or to legislate in the best possible way. Making good laws is not exactly like making good coffee, but like making good coffee, the art of good law-making involves a *form*, ie sound procedures and the practical knowledge about *how* to continue accordingly which will help achieve the intention of performing the action in the best possible way.

Let us return to the example of making coffee at your house. When I go into your house, I see all the necessary equipment for making coffee, I see good quality coffee and I listen to your expression of intention 'I will make you an excellent cup of coffee'. All these elements allow me to think that you will make a good cup of coffee. I am now forming my intention to drink the coffee *based* on the presumption that you will make a good cup of coffee. Similarly, the Rule of Law as the *form* of making good law enables us to presume the goodness of legal rules together with the authority's claims of legitimacy (V). We could say that most of the time, law-abiding citizens follow legal rules *based* on a presumption of the goodness of legal rules.

8.6.3 Authorities' Claims of Moral Authority and Correctness

The connection between our analysis in Chapter 7 of the authorities' claims as expressions of intentions and the notion of the presumption of authority is now clear. The authoritative character of law is *possible* because both legal authorities and citizens intend to act. This is why Raz's example of the arbitrator is so appealing: we give to the arbitrator the power to decide over our actions. In some sense, 'we surrender our intention to act'. But this intention is not a mental state as an acceptance,[71] on the contrary, intention to act cannot be understood unless it is connected to the good that the authority aims to instantiate. We surrender our intention because we can either (a) avow the goodness of the authority, or (b) avow the grounding reasons as good-making characteristics of rules.

I have defended the view that authorities' claims of moral correctness and legitimate authority are expressions of intentions that authorities will perform their legal acts in a morally correct and legitimate manner. They reflect practical knowledge as they are not *merely true* propositions about current or future states of affairs or events, they are intentions that are known by the legal authorities in a *transparent* way (sections 3.3 and 5.3.1) and they enable us to rely on their performance to coordinate and act accordingly. They are insuf-

---

[71] Arguably, 'consent' theories rely on 'acceptance' as a mental state to justify authority. For a discussion of Hobbes' implicit reductive psychologism and his political theory of 'acceptance' of authority in order to guarantee survival, see S Darwall, 'Normativity and Projection in Hobbe's *Leviathan*' (2000) *Philosophical Review* 313.

ficient evidence that the action will be performed in a moral and legitimate manner and enable us to create a presumption of the goodness of the authority and its legitimacy.

To summarise, I have defended an 'ethical-political' account of legal authority in which authorities create legal rules or authoritative directives based on grounding reasons as good-making characteristics that are *transparent* to the addressee of the legal rule or authoritative directive so that their will is engaged with it. Authorities create a *presumption* of legal authority through their claims of moral correctness and legitimacy together with compliance with the eight desiderata of the Rule of Law. Thus, the service that law provides us accords with the weak reading; that is to say, legal authorities show us the legal rule to be followed and the grounding reasons as the good-making characteristics of the legal rules to be engaged with.

9

*The Epistemology of Modestly Objective Values and Robust Value Realism**

9.1 A THEORETICAL RESPONSE TO A DELIBERATIVE QUESTION

IT MIGHT BE argued that because we occupy the deliberative standpoint we cannot detach ourselves from our own values. In one sense, this is true, we cannot dissociate entirely from our values without losing our identity as agents. However, we can revise and correct our values whilst holding to other values at the same time. The fact that we submit our values to correction and revision does not mean that we forfeit all standpoints.

This view might be interpreted as the position that there are no objective answers in terms of what is valuable. We are condemned to our particular perspective, to what is good *for us*. However, this interpretation seems to me incorrect. What this view is trying to convey is that the question 'what should I truly do?', the deliberative question, can be answered from the reasons that I have, ie from the first-person perspective. The reasons are transparent to me and they are related to what appears valuable to me, but this does not mean that reasons for actions are merely *from my point of view or from the relative point of view of 'religion',' morality' or 'law'*.[1] The deliberative matter might be about a moral, religious or legal issue, but the deliberative point of view is only one. I-myself is posited to the question 'what should I truly do?'. It is from the first-person perspective, but the search for the answer is not *from my point of view or good relative to my point of view*. On the contrary, the search is in terms of the state of affairs in the world, what should I do in terms of what is the case and in terms of judging and valuing this state of affairs. Thus, when my will or intention is directed at achieving a particular goal and after a series of responses to the question 'why?' I articulate a reason for action that gives unity to the series of successive steps

---

* This chapter relies on material first published as 'If You Cannot Help Being Committed to It, then It Exists: A Defence of Robust Normative Realism' (2012) *Oxford Journal Legal Studies* 823.

[1] For example, Gardner interprets that the 'religious' or the 'moral' points of view are relative because of the issues that these are concerned with. 'Within each point of view there are reasons, but there are no further independent reasons to take one or the other point of view', J Gardner, 'Law as a Leap of Faith' in P Oliver, S Douglas-Scott and V Tadros (eds), *Faith in Law* (Oxford, Hart Publishing, 2000) 1.

towards the action; I do not think *this is my good* or '*this is good for me*'. The object of my intention is presented to me transparently as *good simpliciter*. It is, in one sense, *absolutely good for me now*. In this way, it involves a commitment to avoiding error and to finding out what I should truly decide. This takes us then to a distinction between *intelligible* reasons and *justified* reasons.

One consequence of the 'guise of the good' model and its focus on the deliberative viewpoint is arguably the recalcitrant asymmetry between the first- and third-person perspectives. We cannot perceive in ourselves what we sometimes see clearly in others, ie an evil will that we cannot recognise because we act purely on what *appears* good to us:[2] 'light outside and darkness within'. The objection that we are trapped within our *own view of what is good* seems to me fatal to our project of applying the 'guise of the good' model to legal rules and the possibility of objective values embedded in legal rules. However, I argue that we have the practical and conceptual capacities for acting according to what is of value and not merely according to what *appears* good or valuable. 'Intentional action to pursue values' should be understood in its paradigmatic sense and this paradigmatic sense of 'intentional action' is what produces objectively good laws that entail objective values, good acts, good communities, good schools, good cathedrals, good paintings, good pieces of music, and so on.

What is the answer to the question of how we determine or identify the *objective* grounding reasons as good-making characteristics of legal rules? An answer to this question is also an answer to the question of *what a legal rule is*. There could either be a theoretical or a deliberative answer. It is a theoretical answer if my aim is to explain what the rule is. It is the latter if I intend to make up my mind about how to act or what I should do. An answer to the theoretical question is formulated in terms of what I am to believe about a specific rule, but is not *primarily* about my mental states or those of my community, ie whether members of the community accept the rule, whether they act according to self-interest or according to morality, and so on. This kind of explanation is not about the rules, but about *beliefs* concerning *what the rule is*. Thus, for example, if someone asks me whether 'Simón Bolívar was a revolutionary', I need to determine whether it is the case that he was a revolutionary, I need to read history books, carry out research in the archives, or ask experts in the field of nineteenth Latin American history. I do not examine my *beliefs* or those of the community about whether 'Simón Bolívar was a revolutionary'. Similarly, a description of a rule is about the content of the rule and includes the grounding reasons as good-making characteristics of the rule. In one way, we might say, to learn about legal rules is to learn about the grounding reasons as good-making characteristics of such rules.

---

[2] A Gombay, 'The Paradoxes of Counterprivacy' (1988) *Philosophy* 191.

Interestingly, if I ask the question 'what is the legal rule?' and my aim is to act upon the rule, ie I search for a deliberative answer, I need to rely, in some sense, on the theoretical answer.[3] Let us suppose that I intend to make an espresso; I need to know whether to boil the water, how to turn on the espresso machine, which coffee to put inside the machine, and so on. There is no difference between this explanation and the explanation that I will give if someone asks me to write a manual on how to make an espresso (see Chapter 3). Let us suppose that you ask me about the rules on driving in England. I explain to you that drivers in England drive on the left and that they stop at traffic lights and at zebra crossings when pedestrians are walking. But in this explanation either the grounding reasons as good-making characteristics are implicit or I actively inform you about them. Let us go back to the example of making an espresso. The best way of guiding you about the rules of making an espresso is to tell you about the grounding reasons as good-making characteristics. I will tell you that you need to put the coffee in 'this way', rather 'that way' but I do not need to tell you *why* we turn on the machine and *why* we boil the water. You master the necessary concepts and practical abilities to understand and be guided by this part of the rules (Chapter 4 and section 9.2). Similarly, if you do not know *why* drivers stop at zebra crossings, I will tell you that it is to avoid running into pedestrians, and that the speed limit around schools is 20 miles per hour because research has shown that a child can survive if a car runs into him or her at 20 miles per hour, but not at 30 miles per hour, and that we stop at traffic lights to avoid colliding with other vehicles, and that we have all these rules in order to protect human lives, because human lives are valuable.

But there are legal rules that are more complex than those applying to road traffic. For example, if a solicitor has been negligent for misstatements he will be liable to his client and to third parties who have suffered economic loss by his negligent actions.[4] This rule is based on the idea that the solicitor has 'assumed responsibility' and this creates a presumption of a close relationship between the third party and the solicitor. A possible response to the question 'why is this so'? and 'what is the grounding reason of such a legal rule?' is that the grounding reason is that it is a good thing for legal professionals to be responsible for their negligent statements if other persons have relied upon them. The grounding reason as a good-making characteristic is the value of reliance. Let us suppose that you disagree with me and argue that such a

---

[3] Raz asserts that there are similarities between the structure of practical and theoretical authorities. J Raz, *The Morality of Freedom* (Oxford, Clarendon Press, 1986) 53. However, Anscombe has emphasised the differences between practical and theoretical knowledge, E Anscombe, *Intention* (Cambridge, MA, Harvard University Press, 2000) paras 39–40 and this analysis has important implications for the structure of practical and theoretical authorities (see Chapter 3).

[4] *Hedley Byrne & Co Ltd v Heller & Partners Ltd* [1966] AC 465 and *White v Jones* [1995] 2 AC 207.

grounding reason has no good-making characteristics. Professionals such as solicitors, you might continue, already have an excessive burden of responsibilities which they have voluntarily assumed simply through the contractual nature of the service they provide, and why should we impose on them further responsibilities for third parties to the contract? Doing so will have, in your view, detrimental economic implications for society as a whole (specifically a wholesale increase in legal fees). You think that the grounding reason of the rule of tort law for negligent misstatements, ie it is a good sort of thing that legal professionals are accountable to others, including third parties, when it comes to statements, is not a good-making one and you find no reason to follow the legal rule. However, I can still argue that law in general is a good sort of thing and that this gives you a reason to comply with legal rules (section 8.6.1). Let us suppose that you agree that law is a good sort of thing, but disagree that this specific rule is grounded on a sound good-making characteristic. How can we resolve the disagreement? One needs to be attentive to particulars, and specifically, to the multiple instantiations of the good. The core argument is that the right exercise of our conceptual and practical capacities enables us to determine the grounding reasons as objective good-making characteristics of legal rules. The following two formulas for the *identification* of the grounding reasons as objective good-making characteristics are adumbrated. They will be called in abbreviated form the 'identifying formula for acts' (IA) and the 'identifying formula for prohibited acts' (IPA):

> (IA): 'A grounding reason as a good-making characteristic of a legal rule is *objective* if the addressee of the legal rule or authoritative directive cannot reasonably *refuse* to intend to act under a certain hypothetical description of the grounding reason'.

> (IPA): 'A grounding reason as a good-making characteristics of a legal rule is *objective* if the addressee of the legal rule or authoritative directive cannot reasonably intend to act under a certain hypothetical description of the grounding reason'.

Before explaining the 'identifying formulas', I will explain what I mean by 'conceptual and practical capacities'.

9.2 CONCEPTUAL AND PRACTICAL CAPACITIES

I have emphasised the asymmetry between the first- and third-person perspectives and have argued in favour of the primary role that the first-person perspective should have in our understanding of intentional actions and the rule-following phenomenon. However, one result of this is that we have an explanation of action and legal rule-following rules that is purely from the perspective of the agent, and this could justify perverse actions if the perverse or evil reasons for actions are presented as good-making characteristics. Could we evaluate from the third-person perspective these actions and attempt (as agents) to reconcile the first- and the third-person perspectives? The grounding reasons as good-making characteristics of legal rules can be criticised as perverse or wrong; this perversity or wrongness might be explained by different factors. It might be due to ignorance about the good-making characteristics of the particulars, ie things, events, state of affairs, etc. It could result from lack of attention to the features of the human good. It could result from self-deception on the part of legal authorities and officials who are confined to habits of thoughts that are wrong or perverse. When we ask the agent or legal authority why she or he has acted in a certain way, the answer invites reflection but such reflection is not directed inwards, it is directed outwards to the world; in this sense we can say that it is 'world-guided'. The agent is able to make a transition and to take a theoretical perspective of his own action, detached from the experience of performance, and he can see things that he could not see before. Practical imagination, literature and the arts in general play a key role and help us to see the complexity of objective goods and their instantiation in particulars.

When we talk about the groundless and practical character of first-person statements (see Chapters 2 and 3) this does not mean that they can only be formulated in an absolutely private language. Expressions of intention take place within a conceptual network together with what are practical learnings in a social context. It involves the learning of roles and the learning of rules with the grounding reasons (*logos*) as good-making characteristics.[5] Furthermore, the grounding reasons of rules are not static or ahistorical. We learn new ways of looking at and describing things and we use our practical imagination to learn a new *logos* or a new grounding reason as good-making characteristic. *It is because intention is thought-dependent that we can imagine new ways of acting and describing our actions.*

Because law is the actuality (Chapter 4) of a human capacity, ie practical reasoning, it is inevitable that the legal authorities in certain legal systems will fail in advancing legal rules grounded on objective good-making characteristics. It is also possible that some citizens of certain legal systems will be alienated from what is valuable and fail to avow the grounding reasons as objective good-making characteristics of legal rules.[6] It is also likely that the legal

---

[5] Hampshire points out: 'He could not lend his action an altogether private significance, as having a character that no one else would recognise in it, any more than he could endow his words with a private significance independent of their normal meaning' (S Hampshire, 'A Reply to Walsh on Thought and Action' (1963) *Journal of Philosophy* 410, 418).

[6] Stone very helpfully points out that the purpose of Fuller's critique of Hart is to criticise a conception of morality as 'principle' or 'maxims'. Morality, thus should be understood as related to differences and the perception of the particular. Law has no filter against immorality. There is

authorities of some legal systems will pursue what they think are good-making characteristics but which are not. Law as an *actuality* can be carried out for evil or good reasons and the outcome of their actions can therefore be either evil or good. Law in the paradigmatic sense, ie in the exercise of full agency with a view to achieving objective values, enables us to understand law in the marginal or non-paradigmatic sense, ie in the exercise of full agency with a view of achieving what seems good but what truly has no value.

It is tempting to say that in order to grasp or discover the grounding reason or *logos* of legal rules we need to engage in constructive interpretation as, for example, along Dworkinian lines.[7] We need, however, to resist this temptation. Interpretation is usually a passive and theoretical exercise.[8] As Finnis puts it: Dworkin's concept of interpretation is endowed with all the richness of 'practical reasoning's creative engagements with goods (including of course their privation: harms) ends or purposes'.[9] However, we should not read Dworkin, as Finnis warns us, as being the unmitigated enthusiast of practical reason. In spite of Dworkin's recognition of the importance of the point or end of practices, he is clear in the view that the point or end of our social practices is to be 'imposed'. He says, moreover, that the 'point' or 'end' is not assessed in terms of the world and hypothetical goods. The core of Dworkin's legal theory is not intentional action and practical reason (see section 10.6 for a detailed defence of this point).

The agent has certain conceptual and practical capacities (Chapter 4 and section 9.2) and this is evidenced by the activity of the agent in his or her exercise of practical reasoning (Chapter 3). The agent *knows how* to follow the successive steps of an action and learns how to follow rules because he or she knows how to follow the grounding reasons or *logos* of the legal rules. Anscombe links practical knowledge and our capacity for doing things as follows:

> When we ordinarily speak of practical knowledge we have in mind a certain sort of general capacity in a particular field; but if we hear of a capacity, it is reasonable to ask what constitutes an exercise of it. In the case of practical knowledge the exercise of the capacity is nothing but the doing or supervising of the operations of which a man has practical knowledge; but this not *just* the coming about of certain effects, like my recitation of the alphabet or of bits of it, for what he effects is formally characterised as subject to our question 'Why?' whose application displays the A-D order which we discovered. Although the term 'practical knowledge' is

no maxim, principle or 'recipe' in action that we can follow to filter out bad laws (M Stone, *Positivism as Opposed to What? Law and the Moral Concept of Right*, Cardozo Legal Studies Research Papers No 290, available at http:// ssrn.com/ abstract=1554500).

[7] R Dworkin, *Law's Empire* (Cambridge, MA, Harvard University Press, 1986).

[8] See J Finnis, 'On "Reason" and "Authority" in Law's Empire' (1987) 6 *Law and Philosophy* 357, 358–61 for a discussion of the predominance of the theoretical element in Dworkin's legal theory.

[9] ibid 359.

most often used in connexion with specialised skills, there is no reason to think that this notion has application only in such contexts. 'Intentional action' always pre-supposes what might be called 'knowing one's way about' the matters described in the description under which an action can be called intentional, and this know-ledge is exercised in the action and is practical knowledge.[10]

When we follow legal rules we refer to what we believe are the grounding reasons of the rules and we characterise them as being good. Thus to say that we follow road traffic rules is to say that we '*know our way about*' the matter, ie driving on the left side of the road, pressing the brake pedals and stopping at the zebra crossing and traffic lights. Furthermore, we can adjust our conduct to different circumstances on the road because we act under the description in terms of reasons for actions as good-making characteristics. We have learned that the grounding reasons, ie *logos*, of road traffic rules is the safety of pedes-trians, drivers and all users of the road. I exercise my practical capacity and 'practical reason shows itself' when I provide answers to the question 'why?'. For example, if you ask me 'why did you press the brake pedal?', I answer 'because I intended to stop the vehicle'. My answer to your question 'why did you want to stop the vehicle?', is 'because the traffic light is on red'. In response to the question 'why did you stop the vehicle because the traffic light is on red?' my answer is 'because I intended to avoid colliding with other vehicles coming from the opposite direction'. You can then ask me 'why did you intend to avoid colliding with other vehicles?', and I answer 'because I want to protect my life and the lives of other human beings and because I consider them valuable'.

Following the criticism of the two-component model on intentional action advanced at the outset of this book (see Chapters 2, 5 and 6), I assert that we do not follow legal rules primarily because of our *beliefs* or *desires* about legal rules. In following legal rules, our movements are governed and controlled by us, but they are interlinked and the reason for the action gives unity to the successive steps of the action (Chapter 3).

A practical capacity involves a 'knowing how'. Knowing *how* should not be reduced to knowing *that*.[11] In other words, knowing how to φ cannot be identi-fied with propositional knowledge. Although intentional action is usually accompanied by the knowledge of *how to,* there are instances when I intend to act, but I do not know how. Let us suppose that a man intends to disconnect a bomb, but he does not know how. He is faced with many coloured wires, which one should he disconnect? In despair, he cuts the red wire and succeeds in defusing the bomb. In spite of his uncertainty and his lack of knowledge in

[10] Anscombe (n 3) paras 48–49.
[11] G Ryle, *The Concept of Mind* (London, Hutchinson, 1949) ch 2. Cf J Stanley and T Williamson, 'Knowing How' (2001) *Journal of Philosophy* 411.

defusing a bomb, he has some knowledge of relevant means.[12] He is able to deliberate as *he acts* and in one sense we can say that he 'knows how'.

Concerning conceptual capacities, the agent in the case of following the road traffic rules, understands concepts such as 'safety and protection of my own life and the lives of others', 'stopping the vehicle', 'crossing the street', and so on. In more complex examples, concepts can be connected to other concepts but we do not need to master all the interlinked concepts to follow legal rules such as 'compensate an employee for foreseeable psychiatric injury caused by a negligent act as a employer' or 'respect for human dignity'.[13]

A sceptical theorist on objective values might argue that it is possible to accept the 'guise of the good' model and still hold to the view that there are no objective values. Agents can perform actions believing that the action is a good sort of thing, event or state of affairs. Different agents can have different perspectives about what good is. Furthermore, an objector might argue, there might be collective self-deception among legal authorities. Agents can collectively believe that certain values and states of affairs are good, when they are actually evil.[14] However, these are cases in which the 'guise of the good' model is confirmed. They show that intelligibility is not sufficient to determine the objectivity of the good. A caveat should here be mentioned. The guise of the good model does not aim to show that there are absolute and universal objective goods. The guise of the good model can only show that there are goods *from the point of view of creatures like us.* Our understanding of 'creatures like us' is not limited by social and historical contexts, but rather in continuity with our learning of values in social and historical contexts. Our values are dynamic. This means that we are able to change and transform our values and adjust our institutions such as law accordingly.

The epistemology of value defended so far is not ambitiously objective but, rather, modestly objective. The idea of particulars that have good-making characteristics plays a mediating role between objective values and our subjective value judgements. The way to understand and grasp values is through our value judgements and conceptions of the good. Value judgements are directed towards objective values which are instantiated in particulars. The epistemology of objective values as construed by the 'guise of the good' model is not ambitious and is not completely independent of our evaluative stance. The metaphor of Neurath's boat[15] seems compelling: we cannot revise and correct all our values at the same time. The good is instantiated in the particulars and it is known through them. The difficulty is that we might tend to

---

[12] K Setiya, 'Practical Knowledge' (2008) *Ethics* 388, 404.

[13] See J Raz, 'Two Views of the Nature of the Theory of Law' (1998) *Legal Theory* 249.

[14] See H Pauer-Studer and D Velleman, 'Distortions of Normativity' 14 (3) *Ethical Theory and Moral Practice* (2011) 329 for a discussion of the complete inversion of values.

[15] WO Quine, *Word and Object* (Cambridge, MA, MIT, 1960) 3.

value only what is familiar.[16] Raz recognises this difficulty in the 'guise of the good' model *a propos* of an example of a racist person who attacks a foreigner:

> But assume that, as in our previous examples, our racist does not have our philosophical concept of the good. He does not admit to a belief that preserving purity is of value. In fact preserving racial purity has no value. What grounds do we have to attribute to him a belief which neither he nor we admit to?[17]

If racial purity is instrumental in relation to other values, ie excellence, we can show the racist that his view is mistaken. What happens when the culture is alien to or radically different from ours? For example, the Aztecs who sacrificed women to the Gods in the belief that this would assuage their fury? We do not have sufficient knowledge of the framework of values of the Aztecs to see how the value of devotion to God is coherent with the higher values that they endorsed. My arguments so far have shown that values are limited to the social and historical concepts we master, but that through practical imagination we can expand and revise our concepts, though relying on the conceptual framework that we already have.

9.3 TWO FORMULAS FOR IDENTIFYING THE OBJECTIVE GROUNDING REASONS FOR ACTIONS AS GOOD-MAKING CHARACTERISTICS OF LEGAL RULES

At the outset of this chapter (section 9.1), two formulas ((IA) and (IPA)) for the identification of objective grounding reasons as good-making characteristics of the legal rules and authoritative directives were adumbrated. In the previous section, I argued that the deliberative question requires engagement with the theoretical reason. The agent looks outwards at the features of the world to determine how to act and the formulas help her to determine whether the hypothetical good-making characteristics are objective and therefore justified. They also enable the agent to revise and correct her or his values and develop further her or his practical and conceptual capacities. Practical objective judgements are manifested in one's action. This means that the agent will act for a reason under a certain description and this description is objective if the corresponding formula is satisfied. An example might illustrate this point.

Let us suppose that there is a traffic light in the middle of the dessert. The grounding reason of the rule 'you must stop at the red traffic light' is the

---

[16] For a similar criticism on 'familiarity' levelled against Anscombe's defence of the modest objectivity of values, see E Anscombe, 'Brute Facts' (1958) *Analysis* 69 and DZ Phillips, 'Miss Anscombe's Grocer' (1968) *Analysis* 177.

[17] J Raz, 'The Guise of the Good' in S Tenenbaum (ed), *Desire, Practical Reason and the Good* (Oxford, Oxford University Press, 2010).

protection of lives. Is (IA) satisfied? Can we say that an agent cannot reasonably refuse to intend to stop at a red traffic light in the middle of the dessert in order to protect her life and the lives of others? The answer is positive. An objector might argue that in the circumstances there are no lives to protect as the driver can observe that there are no pedestrians or other vehicles around and about. Therefore, the grounding reason of the action 'to protect human lives' does not apply in this case. It is reasonable, the objector might continue, to refuse to stop at the red traffic light in the middle of the dessert. But this objection confuses two different things. First, there is the subjective evaluation to determine whether the description of the act under the rule, ie to protect human lives, is fulfilled in the circumstances. Secondly, there is the objective characterisation of the good-making characteristics of an event, thing or state of affairs that constitutes the grounding reason of the rule. Our focus is on the latter. We say that the agent has objective reasons as good-making characteristics to follow the rule of stopping at traffic lights in all circumstances. The agent can disagree because she avows the objective reasons as good-making characteristics, but does not believe that these objective reasons apply in the circumstances. The agent needs then to engage in deliberation; in other words, she needs to decide whether her subjective assessment is sound and not prone to error, for example, that a child is not hiding in the bushes or that a very fast motorcycle will not pass by at the moment she decides not to observe the red traffic light.

Imagine a citizen who is asked to pay council tax as a contribution to the services provided by the local council, ie collection of the rubbish, control of the local traffic, provision of good quality homes for low income families, and so on. Is (IA) satisfied? Can the citizen reasonably refuse to intend to pay council tax and therefore to follow the legal rule under the relevant descriptions of the grounding reasons as good-making characteristics of the tax rule? My argument is that this is the question that needs to be advanced in order to determine whether the grounding reason is modestly objective.

Similarly, legal rules prohibit certain acts, for example, 'do not steal', 'do not kill', 'do not torture human beings'. The objective grounding reason of the rule 'do not torture human beings' might be described as 'to prevent the violation of the physical integrity of others'. Following (IPA), can we reasonably intend to act under such a description of the grounding reason? Is it reasonable to state 'I intend to torture you because it is a good sort of thing to violate your physical integrity'? The answer is negative and we see that IPA is satisfied. The afore-mentioned grounding reason as a good-making characteristic of the rule 'do not torture human beings' is objective.

Judges and legislators in creating legal rules also need to engage their practical and conceptual capacities and, in the light of the two formulas, to reflect on the objective good-making characterisations that ground legal rules.

Values and the grounding reasons as good-making characteristics of legal rules are learned through our concepts which have a social nature. Our practical and conceptual capacities are developed, refined and revised with other creatures like us who share our biological, psychological and spiritual constituency, in a community that emphasises certain practices and their values, and disregard or forget other values enshrined in traditions. Correction and error is possible within the web of social practices, personal and collective histories, and different ways of imagining ourselves within the deliberative standpoint, following the Neurathian methodology. This does not mean that evaluations are merely social. On the contrary, the individual needs to face the justificatory question 'why?' which is posed from the deliberative point of view, but answer with an outward looking approach as if it were a theoretical question.

9.4 ARE THERE *REALLY* ROBUST OBJECTIVE VALUES? A DEFENCE OF NORMATIVE AND VALUE REALISM

One might object that a modest epistemology of values as construed in this chapter presupposes *the existence of* robustly normative truths or values. In other words, it presupposes normative and value realism. Thus, the implicit idea of a modest epistemology of values is that we can always *progress* and *improve* our understanding of what is valuable, dutiful, obligatory, and so on. The modest epistemology that I have defended argues that we can only know values and normative truths through our beliefs and conceptual capacities. Furthermore, correction is only possible within our beliefs and conceptual capacities; however, values and truths *exist* independently of our beliefs and concepts. Our concepts expand and we are able to reach a better and more accurate understanding of what is good and valuable. Contra this position, an objector might argue that the possibility of the *existence of* objective values and the so-called 'first-person point of view' are merely illusory since they cannot easily be compatible with our scientific understanding of the world.[18] Therefore, normative and value realism might be false.

A full philosophical defence of normative and value realism would be beyond the scope of this book. It requires serious engagement with metaphysical problems. However, I will gesture towards an argument that defends normative and value realism. The argument is 'the deliberative indispensability of irreducibly normative truths' advanced by Enoch in his book *Taking Morality Seriously*. I will show that this important and original argument as it stands fails. I will also show that if Enoch had embraced all the consequences of his argument, then a more promising line of argument would have opened up via

[18] See especially JL Mackie, *Ethics: Inventing Right and Wrong* (London, Penguin, 1977).

which to defend the robust realism of values and normative truths. I will, therefore, attempt to defend a modified version of robust value and normative realism.

9.4.1 The Story of a Philosophical Problem: Putting Enoch's Robust Realism in Context

Imagine the following example. Jean is an 18-year-old law student who suffers from a heart condition that requires an immediate operation. A doctor operates on her but negligently overlooks an allergy report that mentions Jean's sensitivity to a certain drug. After the operation, Jean suffers a liver failure that will require treatment for an indeterminate period of time. Evidence shows that Jean had an allergic reaction to a drug administered during the operation and that this reaction caused the liver failure. The administered drug had not been mentioned in Jean's allergy report, however a paper in the little-known academic journal, *Drugs*, had recently reported that the administered drug has a similar chemical composition to the drug identified in the allergy report. The doctor is taken to court and it is alleged that his action has been negligent. Some laymen, judges and legal practitioners might believe that Jean has a right to be compensated independently of our conventions or what we think about it. Normative truths and values, such as 'good' and 'rights', exist in an absolute and robust manner. We might deny their existence, there may be cultures and social practices that do not have rights for wrongs negligently committed, but this does not mean that such rights do not exist. The appropriate metaphor for these normative truths and values is that they are part of the 'furniture of the universe' or that they exist in 'Plato's Heaven'. Philosophers have, however, argued over the nature and existential status of rights and other normative truths. They assert that they *do not exist* in an absolute manner; that they *do not exist* independently of our agreements, beliefs, practices or conventions.

Dworkin,[19] for example, has famously rejected the idea of robust and absolute normative truths since it entails an implausible worldview that conflicts with our scientific and empirical understanding of the world. Thus, normative truths cannot be verified or observed scientifically. Furthermore, Dworkin asserts, normative truths depend on our moral theories and morally substantive claims. Thus, if I assert that 'the killing of animals for consumption is morally wrong', this statement depends on the substantive moral claim that it is always wrong to kill a living being and to inflict pain on living creatures.

---

[19]   R Dworkin, 'Objectivity and Truth: You'd Better Believe It' (1996) *Philosophy and Public Affairs* 87.

But, one might ask, what makes these substantive moral claims true and objective? Apart from asserting that the truth of such statements is not independent of our moral theories and beliefs, Dworkin does not tell us *why* or in virtue of *what* they are objective moral truths. Dworkin[20] tells us that judges disagree genuinely over the nature of law and more specifically over what the law is. According to Dworkin, legal practitioners advance different conceptions of the point of the law. The task of the judge is to advance the best possible interpretation of the point of the law, which at the pre-interpretative stage emerges due to practice and at the interpretive stage is constructed and refined in light of the two criteria of moral appeal and fit with the bulk of the past legal material. Let us take the case of Jean: judges and legal practitioners might disagree about whether Jean has a right to be compensated. Some judges and legal practitioners might think that the doctor has not breached his duty of care (the standard of duty) since a responsible body of medical opinion has stated that common medical practice is to rely on reports provided by laboratory tests. Furthermore, there was no knowledge at the time of the operation that the pharmaceutical drug that was administered belongs to the family of pharmaceutical drugs to which Jean is allergic as identified by the allergy report.[21] The common practice of medical doctors is to learn about pharmaceutical drugs from prominent journals. Medical doctors are not pharmacologists or chemists and they should not be expected to know about recent and little heard of discoveries relating to pharmaceutical drugs. By contrast, some other judges and legal practitioners might disagree and consider that it is a matter of diligence and logic to learn about the most recent advancements in the field in this case, particularly in light of the fact that that the patient is known to be allergic to an identified drug. Furthermore, Internet and electronic resources make available to medical doctors knowledge that in the past was only accessible to specialists in the field. It seems unjust to deny compensation for foreseeable damage just because a responsible body of medical opinion has established that medical doctors usually rely on reports from laboratory tests and learn about advancements in pharmaceutical drugs from well known academic journals. Thus, they might argue, judges need to pay attention to what the practice *should be* rather than to what it *is*.[22]

According to Dworkin, in the case of Jean, the judge exercises what he calls 'constructive interpretation'. As such he will decide according to what is morally appealing and fits the bulk of past legal material. The starting point of the judge will be the different conceptions of the legal practice and the point of such practice. Arguably, in this case, it is morally appealing to advocate the view that – despite the fact that it did not reflect the common practice of

---

[20] Dworkin, *Law's Empire* (n 7).

[21] *Bolam v Friern Hospital Management Committee* [1995] 1 WLR 582.

[22] *Bolitho v City and Hackney Health Authority* [1997] 4 All ER 771.

medical doctors – Jean has a right to be compensated because the medical doctor ought to have been aware of recent discoveries in the field of pharmaceutical drugs. This also fits the bulk of past decisions where the test of the standard of duty is tempered by the logic of what typical medical practice ought to be. It is apparent then that there is clear continuity between Dworkin's rejection of robust normative truths and his legal philosophy. Jean's right to be compensated does not exist independently of our morally substantive conceptions, and rights are neither part of 'the furniture of the universe' nor are in Plato's Heaven. It is not the task of the judge, Dworkin tells us, to engage with the *nature or concept* of rights, duty, responsibility or obligation to determine their robust truth. On the contrary, the judge engages with different conceptions about the point of law that emerges in legal practice and aims to find the best possible interpretation in light of what seems to him or her morally sound and fits the bulk of past legal material. The judge does not need to ask the morally practical question 'what ought I to do?', but rather look at the different conceptions that emerge from our views about the point of the practice (for a full criticism of Dworkin's constructive interpretation see section 10.6).

Contra Dworkin, many contemporary legal theorists have recognised the significance of showing that there are absolute and robust normative truths and values. If there are no normative truths and values, then a contradiction between our more abstract philosophical thinking and our practices and experiences seems inevitable. For example, if there are no normative truths and values, then how can we explain the phenomenology of our legal practices and adjudication, ie when we engage in trying to find the 'right answer' to a legal dispute, we seem to genuinely disagree as to what the law is. Furthermore, if there are no normative truths, then there is no right answer regarding whether the judge has decided correctly or incorrectly, and there is no point in engaging in doctrinal analyses to determine the sound principles that ground legal notions such as rights, obligations, negligence, duty of care, breach of duty of care, legal responsibility, sovereignty, and so on. If there are no robust normative truths and values, then legal analyses and legal thinking fall prey to relativism, subjectivism and scepticism. Let us think about Jean's case again. If there are no robust normative truths then, arguably, the disagreements over whether she has a right to be compensated is relative to the substantive moral claims of judges and legal practitioners and not to whether she truly and robustly has this right. We might say that in some sense all legal practitioners and judges are correct in their decision-making to the extent that their decisions are coherent with their moral substantive claims and perspectives.

Let us imagine another example. Susan, who lives in England with her spouse Peter, is raped by him. Nowadays we say that Peter has committed a moral wrong and, under criminal law, he has committed a legal wrong.

Pre-1991,[23] however, Peter's wrong would not have been a legal wrong. Furthermore, philosophers like Dworkin, who do not endorse the view that there are robust normative truths, might suggest that pre-nineteenth century the rape of a spouse was not morally wrong because the wrongness of rape depends on the moral claims, theories and perspectives of the time. By contrast, some philosophers, laymen and legal participants believe that the rape of spouses is and has always been morally wrong, that Peter has committed a wrong, and that the law before 1991 was mistaken. So how can we explain this phenomenology without absolute and robust normative truths? The phenomenology of our legal practices becomes merely illusory and the only task left is to unmask the myth of 'the truth in law'. Some have argued that literary and historical scholarship are better equipped than philosophical and doctrinal analyses to perform the task of unmasking this myth. For a less radical project concerning 'truth in law', and if Dworkin is correct in rejecting robust normative truths, then constructive interpretation seems compelling.

David Enoch aims to defend robust realism of normative truths, ie a full meta-ethical position. Such a position is, as we shall later see, the only way to 'take morality seriously'. Enoch adumbrates two core arguments to defend robust realism of normative truths. The first argument is a refinement of an idea found in other ethical realists on the moral significance of moral disagreement.[24] Enoch argues that in our daily life we disagree 'genuinely' on what should be done and only robust realism can provide a satisfactory explanation of our experiences. Furthermore, a neutral or impartial perspective on what ought to be done distorts the experience of 'genuine' disagreement that morality involves, ie that one party to the dispute *must* be wrong and the other *must* be right. Enoch calls this argument 'the deliberative indispensability of irreducibly normative truths'. I will concentrate on the discussion of this important argument and will show that this argument fails as it stands.

9.4.2 Harman's Challenge

For Enoch, normative truths are universal, objective, absolute and independent of how we conceive them and of whether we desire them or not.[25] In a

---

[23] *R v R* [1991] UKHL 12, [1992] AC 599.

[24] His argument is a refinement of views on the capacity of realism to explain the phenomenology of moral disagreement. (See D Brink, *Moral Realism and the Foundations of Ethics* (Cambridge, Cambridge University Press, 1989, 24). See also F Tersman, *Moral Disagreement* (Cambridge, Cambridge University Press, 2006) and my article 'Genuine Disagreements: A Realist Reinterpretation of Dworkin' (2001) *Oxford Journal of Legal Studies* 649, where I argue that Dworkin cannot avoid being committed to a moral realist view if he wishes to make sense of his distinction between 'genuine' theoretical disagreements and semantic disagreements.

[25] D Enoch, *Taking Morality Seriously: A Defense of Robust Realism* (Oxford, Oxford University Press, 2011) 3.

metaphorical sense, we could say that they are in Plato's Heaven, ie they are outside of our limited perspective and conceptions. We would say, in the examples above, Jean truly has a right to be compensated and Peter has committed a wrong independently of our moral substantive claims, moral theories, beliefs, desires, cultural and social practices or conventions. Thus, Enoch argues that these normative truths are not reducible to natural facts and therefore he aims to defend non-naturalist robust normative realism.[26] Normative truths refer to what should be done or what is valuable.[27] They are present in our everyday experiences. Gilbert Harman,[28] however, has questioned the intelligibility of the idea that there are absolute and robust normative truths and values since they cannot exist in our empirical or scientific world. Harman asks: how do we know that things like stones, cats or electrons exist? Harman answers that they exist because either we can observe them or they play an explanatory role in our best scientific theories. By contrast, in response to the question about the explanatory role of objective and universal moral truths and values, Harman answers that there is no explanatory role. For example, if you saw a child burning a cat you would say, 'It is wrong to do that'. The best explanation of this judgment, according to Harman, is sociological, psychological and/or cultural. An apparently irreducible, objective and universal normative fact can be eliminated and is not needed to provide the best possible explanation of our moral experiences. Similarly, if electrons can be eliminated from explanations of our physical phenomena, then we are not justified in believing in them. However, our best physical theories need a commitment to 'electrons' to explain physical phenomena, hence we cannot eliminate them in the way we can eliminate irreducible moral facts. Therefore, according to Harman, we are justified in believing in electrons, but we are not justified in believing in irreducible moral or evaluative facts. The latter are redundant for our explanations.

Enoch aims to undermine views similar to the ones defended by Harman, because they only focus on explanation. According to Enoch, views like the one advocated by Harman give privilege to the explanatory enterprise, ie they give privilege to the idea that our task is to explain what the world is like, and that any other enterprise is justified to the extent that it is part of or contributes to explanations of what the world is like. This approach ignores other human enterprises, such as the need to make intelligible and meaningful our

---

[26] I doubt whether he succeeds in separating his view from non-reductivist naturalism regarding normative truths. His defence of strong supervenience, ie the idea that it is impossible for there to be two things that are indistinguishable in their natural properties but are distinguishable in their normative ones (136) might entail a commitment to some kind of naturalism. Enoch himself seems to recognise that this view entails non-reductive naturalism (Enoch (n 25) 101, n 2).

[27] ibid 3.

[28] G Harman, 'Moral Explanations of Natural Facts: Can Moral Claims be Tested Against Moral Reality?' (1986) *Southern Journal of Philosophy* 57.

existence, the need to act according to what seems right, just or good. Thus, in the examples above, there is nothing that gives Jean a right to be compensated, except for the fact that it is part of our moral beliefs and practices to give compensation in cases of physical harm caused by negligent wrongs. According to Hartman, it is nonsense to postulate robust normative truths to show the wrongness of Peter's act of rape and Jean's right to be compensated as absolute and true. These normative truths do not help us to explain how the world is. We can eliminate them without losing sense of the world. Thus, the explanatory enterprise becomes omnipresent. We therefore only need social and biological facts to explain our behaviour and emotions regarding the wrongness of rape and the rightness of compensation for medical professional negligence. For example, one might explain the fact that we feel very strongly about Jean's right to be compensated because our evolutionary history has shown that harm and pain is avoided by our animal nature. Similarly, our feeling that there is genuine wrongness in Peter's act is due to the fact that the mutual trust and respectful caring that develops between two human beings who live together has been undermined. We do not need to talk about 'the wrongness of marital rape' or the 'right to be compensated' as these normative categories, ie right and wrongness, can be eliminated from our explanations. We only need to be engaged in an explanatory enterprise.

9.4.3 The Deliberative Indispensability Argument: Can It Stand?

Enoch asserts that those who, like Harman, advance the priority of explanation are really concerned with parsimony. In other words, they are concerned not to multiply entities without *sufficient* reason. Thus, in our examples, the key concern is with not multiplying categories such as 'right' or 'wrongness' without sufficient reason. They might ask, 'why do we need these concepts if they do not refer to anything in the world?'.

Contra Harman, Enoch points out that being explanatorily useful is not the only good and sufficient reason and that we can multiply entities when they are *indispensable*.[29] Enoch's first strategy is then 'a separatist strategy' concerned with severing the connection between the view that explanation has priority over any other enterprise, eg the need to make intelligible and meaningful our actions and the actions of others, the need to decide what we ought to do or how we ought to act. Thus, according to Enoch, the existence of some entities seems indispensable for the purposes of our activities and different enterprises in the world. For example, it seems indispensable to be committed to making intelligible the actions of others. It is equally indispensable to believe that

---

[29] Enoch (n 25) 52–54.

something makes things and acts right, good and just to make sense of our moral decisions.

How does a judge decide how he ought to decide in Jean's case or Peter's case if the answer is already predetermined by the explanatory enterprise, ie our biological, sociological or cultural natures? Furthermore, how can we attribute legal and moral responsibility?

Enoch relies on recent views advanced in the philosophy of mathematics and particularly on the view of Colyvan[30] who defends a Platonist or robust realist position in mathematics on the basis of the indispensability argument. However, as I will show below, the indispensability argument for mathematical realists is anchored in the priority of explanation due to its commitment to naturalism and confirmational holism. Naturalism means that we abandon the idea that the philosophical method occupies a privileged position: we do not rely on anything that is beyond experience and can be known by the merely hypothetical-experimental method of science to determine the truth of our propositions. This means that merely theoretical or conceptual ideas that cannot be assessed empirically cannot be part of our theories. Confirmational holism entails that we cannot test our propositions individually and that we can only test whole sets of propositions. Thus, let us suppose that we have the following scientific propositions: 'sunlight is composed of seven different wavelengths which can be detected by looking through a prism' and 'light has a dual existence: as a wave and as a particular'. These propositions need to be confirmed holistically and not individually. If an experiment shows that the first proposition is false, this is not sufficient to reject it. To reject the proposition it is also necessary to show the falsehood of other interrelated propositions.

Colyvan does not separate the indispensability and the explanatory arguments. On the contrary, for mathematical realists explanatory priority and indispensability cannot and *should not* be separated, they are inevitably interconnected.[31] Let us call this position the 'inseparability' thesis and the mathematical realists and philosophers who advocate this view 'inseparatists'. According to Enoch, a philosopher who advocates the view that explanation is an indispensable activity is unable to show that other kinds of indispensability are not equally respectable.[32] They cannot discriminate between respectable and non-respectable types of indispensability. Thus, for Enoch, if the existence

---

[30] M Colyvan, *The Indispensability of Mathematics* (Oxford, Oxford University Press, 2001) and 'In Defense of Indispensability' (1998) *Philosophia Mathematica* 39.

[31] Colyvan establishes that naturalism and confirmational holism ought to be compatible with the indispensability argument: 'In particular, I will be defending the Quine/Putnam version of the argument against Maddy's claim that there are internal tensions between the doctrines of naturalism and confirmational holism. As we shall see, both these doctrines are crucial to the indispensability argument, so it is important that they be mutually consistent' ('In Defense of Indispensability' (n 30) 39).

[32] Enoch (n 25) 55.

of normative truths is indispensable for making sense of our moral decisions, and the existence of prime numbers is indispensable for making sense of our mathematical theories, then normative truths and prime numbers are equally indispensable. Thus, the existence of normative truths such as 'rights' or 'wrongness' are indispensable to our engagement with legal deliberation and decision. According to Enoch, one cannot argue that normative truths can be eliminated because they play no explanatory role in how our empirical world is. Moreover, Enoch tells us that philosophers who advocate the 'explanatory indispensability' thesis cannot advance a principle to demarcate explanatory indispensability from other types of indispensability. Therefore, as long as no one has advanced such a principle, or because *such principle cannot be advanced* (I am not sure which view Enoch takes on this) explanatory indispensability and other kinds of indispensability have equal status.[33]

I believe that Enoch is mistaken on this. It is true that the defenders of explanatory indispensability cannot show that explanatory indispensability *qua* indispensability is privileged over other kinds of indispensability, but they have shown that explanatory indispensability *qua* explanation is privileged.[34] In consequence, the *additional* principles advanced by mathematical realists that enable them to separate the wheat from the chaff, ie to differentiate between different types of indispensability, are naturalism and confirmational holism. Mathematical realists rely on the works of Quine and Putnam's work. According to Quine[35] and Putnam,[36] if our *best* scientific theories need to be committed to the existence of certain entities to make sense of the empirical world, for example, our best biological theories are committed to DNA and our best physical theories are committed to 'electrons', and if they cannot be eliminated without losing intelligibility, then, by inference to the best explanation, such entities exist. For example, if we attempt to reduce electrons to non-theoretical or empirical entities or to eliminate them, the physical data will not be coherent and our physical theories will be unrecognisable and probably unintelligible. Similarly, if we attempt to eliminate differential equations from our mathematical and physical theories, the physical and mathematical data will be incoherent. What we call our 'best scientific theories' are the *best* because they have proved themselves to be successful and have passed holistically the tribunal of experience (confirmational holism). Therefore, contrary to Enoch's view, mathematical realists can discriminate among different indispensabilities.

---

[33] ibid 11, 50, 56.

[34] Colyvan (n 30).

[35] WO Quine, 'On What There Is' in *From a Logical Point of View*, 2nd edn (Cambridge, MA, Harvard University Press, 1980) 1.

[36] H Putnam, 'Philosophy of Logic' in *Mathematics, Matter and Methods: Philosophical Papers* (Cambridge, Cambridge University Press, 1979) vol I, 323.

Enoch, however, advances a refinement of the indispensability argument. According to Enoch there is an additional type of indispensability called 'deliberative indispensability'. Enoch distinguishes between instrumental indispensability and essential indispensability. Thus, something is instrumentally indispensable if it cannot be eliminated without undermining whatever reason we have to engage in that project.[37] For example, if I engage in a religious project then I cannot eliminate the entity of God, or some kind of deity or some kind of perfect state. To eliminate these things undermines the reasons for engaging in that project, eg to reach unity with God or some kind of deity or reach a state of perfection. However, Enoch tells us that something being instrumentally indispensable cannot guarantee justifiably ontological commitments. A further essential indispensability is also necessary. *According to Enoch, a project is essentially indispensable if it is rationally non-optional. This means that we cannot rationally disengage from such projects.*[38] Enoch advocates the view that we are essentially deliberative creatures, ie we cannot help but ask ourselves what we should do, believe, act, reason or care about.[39] This deliberative stance is from the first-person perspective.[40] We are engaging in deliberation that presupposes 'good', 'valuable', 'duty' and 'obligation'. Arguably, Enoch tells us, these are rationally non-optional activities because of the kind of creatures that we are. *Contra Enoch*, my interpretative point is that mathematical realists argue that explanatory indispensability is privileged over other types of indispensability and, furthermore, that these other types of indispensability cannot show the ontological existence of the entities to which they are committed *unless* they are anchored in naturalism and confirmational holism. But Enoch cannot avail himself of this strategy because he aims to be a non-naturalist realist.[41] Enoch completely ignores this important point which has equally been raised by mathematical realists and 'inseparatists'. A philosopher who advocates the 'inseparability thesis' will claim that it is fallacious to say that if deliberation is a rational non-optional project for creatures like us, and if normative entities are *indispensable for* the success of deliberation, then by inference to the best explanation, such normative entities – values and oughts – do exist. But where, exactly, does the fallacy lie? The 'inseparatist' philosopher will say that the fallacy lies in thinking that because the project is 'rationally

---

[37] Enoch (n 25) 69.

[38] ibid 70.

[39] ibid 70.

[40] Enoch says the following, *a propos* of an example about choices between doing philosophy or law: 'Even with answers to most – even all – of these questions, there remains the ultimate question. "All things considered", you ask yourself, "what makes best sense for me to do? When all is said and done, what should I do? What shall I do?"' (n 25) 72.

[41] Arguably, there are aspects of Enoch's view that gesture towards non-reductive naturalism, though he rejects that he is a non-reductive naturalist since he gives a different interpretation of naturalism to the one advanced by the Cornell Realists, for example.

non-optional' we are 'necessarily committed to its existence' in the same way that we are committed to 'electrons', 'DNA' or 'differential equations', and therefore the project or activity must 'exist'. Therefore, for Enoch, if the activity is committed to normative entities, these entities also exist. This is a mistaken conclusion, the 'inseparatist' might argue, and he might also insist that the existence of mathematical and physical entities is not due just to theorists who are committed to them, but due also to theories that have proved themselves to be the *best available theories*. They have passed holistically the tribunal of experience. There is coherence and systematicity between our mathematical theories and scientific theories. The 'inseparatist' could continue with his argument by saying that Enoch's view of 'deliberation' as rationally non-optional is not the best available theory to explain our deliberative experiences, ie our first-person experience when faced with questions such as 'what I ought to do', and that this view does not cohere holistically with our other beliefs about science and the natural world. Thus, the 'inseparatist' might argue that 'deliberation' is an evolutionarily adaptive behaviour and this explanation is the best possible explanation that coheres (confirmational holism) with our other beliefs in science (naturalism). The objection could take the following formal reasoning:

Premise 1: Normative truths are indispensable for the success of deliberation.

Premise 2: Deliberation is rationally non-optional. This means that every human being, as long he or she is rational, 'ought' to deliberate.

Premise 3: By inference to the best explanation, normative truths exist.

Premise 4: Only if an experience, theory or entity coheres with our best scientific truths are we committed to it and only then does it exist.

Premise 5: The experience of 'deliberation' from the first-person perspective does not cohere with our best scientific theories; therefore we need not be committed to it.

Premise 6: The experience of 'deliberation' from the first-person perspective does not exist (from premises 4 and 5).

Premise 7: Normative truths are indispensable for the success of 'deliberation', but 'deliberation' does not exist (from premises 6 and 1).

Premise 8: If we need to be committed to normative truths for the success of deliberation, by inference to the best explanation, then normative truths exist.

Conclusion: 'Normative truths' do not exist since we do not need to be committed to deliberation (from premises 5–8).

There is something peculiar about this reasoning. Enoch could argue that the key premise is premise 2. It is a 'normative' premise and therefore it cannot be the subject of empirical refutation in terms of coherence with our *best scientific theories*. Therefore, Enoch might argue, premise 5 is false. Is Enoch begging the question? In order to show that there are 'normative truths' he argues that we need a 'normative proposition'.[42] *But perhaps his argument is concerned not with 'indispensability' but with the difference between the two domains: the normative and the empirical or the first-person and third-person perspectives.* Faced with this argument, the 'inseparatist' will remain unconvinced. He or she will demand an explanation in terms of coherence with our other beliefs, including our scientific beliefs. The 'inseparatist' will affirm that the indispensability argument cannot be separated from confirmational holism and naturalism. It seems, therefore, that we have come full circle and find ourselves back again at Harman's challenge, ie normative entities are dispensable because we do not need them to explain our normative judgements.

But perhaps Enoch is saying something more sophisticated, though full of ambiguities. Enoch asserts that deliberation is from the first-person perspective and therefore the deliberative indispensability of normative entities is *for the concern of the deliberator, and not of the bystander, observer or theoretician who aims to explain moral or normative judgements.[43]* In other words, one might say, Harman and the 'inseparatist' mathematical realists take the third-person perspective and fail to grasp the first-person perspective of the deliberator.

Thus, let us suppose that I am a judge in an appellate court in 1990 facing the decision as to whether Peter has committed a wrong by raping his spouse. I am faced with two choices: either I follow the case law and decide that Peter has committed no wrong or I decide that Peter has committed a wrong since he had no right to violate the physical integrity and autonomy of his spouse. I assert that the law has been mistaken and I change the law on this matter. There must be something, *from my deliberative point of view*, of value in not violating others (preserving physical integrity and being autonomous). It is not that preserving physical integrity and being autonomous is valuable 'from my point of view' since this entails that I take a theoretical stance – I see myself as having a 'point of view', so to speak – but rather that preserving physical integrity and being autonomous is, 'as I see it' valuable, good or what ought to be done *simpliciter* (sections 3.3 and 5.3.1).

Let us suppose that a number of scientists engage in a super-experiment in the cosmos and successfully demonstrate that there are no entities such as 'values', 'oughts' or any kind of normative truths. They discover that there is a set of particles in the universe that are activated every time a human being thinks or pronounces the words 'value' or 'ought to be done'. Because of this set of particles, we experience the feeling that something ought to be done or

[42] Enoch (n 25) 62, n 33.
[43] ibid 76 n 62, 79.

that there is genuine value in something, and at the same time this mere feeling (or intuition) is linked to the stronger thoughts that we actually happen to have. The particles are called Kalons and because of this crucial experiment we discover that there are not really values or normative truths. In books, thoughts and articles, 'value' is replaced by the word 'Kalon-value', and 'Kalon-ought' refers to the particles and their effect on us. Because of this justified belief – it coheres with our best scientific theories – it no longer matters whether or not, as a judge, I decide that Peter has committed a wrong. *From the theoretical or third-person perspective* deliberation is meaningless. We live in this new world where Kalons exist, but nothing else has changed, and we still have the 'feeling' or 'experience' of choice and freedom from the *first-person perspective*. However, the discovery has not changed our deliberative phenomenology. I, as a judge in an appellate court, need to engage in deliberation from the *first-person perspective* and assess whether I ought to preserve physical integrity and autonomy of all human beings or preserve the value of legality and continuity with preceding cases. I need to assess what gives a legal decision *worth*, and what is valuable. I need to *direct* my actions towards the chosen value and persist over time towards achieving my goals, eg changing the law according to what I think is just and right, even if I know that (in my theoretical moments of reflection) Kalons are always there, working away in the background. My deliberation is intelligible to me because there are things that are of 'value' and are 'just', and that represent 'duty' and 'obligation'. However, from the third-person perspective I know that 'Kalon-value' and 'Kalon-ought to be done' is doing the work. My theoretical knowledge does not change how I 'naively' operate in the world of my actions and values.

Science has not, however, succeeded in discovering Kalons and therefore the challenge for scientific theories is to explain the deliberative experience as lived and experienced in the first-person perspective. Scientists could design a simulated world that eliminates our first-person deliberative experiences and where Kalons will do all the work, but we still need to 'choose' to live in the simulated world and deliberation concerning 'why?' and 'who?' will begin again. My point is not that science cannot possibly refute our deliberative and moral experiences at the theoretical level/third-person perspective, but rather that the theoretical point of view cannot undermine the phenomenology of the deliberative point of view and agency as lived and experienced by the deliberator. This is the point, in my view, that Enoch needs to emphasise for his argument on 'deliberative indispensability' to succeed. He needs to emphasise that there is an asymmetry between the first-person perspective and the bystander, third-person or theoretical perspective, and that this asymmetry is pervasive in the sense that the third-person perspective is unable to grasp the first-person perspective of the deliberator who is engaged in the question of what he or she should do. Furthermore, because Kalons have not yet been discovered, at the theoretical level we leave open the hypothesis that these values and what ought to be done 'really' exist. The result is Hypothetical Robust Realism for normative truths. This means, so far, that the best possible explanation of the phenomenology of the first-person deliberative stance entails a commitment to the existence of normative entities. Furthermore, the phenomenology of the first-person deliberative perspective is 'lost' by the theoretical or third-person explanation. Normative entities seem to persistently appear in the best story of the phenomenology of our deliberation. I will call this argument 'the best possible explanation of the phenomenology of the deliberative stance'. This explanation is, moreover, the best possible to explain the phenomenology of the deliberative experience, because it grasps the 'first-person perspective'. Consequently, contra Enoch, I advocate the view that explanatory indispensability has priority over other kinds of indispensability, including deliberative indispensability. However, contra reductive naturalists, I argue that explanations cannot be reductive and need to preserve the distinctiveness of different domains, eg deliberative/practical and theoretical. This view finds its basis in the distinction between theoretical and practical reason and the relative autonomy of the latter. But the deliberative stance also implies that we are agents in the world, that our intentions and ideas change in a complex way our empirical and material world. We transcend our empirical constitution and material world to transform it as we plan and intend it. Thus, as sculptor, I can plan and buy a piece of marble, draw up a plan, take a hammer, chisel and mallet and carve the stone to make a sculpture as I imagined and sketched it. This process requires the engagement of my will and the continuous effort of my intentional action. Before starting the task, I ask myself, 'Why do I want to carve something? Should I carve a "David" or a "Hercules"?, and why should I carve this?'. In answer I might say 'because I am a sculptor' and if I am asked why I am a sculptor I might say 'because it is fulfilling and beautiful' or 'because it makes life worth living'. It seems, then, that to engage successfully in deliberation and acting, I need to be committed to normative truths, ie to 'the beautiful' and 'the worth living'.

In the example of Peter, the appellate judge needs to decide whether it is wrong for a husband to force sex upon his wife. The judge faces the moral challenge of determining the truth of the matter and this entails weighing up normative truths. This exercise is undertaken from the deliberative or first-person perspective; it is not an explanatory exercise of describing what the law is from the theoretical or third-person point of view and nor is it an exercise on identifying the different conceptions of the point of law advanced by legal participants, ie what legal participants have in their heads or consciousness. It is an engagement with the normative furniture of the world and with 'Plato's Heaven', and is aimed at transcending our legal practices, cultural, social and moral beliefs through our conceptual and practical capacities (section 9.2 and

Chapter 4). Normative truths and values are indispensable to our understanding of what judges do and we need to think about these normative truths and values as absolute and independent of our moral theories, social and cultural beliefs, convictions or conceptions of legal practices. At the same time, however, *these normative truths and values are the best possible explanation of our deliberative phenomenology*. We truly believe, engage and act as if there were normative truths and values and we disagree with others about whether, for example, Peter has violated his wife's autonomy and integrity by raping her. When we talk about 'integrity' and 'autonomy' we believe that we are referring to things that are independent of our cultural or social beliefs and we argue, theorise and philosophise in an attempt to grasp the nature of these things. Similarly, we debate whether Jean has the right to be compensated for a doctor's negligence. In the same way as we create cathedrals, sculptures, novels and pieces of music, judges change our world with their decisions and they do so in accordance with what they believe to be 'right', 'good', 'dutiful' or 'obligatory'. Of course, as the history of slavery, exploitation and despotic laws show, judges can completely fail to grasp the nature of normative truths. But the fact that we scrutinise and criticise the legal regimes of other times and cultures is possible precisely because of the existence of normative truths. How do we explain this phenomenon? *Contra* Enoch, I have argued that explanation is still privileged, but that *what* we need to explain is the phenomenology of the first-person or deliberative point of view.

The contrast between Enoch's argument and my argument as I have outlined it is now apparent. Enoch rejects the partial autonomy of the practical or deliberative domain and argues that we should blur the distinction between practical/deliberative and theoretical reason.[44] Consequently, he is left vulnerable to the attacks of Harman and the mathematical realists who advocate the 'inseparability' thesis. Enoch complains that he does not understand the distinction between the practical/deliberative and theoretical reason, and the role that the latter plays in forming and revising the relevant normative beliefs. We discover normative beliefs, Enoch tells us, by using our theoretical reason. According to Enoch we do not need the notion of practical reason and it is unclear what it amounts to. If Enoch's view on practical reason is correct, what should we make of Enoch's claims about the first-person deliberative stance? If we decide to blur the distinction between practical and theoretical reason, why not also blur the distinction between the first-person deliberative and the third-person theoretical stances? Why not collapse the first-person deliberative stance into the third-person theoretical stance? According to Enoch we use theoretical reason to form and revise our normative beliefs, and thus it appears that intentional action is a matter of 'being responsive to the

---

[44] ibid 241.

relevant normative truths'.[45] Contrast this view, for example, with the views of Aristotle or Aquinas on the need to have 'an operative' principle or an *arkhé* for an agent to be engaged in intentional action. For Aristotle and Aquinas, the relevant normative reason is formed by theoretical reason, but the reason is *in the action* and *when* the agent acts. Like Aristotle and Aquinas, Enoch considers that we are the kind of creatures who respond to relevant normative reasons. Unlike Aristotle and Aquinas, however, he does not consider that we respond on the basis of our practical capacities, ie practical reasoning. According to Enoch, my actions have been caused by my belief in the normative reasons involved in my action.[46] It is mysterious, however, how actions are caused in the *right* way by my beliefs about normative truths without the participation of the *agent's* practical capacities and practical point of view.

Let us suppose that I am a sculptor and that I decide to carve a 'David' from a piece of marble. One might conclude that, for Enoch, the movements of my hand on the marble are caused in the right way by my belief in the beauty (normative truth) of my planned sculpture, but I am not the one who controls the movements. Enoch cannot explain how mere beliefs can control the movements of my hands and the persistence over time of my actions. Consider the following example: I lose my chisel and look for it in all the cabinets of my workshop; I go to the store to try to buy a chisel and realise that I have no money or card to pay for the chisel. I return home to get some money, go back to the store and pay for the chisel. I return to my workshop and continue carving the sculpture. Arguably, for Enoch, this series of actions is *caused in the right way* by a mental state, ie my belief in the beauty of the planned sculpture.[47] This is an implausible view that does not answer the questions of how I have achieved the planned sculpture or of how I have obtained what I have intended, ie a sculpture of a particular size and with particular features (for a full discussion of this point see section 10.3).

In the context of legal decision-making in the case of Peter, Enoch will say that the belief (as a mental state) in the integrity and autonomy of Peter's wife caused the judge to decide that Peter has committed a wrong in raping her. It is not that Peter's wife possessed integrity and autonomy as any other human being, but rather that the judge was in the mental state of believing in these normative truths and that this mental state caused his decision. Why, then, does Enoch need to argue that normative truths are indispensable for engaging in the activity of judging? Would it not be sufficient to explain the judge's decision in terms of an explanation of the judge's mental state (ie a psychological or social explanation)?

---

[45] ibid.

[46] ibid.

[47] For a sceptical view on the possibility of 'beliefs' causing actions, see L Wittgenstein, *Philosophical Investigations* (E Anscombe (trans), Oxford, Blackwell, 1953) para 645.

In my view, Enoch's extremely theoretical view entails the dissolution of our first-person deliberative experiences, ie the idea that I am the agent who moves (not that I am moved by my beliefs and therefore by some 'part' of me) and who causes changes in the world according to what I intend and understand. Enoch seems too impatient with the practical/theoretical distinction and succumbs too quickly to the dominance of the theoretical domain, where Harman's argument predominates. I have argued that Enoch's insight concerning the importance of deliberative indispensability could undermine Harman's challenge, but only if the most powerful underlying view of Harman's argument is also weakened, ie Harman's belief that practical reason can collapse into theoretical reason, or rather that the first-person deliberative stance should be reduced to the third-person perspective. *Contra* Harman and Enoch, I have argued that we should resist the colonisation of the theoretical domain over the practical one.

10

Possible Objections and Concluding Note

10.1 *FIRST OBJECTION*

THE FEAR OF sanction. It could be argued that the 'guise of the good' model is an ideal model of law-abiding citizens interacting with one another in optimum conditions. Reality, however, differs substantially from this ideal model and the reason for this is that the majority of citizens in 'real' legal systems follow legal rules because and only because they fear the sanctions established in the law. They are coerced to act in certain ways and fear the consequences if they do not. It could be argued, further, that the 'guise of the good' model is too demanding for the normal citizen who merely follows legal rules without deliberation and without being guided by them. Consequently, citizens do not normally avow the grounding reasons as good-making characteristics of legal rules (Chapter 1) nor of the goodness of the legal authority (section 8.6.1).

My reply to this objection is that sanctions are auxiliary reasons and that they help us to understand that legal rules are grounded on reasons as good-making characteristics. They draw our attention to the importance of rules and their grounding reasons. If the majority of a population systematically follows legal rules because it fears those rules, and cannot understand or avow the grounding reasons as good-making characteristics of the legal rules, then those legal rules are part of a legal system that has marginal agency and fails to provide and engage citizens with the *logos* of the legal rules. Imagine a legal system where citizens stop at traffic lights not because they aim to protect lives, but because they fear the punishment which will result if they do not stop at the lights. Imagine, similarly, a legal system where citizens do not throw litter in the streets and teach their children not to do so purely because they fear being sanctioned and not because they believe that it is a good sort of thing to live in an unpolluted and clean city. This view does not contradict the point that some citizens in different kinds of legal systems might *occasionally* be alienated from the legal system and will have no capacity to avow either the grounding reasons of the legal rules or the goodness of legal authority. However, it seems possible that only a few will be *systematically* alienated in this way.

10.2 *SECOND OBJECTION*

Legal rules are redundant and there is nothing distinctive about law's normativity. I have explained legal normativity in terms of the normativity of goodness, but then, an objector might argue, there is nothing distinctive about law's normativity.

The arguments of the book do not aim to challenge the legal positivist view that law is identifiable by its sources. Furthermore, we recognise the importance of social sources and norms, but this study does consider that a *complete* and sound understanding of the normativity of law requires a further investigation on the character and nature of legal rules. I have argued that justificatory norms in terms of goodness are *primary* to norms socially construed. This approach involves the idea that the mere social fact of posing a legal rule does not explain the legal rule in all its complexity. It is argued that legal authorities' directives and legal rules need to engage with the good-making characteristics of actions, states of affairs and objects in order to guide the addressees' actions and gain normative status. Legal authorities make salient the reasons for actions as good-making characteristics that are required to live well in communities of creatures like us.

Imagine a legal system that does not engage at all with the grounding reasons as good-making characteristics of legal rules; worse, engages with grounding reasons that have (believed) evil-making characteristics, then it seems compelling to conclude that in cases such as these there is not a legal system for *creatures like us*. In this kind of legal system, citizens are asked to follow the rules of traffic, rules of contract, rules of tort law without the authorities engaging in the grounding reasons of such rules and therefore these ungrounded rules will fail to guide the citizens and will fail to gain any normative status. Let us put the following example. One of the legal rules in this legal system might be that parents or guardians are asked to give to their children stone and grass for snacks at the schools since it is believed that not growing is unhealthy. Similarly, road traffic rules are grounded on evil-making characteristics of risking your life and the lives of others and this is believed to be a bad sort of thing. Thus, instead of stopping at pedestrian crossings you must endeavour to run the pedestrians over. These examples show the absurdity of a possible world where there is no engagement with good-making characteristics and only engagements with evil-making characteristics which are believed to be bad or unreasonable by both the authorities and the addressees of the legal rules.

The view defended in this book does not commit us to the idea that legal authorities will always decide according to objectively good-making characteristics. There is plenty room for mistake and error on the part of the legal authorities (as has been clearly shown in Chapter 9). There will be occasions when legal authorities have mistaken beliefs about the grounding reasons as good-making characteristics of the rules, but even on these occasions there is engagement with grounding reasons which are believed to be good-making characteristics.

10.3 *THIRD OBJECTION*

Being in the world entails the triggering of reasons for actions, therefore, there is nothing special about legal normativity. David Enoch has denied that the normativity of law poses any substantial challenge to theories of law.[1] He argues that law provides reasons for actions in terms of what he calls 'triggering reasons' and argues that robust reason-giving, eg in the ethical domain and in law, are kinds of reason-giving as triggering reasons. Consequently, because there are many circumstances in which reasons are triggered, the law does not pose a special challenge. Once we understand the way that triggering reasons operate we can understand how legal directives and legal rules provide us with reasons for actions. Furthermore, according to Enoch, legal positivism is in the best position to explain the reason-giving character of the law in terms of what he considers the sound account of reason-giving, ie triggering reasons.

Let us begin with the following example provided by Enoch (with some expansion and variations):

'Buying milk': On most Mondays, you wake up in the morning, you wake up your friend, take the keys to your vehicle, and you both drive to the local grocery store. You get out of your vehicle, enter the grocery store, find the milk in the fridge and buy two bottles. But today is different. You and your friend drive to the local grocery store and in an unusual move, you choose to buy one bottle of milk instead of two. When your friend sees that you have chosen one bottle of milk instead of two, he asks you '*why*?'. Your answer is that the price of milk has risen and you wish to save money. Your friend asks you *why* you wish to save money and your answer is that you intend to travel to South America in the summer. He asks you again '*why*?' and you answer that you find travelling attractive and a good learning experience. The elucidation of the reasons for action from the point of view of the agent, ie the deliberative point of view, can now stop or rest. The series of complex actions, ie waking up on that Monday, driving to the local grocery store and

---

[1] D Enoch, *Reason-Giving and the Law*, Oxford Studies in Philosophy of Law (Oxford, Oxford University Press, 2011). A further detailed account of Enoch's triggering-reasons approach can be found in his article 'Giving Practical Reasons' (2011) 11 *Philosopher's Imprint* 4. For a clear exposition and defence of Enoch's view see B Bix, 'The Nature of Law and Reasons for Action' (2011) 5 *Problema* 399. For a critical discussion of Enoch's idea see W Edmundson, 'Because I Said So' (2013) *Problema* 41.

buying one bottle of milk, finds an end that is presented to the agent as having good-making characteristics. The reason for buying one bottle of milk is that you intend to save money and you intend to save money because you intend to travel to South America. You intend to travel to South America because you find travelling attractive and a good learning experience.

In this case, the reason for saving money to travel to South America is both a *justificatory* and *explanatory reason* for your series of actions. It is explanatory because it explains why you did what you did and it is justificatory because it can be subject to praise or blame. You can be judged by your friend as financially wise or as not supporting the local economy and caring for local farmers. The reason also *guided* you in your action and therefore the *reason was in the action*. This means that because you intended to save money, you selected one bottle and not two. Let us imagine a slightly different scenario from 'Buying milk'. Let us call it 'Advice from a friend'. Let us suppose that exactly the same things happen as in 'Buying milk', but when you are about to select your bottle of milk, your friend looks at his iPhone and sees that at another store, half a mile away, the milk is half price. Therefore you return the bottle of milk to the fridge, leave the store, drive for a mile and go to the other grocery store to buy the cheaper milk. You do all this because you have the reason of saving money to travel to South America. The reasons are *in* the action and *when* the agent performs the complex action. Because of your reason of saving money, you persist in your actions and are able to circumvent obstacles. Let us suppose that the second grocery store is closed when you arrive. It will open in 30 minutes so you wait until it opens.

The examples that I have given are paradigmatic examples of reasons for action and *reasons in action*, where *justificatory* and *explanatory* reasons for action are one and the same. Reasons *guide* the action of the agent and are present in the agent when she circumvents obstacles and *persists* in her actions over time. Cheap prices give you reasons to buy the items or, as Enoch puts it, the grocer, by putting up the price of milk, has given you a reason to drive until you find cheaper milk.

The example reflects our common-sense view of reasons for action and establishes four different key features or principles of reasons for actions: (a) explanation; (b) justification; (c) guidance; and (d) persistence over time. Let us again concentrate on our example 'Advice from a friend': if you suffer from temporary amnesia and forget that you intend to save money while you are at the first grocery store, then you will not drive to the second grocery store and wait until it is opened, you will *desist instead of persist* in your actions. You will drive home and do something else. Features of the world *guide* you in your actions, you are able to track cheap prices and you are justified in doing so because it is a good thing to save money. Furthermore, in providing the reason of saving money you have made intelligible the unity and continuity of your actions.

In 'Buying milk', according to the common-sense view, you have reason to save money on your milk purchases because of your intention to save money and travel to South America. According to Enoch, the grocer has given you a reason to buy one bottle of milk instead of two. The grocer, Enoch tells us, has given you a reason to minimise your consumption of milk. He has manipulated the non-normative circumstances in such a way as to trigger a dormant reason *'that was there all along independently of the grocer's actions'*. The reason of saving money was a dormant reason. In this scenario, let us call it 'Enoch-buying-milk', your friend asks you why you are buying one bottle of milk instead of two and you answer 'because the grocer has raised the price of milk and this triggers my reason of saving money which, by the way, I have *always* had'. When you are asked by your friend why you intend to save money, you would answer, according to Enoch, that you just have this *normative* reason *for action and it was a dormant* reason all along and the grocer's act of raising the price of the milk has triggered it. There are two parts to Enoch's argument. First, the grocer with his action transforms a non-normative fact (the price of the milk) into a normative fact. But let us suppose that the girlfriend of your friend is with you in the grocery store and she does not care about saving money, and neither does your millionaire uncle nor your wealthy niece: they all intend to buy milk in your local grocery store. Has the grocer transformed a non-normative fact into a normative fact for *all of them*, ie for the girlfriend of your friend, your millionaire uncle and your wealthy niece? For Enoch the reason is there *dormant* for *everyone*, including the girlfriend of your friend, your millionaire uncle and your wealthy niece. But it is *not a trigger* for *everyone*. Furthermore, let us imagine the following example:

> 'Fire at home': You are at home with your two pets, Tookey the parrot and Bubble the dog, and there is a fire downstairs. Following Enoch's argumentative line, you have a normative reason for acting and leaving the house to escape and the reason, arguably, is there dormant. Is it also a dormant reason for action for Tookey and Bubble? How can Enoch distinguish between me, Tookey and Bubble? Arguably, Enoch might say, the world has dormant reasons for all creatures, including animals. A firefighter enters the lounge where you are sitting with Tookey and Bubble and orders you to escape.

According to Enoch, the firefighter has triggered a reason for action by giving you the order. Does he also trigger a reason for action for Tookey and Bubble? It would seem absurd to say this. Enoch needs therefore to restrict the scope of the reason-giving *act*. The restriction can be found in his defence of a Gricean theory of intention in the context of showing how robust reason-giving is a sub-species of triggering reason-giving. According to Gricean theory, intentions are mental states and we say, following Enoch, that A attempts to robustly give B a reason to φ just in case (and because):

(i)   A intends to give B a reason to, and A communicates this intention to B;
(ii) A intends that B should recognise this intention;
(iii) A intends that B's reason depends in an appropriate way on B's recognition of A's communicated intention to give B a reason to.

However, if intentions are mental states, how they can cause in the *right sort of way* the recognition of A's communicated intention? In other words, how can we recognise *in the right way* the mental states of others? Enoch reckons that deviant causal chains generate problems for all causalist accounts of mental states. He states that for robust reason-giving to occur, there must be a reason that exists *prior* to the attempt to give robust reasons and he states, concerning the condition of 'appropriate way':

> I am not sure what more to say about the 'appropriate way' qualification in (iii). It is meant to rule out deviant causal (and perhaps other chains) chain. It would have been nice to have an account of how exactly to do this. But I will have to settle for noting that usually we know a deviant causal chain when we see one, and for claiming companions in guilt – for almost anyone needs an account of deviant causal chains. This qualification in (iii) thus doesn't make (iii) (or the account of which it is part) empty, nor does it raise any new problems that are peculiar to my account of robust reason-giving.[2]

In the example of 'Fire at home', the firefighter's orders give me a robust reason that exists independently of the firefighter's order. Arguably, for Tookey and Bubble the reason was there independently of the attempt at robust reason-giving by the firefighter. For 'Tookey' and 'Bubble', however, the reason has not been triggered because Tookey and Bubble could not recognise *in the appropriate way (whatever this means)* the intention of the firefighter. However, it seems absurd to say that Tookey and Bubble have *reasons* for actions, though *dormant* reasons for actions. Of course, I am not saying that Enoch's account is committed to the view that facts in the world give reasons to all creatures, independently of their practical reasoning capacity. But he needs to explain *how* the facts of the world *enter into* our practical reasoning. In this way, he can restrict the scope of reason-giving. He needs to provide an account of reasons for action and *reasons in action*. The crucial part of the explanation remains unexplained, ie *how* we as agents have reasons *during* the action. The notion of the 'appropriate way' aims to fill this explanatory gap, but it is left mysterious how this is done.

In his book *Taking Morality Seriously*,[3] Enoch addresses the issue differently and for the second part of his argument he seems to argue that the belief in your reason for action causes the action. However, merely mental states such

---

[2] Enoch, 'Giving Practical Reasons' (n 1) 17.
[3] D Enoch, *Taking Morality Seriously* (Oxford, Oxford University Press, 2011).

as beliefs cannot cause in the *right* way complex actions such as the drafting of a constitution, the enactment of the Human Rights Act, building cathedrals, writing novels, carving a sculpture, and so on. These activities require the engagement of our intentions (the will) within successive actions and entail continuous practical efforts. The idea that only mental states, ie beliefs, are the causes of our intentional actions that persist over time is weakened by the view that mental states do not have the required stability and directiveness for such endeavours. The empirically mental causal story is too simple to explain and make intelligible the complexity of human endeavours. Furthermore, if Enoch is right, it is a mystery how you *come to* have this justificatory reason. One possible explanation is that it is mainly a theoretical exercise. Enoch asserts:

> The way in which A's φ-ing can be responsive to R's being a normative reason, I suggested, was by being caused (in the appropriate way) by A's belief that R is a normative reason.[4]

But if this is the case, the question that arises is how this belief can guide you and make you persist in your action. In 'Fire at home', following the orders of the firefighter, I go upstairs and try unsuccessfully to open a window, I then run up to the roof of the building and manage to jump down onto the fire-fighters' safety net.

According to Enoch, my performance of all of these actions *is caused by* my mental state of believing that there is a fire in the house and that the firefighter has triggered a dormant reason that I already had, ie to escape from the fire. Deviant causal chains plague these examples. Let us suppose that I am in the mental state of believing that there is fire in my house and the firefighter has triggered a reason that was dormant, ie to escape from the fire. However, I habitually experience an impulse to run up to the roof of my house and jump off. On this occasion, I merely followed my habitual impulse. I am in the mental state of believing that the firefighter has given me a reason, ie he has triggered a dormant reason for action, but it *did not cause* my action. What actually caused my action of jumping from the roof of my house was a habitual impulse.

Thus, guidance and control by *reasons in actions* and persistence in performance *because of reasons in actions* remain unexplained in the normativist view of Enoch's reason-giving. Can the world give you reasons without the intention to act and independently of your practical reasoning and practical capacities? *Mere belief cannot make you to intend to act.*

---

[4] ibid 241.

10.4 *FOURTH OBJECTION*

The possibility of complete error in grasping the grounding reasons as good-making characteristics of the legal rules. Can there be a legal system where *the majority* of the grounding reasons as good-making characteristics of the legal rules are mistaken? In other words, can there be a legal system where the grounding reasons are *systematically* evil or bad-making characteristics? This is indeed a possibility and I have not argued that the 'guise of the good' model guarantees acting well and according to the sound exercise of practical reason. In cases such as these (the Third Reich in Germany, South African Apartheid, for example) there is a complete inversion of values. It is asserted that in these cases there is still an exercise of practical reason by the legal authorities (albeit that such exercise is defective). Consequently, in the *paradigmatic* case of law, the exercise of practical reason and the formulation of the grounding reasons of legal rules as good-making characteristics need to be in terms of objective good-making characteristics, and not merely in terms of hypothetical or 'believed' good-making characteristics. In previous work, I have advanced refinements of Finnis' view that the paradigmatic case of law is from the point of view of the man who exercises practical reason soundly.[5] This means that the paradigmatic case of creating and following legal rules is the case of legal authorities and citizens who engage with *objectively sound* grounding reasons as good-making characteristics of legal rules. This approach towards the paradigm enables us to identify a core or paradigmatic case and overlapping instances with mere resemblances to the core or paradigmatic case. According to this model, it might be the case that some instances are only *indirectly* related to the paradigmatic case through intermediate instances, but have no common properties or features with the paradigmatic case. For example, legal authorities or citizens might engage with the grounding reasons of legal rules by engaging with mistaken or non-objectively good-making characteristics as opposed to the objectively good-making characteristics of the paradigmatic case. The non-paradigmatic cases of mistaken good-making characteristics will have no common properties or features with the paradigmatic case. However, non-paradigmatic cases are indirectly related to the paradigm.

---

[5] I challenge Finnis's method of using the Aristotelian notion of the central case to show peripheral and central cases of law. See my article, 'Is Finnis Wrong?' (2007) *Legal Theory* 257. Cf J Finnis, 'Grounds of Law and Legal Theory' (2007) *Legal Theory* 318. However, I agree with the conclusion reached by Finnis, namely, that the paradigmatic case of law is from the point of view of the man exercising practical reason. This book has attempted to show how this point of view (the deliberative point of view) is the central one in following legal rules and it has used the 'guise of the good' model in acting intentionally to show this.

The guise of the good model presents law as an actuality of our special faculty of practical reason (see Chapter 4) and this is the main virtue and advantage of this way of approaching the nature and character of law, including its normative status. Law is presented as an *actuality of our potential capacity to exercise practical reason* that can be performed defectively whose result can also be imperfect due to the unsound exercise of practical reason. Law is not construed as a *mere result or outcome of our performance*, artefact or tool, *produced and caused* by the *minds* of legislators and judges, in a way which can be perfect as well as defective, for example, a knife that does not cut properly. Rather, law is *primarily* an *actuality* that reflects capacities; sometimes virtuous and good, and at other times imperfect and far from good. For example, like the actuality of actions such as cutting, walking, playing an instrument, etc.

10.5   *FIFTH OBJECTION*

Rules are like promises, when we make promises we have reasons for action that are independent of the motivational role of reasons.[6] **however, the 'guise of the good' model conflates the motivational and the normative role of reasons. Consequently, it either collapses into a neo-humean account of legal rules or a normativist explanation of legal rules. The 'guise of the good' model cannot have it both ways.** When neo-Humean and normativists talk about reasons for action they agree that the motivational and the normative role of reasons are different. However, neo-Humeans argue that the motivational role is *primary* and that when we talk about reasons for actions, the idea that such reasons are connected to the motivational or attitudinal set of conditions of the agent, is necessarily involved.[7] By contrast, normativists[8] argue that the question of whether 'x is a reason for action' does not *primarily* depend on whether the agent is motivated to act. An objector could argue that the 'guise of the good' model cannot have it both ways. The 'guise of the good' model, the objector might continue, is not a middle way between neo-Humeans and normativists concerning reasons for actions. In other words, the 'guise of the good' model collapses into either a neo-Humean position or a normativist approach. On the one hand, the 'guise of the good' model is committed to the idea that a reason for action depends on the description of the series of actions as well as

---

[6] See ibid.

[7] B Williams, 'Internal and External Reasons', reprinted in *Moral Luck* (Cambridge, Cambridge University Press, 1993). For recent neo-Humean formulations of reasons for action see M Smith, *The Moral Problem* (Oxford, Blackwell, 1994) and M Schroeder, *Slaves of Passions* (Oxford, Oxford University Press, 2007).

[8] J Dancy, *Practical Reality* (Oxford, Oxford University Press, 2000); T Scanlon, *What We Owe to Each Other* (Cambridge, MA, Harvard University Press, 1999).

the description of the end of the series in terms of the good-making character-istics given by the agent as the unifying factor of the series.[9] It entails, the objector might argue, that such descriptions can only be given by someone who already possesses a certain set of motivational or attitudinal conditions. These motivational or attitudinal conditions *cause* the action. Otherwise, the objector continues, it is mysterious how the action can be caused by a mere description of a series of actions and its end. To negate that mental states cause our actions is to introduce a queer and implausible metaphysics. We cannot change events or states of affairs in the world by mere *reasons as descriptions in terms of good-making characteristics*. How can mere thinking and describing, the objector might ask, transform the world? The 'guise of the good' model seems utterly mysterious on this. On the other hand, it is possible that the 'guise of the good' model simply collapses into a normativist view since the description provided by the agent needs to be intelligible from the third- and second-person perspectives. From these standpoints we engage in evaluating whether 'x as a reason is *objectively* a good sort of thing'. Consequently, the motivations or attitudes of the agent play no determining role in identifying, so to speak, the 'true' reason for action. The objector might point out that legal rules in the 'guise of the good' model are like promises. If the description of the grounding reason as a good-making characteristic of a legal rule is objective, then the addressee of a legal rule has normative reasons for actions, independently of his or her motivations or attitudes.

These objections can be divided into two sub-objections: (a) the question of whether the legal rules under the 'guise of the good' model collapse into a neo-Humean conception of legal rules; (b) the question of whether legal rules under the 'guise of the good' model collapse into a normativist conception of legal rules.

On the first sub-objection, I have argued that the 'guise of the good' model is not the complete story of how we act intentionally when following legal rules. I have defended the 'parasitic thesis' which involves the idea that the 'guise of the good' model is the primary explanation of the legal rule-following phenomenon. According to the parasitic thesis, we need the enabling condi-tions of a body and mental states to act, but a mentalistic, physical or social explanation of the legal rule-following phenomena is *parasitic* on an explana-tion of *why* we are directing ourselves towards certain ends. The position that has been defended aims to reject the simple reduction of intentional actions directed towards ends to mental states that cause an action. Furthermore, we have shown in Chapters 2, 5, 6 and section 10.3 that the neo-Humean con-

---

[9] For an analysis of the difference between Hume's notion of reasons for actions and Aristotle's philosophy of action, see T Irwin, 'Aristotle on Reason, Desire and Virtue' (1975) *Journal of Philosophy* 567. Cf E Galligan, 'Irwin on Aristotle' (1975) *Journal of Philosophy* 579.

ception of intentional action cannot show that desires and beliefs as mental states cause in the *right* sort of way our actions. The issue of how we are able to transform events and states of affairs in the world just by thinking about them is neither solved by neo-Humeans nor by the theorists who advocate the 'guise of the good' model. Therefore, neo-Humeans are not in a better position than 'guise of the good' adherents on this matter. We might need to think harder and more imaginatively about our notions of causation in the philosophy of science and action.

On the second sub-objection, the description of the grounding reason as a good-making characteristic of a rule is given by either the addressees of the rule or the legal authorities. Such descriptions of the grounding reasons of rules can be either objectively good or non-objectively good. In the latter case, the 'guise of the good' model helps to explain the defectiveness of many legal systems and the existence of evil ones. By contrast, a mere normativist view applied to legal rules cannot provide a complete explanation of the existence of evil regimes at the level of the actions of the legal agents. It explains evil regimes through notions such as ideal law or essentialist views of the paradigmatic case of law but this explanation is from the perspective of the theorist.[10] It is true that for Finnis, the man who exercises practical reason soundly should be at the core of the formation of legal concepts by the legal theorist. However, a normativist like Finnis does not articulate the full range of attitudes inherent in the moral psychology of the rule-following phenomenon.

Adherents of the 'guise of the good' model might agree with the normativist theorist that objective grounding reasons ('basic goods' in Finnis' terminology) of legal rules impose on citizens reasons for actions independent of the citizen's motivations or attitudes; however, the guise of the good model goes beyond normativist tenets and aims also to explain and unpack the complexities and richness of *all kinds* of rule-compliance and rule-creating phenomena, including defective ones that result in evil or defective legal regimes. It also aims to establish a conceptual and methodological framework for the sound understanding of the moral psychology of legal-rule compliance. The claim is that the 'guise of the good model' can have it both ways.

In 1958, Anscombe wrote 'it is not profitable for us at present to do moral philosophy; that should be laid aside at any rate until we have an adequate philosophy of psychology, in which we are conspicuously lacking'.[11] Paraphrasing Anscombe, it is not profitable for us at present to do legal philosophy without an adequate understanding of the relationship between key jurisprudential concepts and philosophy of psychology, including under this

---

[10] J Finnis, *Natural Law and Natural Rights* (Oxford, Clarendon Press, 1980) ch 1.
[11] E Anscombe, 'Modern Moral Philosophy', reprinted in *Ethics, Religion and Politics: Collected Philosophical Papers of GME Anscombe* (Oxford, Blackwell, 1981) 26.

rubric philosophy of action.[12] This book aims to be a contribution to this task.[13]

10.6 *SIXTH OBJECTION*

The constructive interpretive theory advanced by Ronald Dworkin is the most attractive view to account for the values and principles that are embedded in legal decisions. We could advance a theory of authority based on Dworkin's account, and argue that legislators and judges construct the best possible interpretation of what the law is according to both criteria of moral soundness and fit with the bulk of legal materials. We have, therefore, authoritative legal reasons based on principles which are addressed to the citizens. Consequently, citizens need to engage with these principles in the way explained by the 'guise of the good' model. Dworkin has given great importance to understanding the 'point' of legal practices and has argued that judges should act as theoreticians to dissolve 'genuine' theoretical disagreements. According to Dworkin, different legal practitioners have different conceptions or interpretations of the point of legal practice. Judges need to engage in constructive interpretation to give the best possible interpretation of the practice according to the two criteria of moral appeal and fitness with the bulk of past legal materials. Dworkin also defends a weak and negative notion of 'objectivity' in which our moral judgements about the 'objectivity' of normative truths presuppose substantive moral claims.[14] In other words, the truth of statements such as 'marital rape is *objectively and robustly* morally wrong' presupposes the substantive moral claim that it is wrong to harm one's spouse or it is wrong to undermine the autonomy of one's spouse. He denies that the truth of such a statement depends on the truth of something robustly normative such as 'autonomy' or 'wrongness' that exists independently of our convictions or moral beliefs at a certain time. Dworkin's view might seem attractive as a means of reconciling our exercise of practical reasoning and robust claims on objectivity. We need, however, to resist this temptation. Despite Dworkin's insistence on the 'practical', his constructive interpretive exercise is a purely theoretically interpretative one,

---

[12] There is currently a flourishing research that aims to understand the nature of 'mind' and 'action' to elucidate the impact of neuroscience on law. See, eg D Patterson and M Pardo, 'Philosophical Foundations of Law and Neuroscience' (2010) *University of Illinois Law Review* 1212.

[13] This book has focused on a defence of the Aristotelian model of moral psychology. Cf L Leiter and J Knobe, 'The Case for Nietzschean Moral Psychology' in L Leiter and N Sinhababu (eds), *Nietzsche and Morality* (Oxford, Oxford University Press, 2007).

[14] R Dworkin, 'Objectivity and Truth: You'd Better Believe It' (1996) *Philosophy and Public Affairs* 87.

where practical reason and the deliberative point of view play no role. Similarly because, for Dworkin, there is no deliberative point of view, robustly objective truths (unsurprisingly) play no key role in his legal philosophy.

Let us recall the distinction between practical and theoretical reasoning to illuminate the deficiency of Dworkin's constructive interpretation. Let us examine the following question: 'what is the colour of snow?'. This is a theoretical question that requires an engagement with theoretical reasoning. Theoretical reasoning involves the idea that to assess the truth of theoretical statements I need to see whether there is any correspondence between the proposition and the world. This means that if I say 'the snow is black' I need to look at how the world *is* to determine whether the snow really is black. If, after observation, I determine that this statement is false, then I need to *change* my beliefs. My beliefs track how the world is. By contrast, in practical or deliberative reasoning the world changes according to what I intend. For example, the question 'what should I give to the Queen on her Diamond Jubilee?' is determined by my intention in action and by my understanding of the matter. If I intend to buy a silver feeding bowl for the Queen's dog and by mistake buy a cat's feeding bowl, I do not need to change my intentions and beliefs about what I should buy for the Queen, I need to *change* my actions and exchange the bowls. Contrary to theoretical reasoning, *I made* the world change according to my intentions and understanding of the matter. The bowls have been exchanged and I now have in my house a dog's silver feeding bowl wrapped up as a present for the Queen. The practical question 'what is the "point" of law from *my deliberative point of view?' requires that I make up my mind about what should I do, what is the best principle, value, duty or obligation to be followed. If after deliberation I make up my mind regarding the best underlying principle, value, duty or obligation and I discover that the principle, value, duty or obligation does not fit with what others practice then I do not change my principles, values, duties or obligations.* On the contrary, as a judge of an appellate court, I shape the law according to how I see the matter, ie according to the principles, values, duties or obligations that should govern the law. If this does not happen then dissenting judgments in appellate courts can neither be intelligible nor explained. Of course, as a judge of an appellate court, I might consider other judges' conceptions and views on the point of legal practice and if they strongly contradict with my views on the underlying values, duties, obligations or rights of the law, then I might change my mind, but not because there were different conceptions as such, but because these conceptions forced me to look again at the subject matter and forced me to form different intentions.

Arguably the question 'what is the point of law from the best possible interpretation?' as formulated by Dworkin is misleading. This is an invitation to theoretical reasoning as opposed to practical or deliberative reasoning. If as a judge or legislator, I need to decide what the 'point' of law is, as Dworkin correctly argues, so that it may guide the actions of citizens and other address-ees, then I need to answer the question *why as a judge I ought to follow this or that precedent*, and why I ought to change it on the basis of this or that 'principle', 'value', 'duty' or 'obligation' *simpliciter*. The answer to the question about the 'point of law' from my deliberative point of view will serve as guide for all addressees. If as a judge I fail to answer the question about the 'point of law', then I fail to guide the citizens in their actions. If the question is formulated from the theoretical point of view, as Dworkin seems to imply it should be, as 'what is the *best possible conception* of the point of law?', then the robust objectiv-ity of normative entities is not necessary. I do not need to look at what is of value and 'ought to be done', I only need to look at the different 'conceptions' as representations or 'mirrors of what reality is' or, in the most extreme case, 'inside' the consciousness of the judges and then decide as to the best possible interpretation of such conceptions. There is no genuine engagement with what is of value or right, or what is duty or obligation. To give greater argu-mentative force to Dworkin's insight regarding the importance and signific-ance of 'the point of law' we need to accept the arguments that Dworkin's constructive interpretation cannot grasp the true 'point' of the law because this 'point' can only be grasped from the first-person deliberative stance. The question 'what should I do?' is continuous with the question 'what should I do as a judge?'. I do not take a theoretical stance on my *role* as a judge and observe myself judging in abstract from what I think is 'right', 'valuable' and 'what ought to be done' (see sections 3.3 and 5.3.1). As a judge and human being, I want to 'get it right' and find the 'right answer' and for this I need to be com-mitted to the ontological existence of normative truths (section 9.4). For example, if as a judge I am asked whether Jean should be compensated for her physical injury that was caused by the accident of her children, I need to engage with the rights that Jean ought to have and the legal rights that are given to her. It is not *sufficient* to engage with the different conceptions or inter-pretive stances of the legal practice and my morally substantive claims on the matter. I do not *only* resort to past legal decisions, the different conceptions of the legal practice and my moral substantive claims, as a judge I engage with what is dutiful, obligatory, right or wrong.

Let us go back to the example of Peter who rapes his wife Susan (see section 9.4.1). Nowadays we say that Peter has committed a moral wrong and, under criminal law, he has committed a legal wrong. Pre-1991,[15] however, Peter's wrong would not have been a legal wrong. If I am asked in 1990 to decide whether Peter has committed a wrong by raping his spouse, I need to engage with the question about whether it is wrong to undermine one's spouse's autonomy and why this is so. If a similar issue arises in 2012, I need to ask

---

[15] *R v R* [1991] UKHL 12, [1992] AC 599.

myself, 'is Peter's act wrong and why?', 'is the current law *mistaken* and *why?*'. I do not *only* resort to past legal decisions, the different conceptions of the legal practice and my moral substantive claims, as a judge I engage with what is dutiful, obligatory, right or wrong. Of course, in the example of Peter, the judge in 1990 might have considered that the law is mistaken; however, she might still insist that she should follow the law since it is not her task to change the law. If you ask her *why* she has decided so, *she will* not answer that 'this is the best possible interpretation' according to the two criteria of moral appeal and fit with past legal decisions. On the contrary, she will say that the value of legality is more important than any other value, eg justice in judging legal cases. Alternatively, she might decide to change the law because *from her deliberative point of view* the value of justice is more important than any other value. In this second scenario, she will assert that previous cases on the matter were mistaken and that Peter has committed a wrong. If you ask her *why* she has decided so, she would not say that 'it is the best possible interpretation of the different conceptions of the point of law at this time'. On the contrary, she will assert that Peter *really did (robustly) and objectively* commit a wrong and that previous cases were *really (robustly) and objectively wrong*.

10.7 *CONCLUDING NOTE*: LAW AS ACTUALITY

The book has shown that legal rules and good things, events or states of affairs are not absolutely distinct from one another. Unsurprisingly, some philosophers have also advanced the idea that the rules of etiquette are connected to what is good and valuable in our lives.[16] This view goes against the common wisdom that legal rules, like the rules of etiquette, are mainly conventional and that their normative force is merely social and therefore not justified. Following this trend of thought, legal philosophers have argued that the internal aspect of legal rules can be elucidated by simply understanding the *beliefs* or other mental states of the agent who follows legal rules. I have resisted and challenged this view.

The study has investigated the nature of the paradigmatic case of action and has attempted to understand how we can follow legal rules whilst preserving our full agency. The thesis presented is action as a continuous process or as series of steps that finalise in a reason that is seen as good by the agent. Under this view, action is understood more like a *gestalt* process than discrete stages of a performance and this view has framed how the book presents the phenomenon of 'legal rules-compliance'. However, this explanation of legal normativity seems to conflict with our intuitions about what legal authority is,

---

[16] S Buss, 'Appearing Respectful: the Moral Significance of Manners' (1999) 109 *Ethics* 795.

such as that law serves us and this, therefore, precludes us from assessing the merits of legal rules when we act following the law. Nevertheless, it has been proposed that there is room for an 'ethical-political' notion of the service that law provides us. Legal authorities show us ways to engage with legal rules by presenting us with their grounding reasons as good-making characteristics. Avowing the grounding reasons of legal rules does not, however, seem an absolute requirement to acting under full agency when following the law. There are occasions when we do not avow the grounding reasons of legal rules but, nevertheless, recognise a presumption of the goodness of legal authority. This presumption arises from the authorities' claims of morally legitimate authority and moral correctness since such claims are the legal authorities' expressions of intentions to perform their actions in a certain way.

The story that has emerged presents the character of law and its normative status as being strikingly similar to other human activities which are shaped by the exercise of practical reason. This approach leaves plenty of room for the defective exercise of human faculties.

The idea that there are laws, legal rules and legal institutions and that they exist as natural or empirical phenomena, ie mental states, instruments or artefacts, can deceive us and take on misleading routes of investigation. The idea makes us believe that the understanding of what law is, is about understanding the concept or the propositional content of statutes, rules and legal institutions. It mistakenly considers that statutes, rules and legal institutions are only *products made or produced* by the beliefs or attitudes of legal participants. But if this is the *primary* way of understanding what law is, then our understanding is incomplete or maybe even incoherent. Following legal rules is *primarily about the actuality of our practical reasoning*.

To regard law as just a concept or a set of legal rules that is merely determined by its propositional content or is the outcome of the mental states, ie attitudes, beliefs of judges or legislators, is to lose sight of the practical or deliberative character of legal rules and the law and fails to understand why law needs to be seen as being in continuity with practical reason. The view of law as a *product or an empirical phenomenon* generates insurmountable difficulties and gives rise to an important paradox: how a *product* or *artefact* that is defective because it does not perform its core function retains its nature. Similarly, concerning law, can legal rules and legal regimes that are not performing their core function because they demand evil or wrong acts still be law? According to this view, law is a simple tool or a means to *produce* something, ie certain desirable or preferential behaviours. If we use the analogy of a knife, can a knife still be a knife if it cannot fulfil its core function of cutting? To think that law is an artefact that produces certain desirable behaviours is like thinking that the movements of my hands and mouth produce my 'playing the flute'. It is true that without my hands I cannot, in principle, play the flute, but there is more to playing the flute than merely moving my hands and mouth. In this book, I have attempted to show that this theoretical framework leads to a mistaken route. If law is understood primarily as *acting (actuality) and therefore deliberating*, no paradox emerges. We fail, on some occasions, to act as we intended, and we fail, on other occasions, to act *well*. However, we are still *acting* creatures who possess conceptual and practical capacities to act well. Even when we act badly, we do not cease to be who we are: creatures whose powers, including practical reasoning powers, can become actuality or fulfilled. Similarly, when legislators and judges create the law, they tell us how we ought to act; the law might ask us to act well but it might, equally, asks us to act in negative or even evil ways. This does not mean that the law stops being law. It is still and primarily *an actuality of our potential capacities*. What, in the common wisdom, are called defective laws (such as the laws of the Third Reich in Germany or the South African Apartheid law) are demands for defective ways of acting, like defective ways of walking, but in both cases it is still *acting*. The sound understanding of *acting (actuality) in the context of rule-compliance* requires the sound understanding of the exercise of our practical capacities in the context of the law and it is this task that the book has concentrated upon. It is also a promissory note on how laws, directives, customary practices[17] and other legal instruments are created as actualities according to practical reason.[18]

It is now apparent that Wolff's anarchist challenge (Chapter 1) emerges due to a narrow and limited understanding of the nature of legal rules. Construing legal rules within the complex and rich framework of the 'guise of the good' model, and thereby demonstrating the intimate connections between legal rules and our practical capacities and inherent rational nature, has enabled us to provide an answer to the anarchist challenge and its puzzling character. It has also helped us to understand the nature of legal normativity and authority.

---

[17] For a discussion on the challenges of a sound understanding of customary practices in the light of practical reason, see A Perreau-Saussine and J Murphy, 'The Character of Customary Law: an Introduction' in A Perreau-Saussine and J Murphy (eds), *The Nature of Customary Law* (Cambridge, Cambridge University Press, 2007).

[18] For a clear formulation of this new approach to natural law see B Bix, 'Natural Law: the Modern Tradition' in *Oxford Handbook of Jurisprudence* (Oxford, Oxford University Press, 2004) 61.

Bibliography

Adler, J and Armour-Garb, B, 'Moore's Paradox and the Transparency of Belief' in L Green and B Williams (eds), *Moore's Paradox: New Essays on Beliefs, Rationality and the First Person* (Oxford, Oxford University Press, 2007)

Adler, M, 'Social Facts, Constitutional Interpretation and the Rule of Recognition' in M Adler (ed), *The Rule of Recognition and the US Constitution* (Oxford, Oxford University Press, 2009)

Alexander, L, '"With Me, it's All or Nuthin": Formalism in Law and Morality' (1999) *University of Chicago Law Review* 530

Alexy, R, *The Argument from Injustice* (S Paulson and B Litschewski Paulson (trans), Oxford, Oxford University Press, 2002)

Alvarez, M, 'Agents, Actions and Reasons' (2005) *Philosophical Books* 45

—— *Kinds of Reasons* (Oxford, Oxford University Press, 2010)

Annas, J, 'Davidson and on the "Same Action"' (1976) *Mind* 251

Anscombe, E, *Intention*, 2nd edn (Cambridge, MA, Harvard University Press, 2000, originally published in 1957)

—— 'Brute Facts' (1958) *Analysis* 69

—— 'On the Source of Authority of the State' in *Ethics, Religion and Politics: Collected Philosophical Papers of GEM Anscombe* (Oxford, Blackwell, 1981)

—— 'Modern Moral Philosophy', reprinted in *Ethics, Religion and Politics: Collected Philosophical Papers of GEM Anscombe* (Oxford, Blackwell, 1981)

Anscombe, E and Morgenbesser, S, 'Two Kinds of Error in Action' (1963) *Journal of Philosophy, Symposium Human Action* 393

Aquinas, T, *Summa Theologica* (Latin and English text, Thomas Gilby (trans), Cambridge, Cambridge University Press, 2006)

Aristotle, *Nichomachean Ethics* (H Rackham (trans), Cambridge, MA, Harvard University Press, 1934)

Aristotle, *Eudemian Ethics*, Loeb Classical Library (H Rackham (trans), Cambridge, MA, Harvard University Press, 1952)

Aristotle, *De Anima* (DW Hamlyn (trans), Oxford, Clarendon Press, 1968)

Aristotle, *Physics, Books III and IV*, Clarendon Aristotle Series (E Hussey (trans), Oxford, Clarendon Press, 1983)

Aristotle, *Metaphysics Book* , Clarendon Aristotle Series (Oxford, Clarendon Press, 2006)

Bertea, S, *Normative Claim of Law* (Oxford, Hart Publishing, 2009)

Bix, B, 'Natural Law: the Modern Tradition' in *Oxford Handbook of Jurisprudence* (Oxford, Oxford University Press, 2004)

—— 'The Nature of Law and Reasons for Action' (2011) 5 *Problema* 399

Blackburn, S, *Spreading the Word* (Oxford, Oxford University Press, 1984)

—— *Ruling Passsions* (Oxford, Clarendon Press, 1998)

Boghossian, P, 'Content and Self-Knowledge' (1989) *Philosophical Topics* 5

Bortolotti, L and Broome, MR, 'Delusional Beliefs and Reason-Giving' (2008) *Philosophical Psychology* 821

Boyle, M and Lavin, D, 'Goodness and Desire' in *Desire, Practical Reason and the Good* (Oxford, Oxford University Press, 2010)

Bradley, GV, 'Comment on Endicott: the Case of the Wise Electrician' (2005) 50 *American Journal of Jurisprudence* 257

Bratman, M, *Intentions, Plans and Practical Reasons* (Cambridge, MA, Harvard University Press, 1987)

—— 'Davidson's Theory of Intention', reprinted in *Faces of Intention* (Cambridge, Cambridge University Press, 1999)

—— *Faces of Intention* (Cambridge, Cambridge University Press, 1999)

Brink, D, *Moral Realism and the Foundations of Ethics (Cambridge*, Cambridge University Press, 1989)

Bulygin, E, 'An Antinomy in Kelsen's Pure Theory of Law' (1990) *Ratio Juris* 29

Buss, S, 'Appearing Respectful: the Moral Significance of Manners' (1999) 109 *Ethics* 795

Byrne, A, 'Introspection' (2005) *Philosophical Topics* 79

Cane, P (ed), *The Hart-Fuller Debate in the Twenty-First Century* (Oxford, Hart Publishing, 2010)

Carman, T, 'First Persons: On Richard Moran's Authority and Estrangement' (2003) *Inquiry* 395

Celano, B, 'Kelsen's Concept of the Authority of Law' (2000) 19 *Law and Philosophy* 173

Charles, D, *Aristotle's Philosophy of Action* (London, Routledge, 1984)

Chisholm, R, 'Freedom and Action' in K Lehrer (ed), *Freedom and Determinism* (New York, Random House, 1976)

Clarke DS, 'Exclusionary Reasons'(1975) *Mind* 252

Coleman, J, *The Practice of Principle* (Oxford, Oxford University Press, 2001)

Colyvan, M, 'In Defense of Indispensability' (1998) *Philosophia Mathematica* 39

—— *The Indispensability of Mathematics* (Oxford, Oxford University Press, 2001)

Coope, U, 'Change and its Relation to Actuality and Potentiality' in G Anagnostopoulos (ed), *A Companion to Aristotle* (Oxford, Wiley-Blackwell, 2009)

Dancy, J, *Practical Reality* (Oxford, Oxford University Press, 2000)

Darwall, S, 'Normativity and Projection in Hobbe's Leviathan' (2000) *Philosophical Review* 313

Davidson, D, 'Actions, Reasons and Events' in *Essays on Actions and Events* (Oxford, Clarendon Press, 1980)

—— 'Freedom to Act' in *Essays on Actions and Events* (Oxford, Clarendon Press, 1980)

Delacroix, S, *The Genealogy of Legal Normativity* (Oxford, Hart Publishing, 2006)

Dennet, D, *Intentional Stance* (Cambridge, MA, MIT Press, 1987)

Dickson, J, *Evaluation and Legal Theory* (Oxford, Hart Publishing, 2001)

Dihle, A, *The Theory of Will in Classical Antiquity* (Berkeley and Los Angeles, CA, University of California Press, 1982)

Donnelan, K, 'Knowing what I am Doing' (1963) *Journal of Philosophy* 401

Dworkin, R, *Taking Rights Seriously* (London, Duckworth, 1977)

—— *Law's Empire* (Cambridge, MA, Harvard University Press, 1986)

—— 'Objectivity and Truth: You'd Better Believe It' (1996) *Philosophy and Public Affairs* 87

Edgeley, R, *Reason in Theory and Practice* (London, Hutchinson and Co, 1969)

Edmundson, W, *Three Anarchical Fallacies* (Cambridge, Cambridge University Press, 1998)

—— 'Because I Said So' (2013) *Problema* 41

Endicott, T, *The Vagueness of Law* (Oxford, Oxford University Press, 2000)

—— 'The Subsidiarity of Law and the Obligation to Obey' (2005) 50 *American Journal of Jurisprudence* 233

Engstrom, S, *The Form of Practical Knowledge* (Cambridge, MA, Harvard University Press, 2009)

Enoch, D, *Reason-Giving and the Law*, Oxford Studies in Philosophy of Law (Oxford, Oxford University Press, 2011)

—— 'Giving Practical Reasons' (2011) *Philosopher's Imprint* 11

—— *Taking Morality Seriously: A Defense of Robust Realism* (Oxford, Oxford University Press, 2011)

Evans, G, *The Varieties of Reference* (Oxford, Oxford University Press, 1982)

Falvey, K, 'Knowledge in Intention' (2000) *Philosophical Studies* 21

Finnis, J, *Natural Law and Natural Rights* (Oxford, Clarendon Press, 1980)

—— 'On "Reason" and "Authority" in Law's Empire' (1987) 6 *Law and Philosophy* 357

—— *Aquinas* (Oxford, Oxford University Press, 1998)

—— 'Law and What I Truly Should Decide' (2003) 48 *American Journal of Jurisprudence* 107

—— 'Foundations of Practical Reason Revisited' (2005) *American Journal of Jurisprudence* 109

—— '"The Thing I am": Personal Identity in Aquinas and Shakespeare' (2005) *Social Philosophy and Policy* 250

—— 'Grounds of Law and Legal Theory' (2007) *Legal Theory* 318

—— 'On Hart's Way: Law as Reason and as Fact' in M Kramer, C Grant, B Colburn and A Hatzistavrou (eds), *The Legacy of HLA Hart* (Oxford, Oxford University Press, 2008)

Frankfurt, H, 'The Problem of Action' (1978) *American Philosophical Quarterly* 157

Frede, M, 'Aristotle's Notion of Potentiality in Metaphysics' in T Scaltsas, D Charles and M Gill (eds), *Unity, Identity and Explanation in Aristotle's Metaphysics* (Oxford, Clarendon Press, 1994)

—— *A Free Will: Origins of the Notion in Ancient Thought* (AA Long and D Sedley (eds), Berkeley and Los Angeles, CA, University of California Press, 2011)

Fuller, LL, *The Morality of Law*, 2nd edn (New Haven, CT, Yale University Press, 1969)

Galligan, E, 'Irwin on Aristotle' (1975) *Journal of Philosophy* 579

Gallois, A, 'Consciousness, Reasons and Moore's Paradox' in *Moore's Paradox: New Essays on Beliefs, Rationality and the First Person* (Oxford, Oxford University Press, 2007)

Gans, C, 'Mandatory Rules and Exclusionary Reasons' (1986) *Philosophia* 373

Gardner, J, 'Law as a Leap of Faith' in P Oliver, S Douglas-Scott and V Tadros (eds), *Leap of Faith* (Oxford, Hart Publishing, 2000), reprinted in *Law as a Leap of Faith* (Oxford, Oxford University Press, 2012)

—— 'How Law Claims, What Law Claims' in M Klatt (ed), *Institutional Reason: The Jurisprudence of Robert Alexy* (Oxford, Oxford University Press, 2010)

Geach, P, 'Good and Evil' (1956) *Analysis* 32.

Gertler, B, 'Do We Determine What We Believe by Looking Outward?' in A Hatzimoysis (ed), *Self-Knowledge* (Oxford, Oxford University Press, 2008)

Gibbard, A, *Wise Choices, Apt Feelings* (Oxford, Clarendon Press, 1990)

Gombay, A, 'The Paradoxes of Counterprivacy' (1988) *Philosophy* 191

Green, L, 'Law, Coordination and the Common Good' (1983) *Oxford Journal of Legal Studies* 299

—— *The Authority of the State* (Oxford, Oxford University Press, 1988)

—— 'Law as Means' in *The Hart-Fuller Debate in the 21st Century* (Oxford, Hart Publishing, 2010)

Grunbaum, T, 'Anscombe and Practical Knowledge of What is Happening' (2009) *Grazer Philosophisches Studien* 41

Halpin, A, *Reasoning with Law* (Oxford, Hart Publishing, 2001)

Hampshire, S, *Thought and Action* (London, Chatton and Windus, 1960)

Hampshire, S and Hart, HLA, 'Decision, Intention and Certainty' (1958) *Mind* 1

Hampshire, S and Morgenbesser, S, 'Reply to Walsh on Thought and Action' (1963) *Journal of Philosophy* 410

Hanser, M, 'Intention and Teleology' (1998) *Mind* 381

Harman, G, 'Moral Explanations of Natural Facts: Can Moral Claims be Tested Against Moral Reality?' (1986) *Southern Journal of Philosophy* 57

—— *Change in View* (Cambridge, MA, MIT Press, 1986)

—— 'Willing and Intending' in R Grandy and R Warner (eds), *Philosophical Grounds of Rationality* (New York, Oxford University Press, 1986)

Hart, HLA, 'Legal Duty and Obligation' in *Essays in Jurisprudence and Philosophy* (Oxford, Clarendon Press, 1983)

—— 'Commands and Authoritative Legal Reasons' in *Essays in Jurisprudence and Philosophy* (Oxford, Clarendon Press, 1983)

—— *The Concept of Law*, 2nd edn (Oxford, Clarendon Press, 1994)

Heal, J, 'Moore's Paradox: A Wittgensteinian Approach' (1994) *Mind* 5

—— 'Moran's Authority and Estrangement' (2004) *Philosophy and Phenomenological Research* 427

Heidemann, C, *Die Norm als Tatsache. Zur Normentheorie Hans Kelsen* (Baden-Baden, Nomos, 1997)

—— 'Arriving at a Defensible Periodisation of Hans Kelsen's Legal Theory' (1999) *Oxford Journal of Legal Studies* 351

—— 'Norms, Facts and Judgements: A Reply to SL Paulson' (1999) *Oxford Journal of Legal Studies* 345

Holton, R, 'Positivism and the Internal Point of View' (1998) 17 *Law and Philosophy* 567

Hornsby, J, *Actions* (London, Routledge, 1980)

—— 'Agency and Action' in H Steward and J Hyman (eds), *Agency and Action* (Cambridge, Cambridge University Press, 2004)

Hurd, H, *Moral Combat* (Cambridge, Cambridge University Press, 1999)

—— 'Why You Should be a Law-abiding Anarchist (Except When You Shouldn't)?' (2005) *San Diego Law Review* 75

Hursthouse, R, 'Arational Actions' (1991) 57 *Journal of Philosophy* 57

—— 'Intention' in R Teichman (ed), *Logic, Cause and Action* (Cambridge, Cambridge University Press, 2000)

Hyman, J and Alvarez, M, 'Agents and their Action' (1998) *Philosophy* 219

Hyman, J and Steward, H, *Agency and Action* (Cambridge, Cambridge University Press, 2004)

Irwin, T, 'Aristotle on Reason, Desire and Virtue' (1975) *Journal of Philosophy* 567

Jhering, R, *Geist des Römisches Rechts*, 4th edn (Leipzig, Breitkopf and Härtel, 1978–1988)

Kant, I, *The Critique of Pure Reason* (P Guyer and A Wood (trans) from *Reine Vernunft* 1st and 2nd edns, Cambridge, Cambridge University Press, 1998)

—— *Groundwork for the Metaphysics of Morals* (TR Hill and A Zweig (eds), Arnulf Zweig (trans), Oxford, Oxford University Press, 2002)

Kelsen, H, *Hauptprobleme der Staatrechtslehre*, 2nd edn (Tübingen, Mohr, 1923, Spanish trans *Problemas Capitales de la Teoría Jurídica del Estado* (México, Editorial Porrúa, 1987)

—— *General Theory of Law and State* (Anders Wedberg (trans), Cambridge, MA, Harvard University Press, 1945)

—— *The General Theory of Norms* (M Hartney (trans), Oxford, Oxford University Press, 1991)

—— *Introduction to the Problems of Legal Theory* (B Litschewski Paulson and S Paulson (trans), Oxford, Clarendon Press, 2000)

Kenny, A, *Aristotle's Theory of the Will* (London, Duckworth, 1979)

—— *Aquinas on Mind* (London, Routledge, 1993)

Korsgaard, C, *Sources of Normativity* (Cambridge, Cambridge University Press, 1996)

—— 'Aristotle and Kant on the Source of Value' in *Creating the Kingdom of Ends* (Cambridge, Cambridge University Press, 1996)

—— 'Acting for a Reason' in *The Constitution of Agency* (Oxford, Oxford University Press, 2008)

—— *Self-Constitution: Agency, Identity and Integrity* (Oxford, Oxford University Press, 2009)

Kosman, LA, 'Aristotle's Definition of Motion' (1969) *Phronesis* 40

Kramer, M, 'Big Bad Wolf: Legal Positivism and its Detractors' (2004) *American Journal of Jurisprudence* 1

Lacey, N, 'Philosophy, Political Morality, and History: Explaining the Enduring Resonance of the Hart-Fuller Debate' (2008) *New York University Law Review* 1059

Lear, J, 'Avowal and Unfreedom' (2004) *Philosophy and Phenomenological Research* 448.

Leiter, L and Knobe, J, 'The Case for Nietzschean Moral Psychology' in L Leiter and N Sinhabubu (eds), *Nietzsche and Morality* (Oxford, Oxford University Press, 2007)

Mackie, JL, *Ethics: Inventing Right and Wrong* (London, Penguin, 1977)

Moore, M, 'Authority, Law and Razian Reasons' (1988–1989) *Southern California Law Review* 827

—— 'Law as a Functional Kind' in R George (ed), *Natural Law Theory: Contemporary Essays* (Oxford, Clarendon Press, 1992)

Moran, R, *Authority and Estrangement* (Princeton, NJ, Princeton University Press, 2001)

—— 'Responses to O'Brien and Shoemaker' (2003) *European Journal of Philosophy* 402

—— 'Replies to Heal, Reginster, Wilson and Lear' (2004) *Philosophy and Phenomenological Research* 455

Moran, R and Stone, M, 'Ascombe on Expressions of Intention' in C Sandis (ed), *New Essays on the Explanation of Action* (Basingstoke, Palgrave MacMillan, 2010)

Moya, C, 'Moran on Self-Knowledge, Agency and Responsibility' (2006) 114 *Critica Revista Hispanoamericana de Filosofía* 3

Murphy, L, 'Concepts of Law' (2005) *Australian Journal of Legal Philosophy* 1

O'Brien, L, 'Moran on Self-Knowledge' (2003) *European Journal of Philosophy* 375

O'Neill, O, *Constructions of Reasons* (Cambridge, Cambridge University Press, 1989)

O'Shaughnessy, B, *The Will* (Cambridge, Cambridge University Press, 1980)

Pasnau, R, *Thomas Aquinas on Human Nature* (Cambridge, Cambridge University Press, 2002)

Pattaro, E, *The Law and the Right: A Reappraisal of the Reality that Ought to Be* (Dordrecht and New York, Springer, 2005)

Patterson, D, 'Explicating the Internal Point of View' (1999) *Southern Methodist University Law Review* 67

Patterson, D and Pardo, M, 'Philosophical Foundations of Law and Neuroscience' (2010) *University of Illinois Law Review* 1212

Pauer-Studert, H and Velleman, D, 'Distortions of Normativity' (2011) *Ethical Theory and Moral Practice* 329

Paulson, S, 'The Neo-Kantian Dimension in Kelsen's Pure Theory of Law' (1992) *Oxford Journal of Legal Studies* 313

—— 'Hans Kelsen's Earliest Legal Theory: Critical Constructivism' (1996) 59 *Modern Law Review* 797

—— 'Four Phases in Kelsen's Legal Theory? Reflections on a Periodisation' (1998) *Oxford Journal of Legal Studies* 153

—— 'The Weak Reading of Authority in Hans Kelsen's Pure Theory of Law' (2000) *Law and Philosophy* 131

Pavlakos, G, 'Non-naturalism, Normativity and the Meaning of Ought' (ms with the author)

Perreau-Saussine, A and Murphy, J, 'The Character of Customary Law: an Introduction' in A Perreau-Saussine and J Murphy (eds), *The Nature of Customary Law* (Cambridge, Cambridge University Press, 2007)

Perry, S, 'Judicial Obligation, Precedent and the Common Law' (1987) 7 *Oxford Journal of Legal Studies* 215

—— 'Interpretation and Methodology in Legal Theory' in A Marmor (ed), *Law and Interpretation* (Oxford, Clarendon Press, 1995) 97

—— 'Holmes versus Hart: the Bad Man in Legal Theory' in S Burton (ed), *The Path of Law and Its Influence: the Legacy of Oliver Wendell Holmes, Jr* (Cambridge, Cambridge University Press, 2000)

—— 'Hart on Social Rules and the Foundations of Law: Liberating the Internal Point of View' (2006) 75 *Fordham Law Review* 1171

—— *Political Authority and Political Obligation*, Oxford Studies in Philosophy of Law vol II (Oxford, Oxford University Press, 2012)

Phillips, DZ, 'Miss Anscombe's Grocer' (1968) *Analysis* 177

Pink, T, 'Purpose Intending' (1991) *Mind* 343

Plato, *The Republic* (A Waterfield (trans), Oxford, Oxford University Press, 1993)

Plato, *Phaedrus* in J Cooper (ed), *Plato Complete Works* (A Nehamas and P Woodruff (trans), Indiannapolis, IN, Hackett, 1997)

Porciuncula, M, 'Razón Práctica y Absolutismo Político: una relación probable -la perspectiva Kelseniana' (ms with the author)

Postema, G, 'Positivism, I Presume? . . . Comments on Schauer's Rules and the Rule of Law' (1991) *Harvard Journal of Law and Public Policy* 797

—— 'Implicit Law' (1994) *Law and Philosophy* 361

—— 'Jurisprudence as Practical Philosophy' (1998) *Legal Theory* 329

Putnam, H, 'Philosophy of Logic' in *Mathematics, Matter and Methods: Philosophical Papers* (Cambridge, Cambridge University Press, 1979) vol 1, 323

Quine, WO, *Word and Object* (Cambridge, MA, MIT Press, 1960)

—— 'On What There Is' in *From a Logical Point of View*, 2nd edn (Cambridge, MA, Harvard University Press, 1980)

—— 'Putting Rationality in Its Place' in *Morality and Action* (Cambridge, Cambridge University Press, 1993)

Rawls, J, *A Theory of Justice* (Cambridge, MA, Harvard University Press, 1971)

—— 'Kantian Constructivism in Moral Theory' (1980) 77 *Journal of Philosophy* 515

Raz, J, *Practical Reason and Norms* (Oxford, Oxford University Press, 1999, originally published Hutchinson & Co, 1975)

—— *The Authority of Law* (Oxford, Clarendon Press, 1979)

—— 'Kelsen's Theory of the Basic Norm' in *The Authority of Law* (Oxford, Clarendon Press, 1979)

—— *The Morality of Freedom* (Oxford, Clarendon Press, 1986)

—— 'HLA Hart (1907–1992)' (1993) 5 *Utilitas* 148

—— *Ethics in the Public Domain* (Oxford, Oxford University Press, 1995)

—— 'The Purity of the Pure Theory of Law' in S Paulson and B Litschenwski Paulson (eds), *Normativity and Norms: Critical Perspectives on Kelsenian Themes* (Oxford, Clarendon Press, 1998)

—— 'Two Views of the Nature of the Theory of Law' (1998) *Legal Theory* 249

—— *Engaging Reason* (Oxford, Oxford University Press, 1999)

—— 'Agency, Reason and the Good' in *Engaging Reason* (Oxford, Oxford University Press, 1999)

—— 'The Problem of Authority: Revisiting the Service Conception' (2006) *Minnesota Law Review* 1003, reprinted in *Between Authority and Interpretation* (Oxford, Oxford University Press, 2009)

—— 'On the Guise of the Good' in S Tenenbaum (ed), *Desire, Practical Reason and the Good* (Oxford, Oxford University Press, 2010)

Reath, A, *Agency and Autonomy in Kant's Moral Theory* (Oxford, Clarendon Press, 2006)

Regan, D, 'Authority and Value: Reflections on Raz's Morality of Freedom' (1988–1992) *Southern California Law Review* 995

Reginster, B, 'Self-Knowledge, Responsibility and the Third Person' (2004) *Philosophy and Phenomenological Research* 433

Rodriguez-Blanco, V, 'Is Finnis Wrong?' (2007) *Legal Theory* 257

—— 'Peter Winch and HLA Hart: Two Concepts of the Internal Point of View' (2007) *Canadian Journal of Law and Jurisprudence* 453

—— 'From Shared Agency to the Normativity of Law' (2009) *Law and Philosophy* 59

—— 'The Moral Puzzle of Legal Authority' in G Pavlakos and S Bertea (eds), *Normativity in Morality and Law* (Oxford, Hart Publishing, 2011)

Ross, WD, *Aristotle's Physics: A Revised Text with Introduction and Commentary* (Oxford, Oxford University Press, 1995)

Ryle, G, *The Concept of Mind* (London, Hutchinson & Co, 1949)

Scanlon, T, *What We Owe to Each Other* (Cambridge, MA, Harvard University Press, 1999)

Schauer, F, 'Rules and the Rule of Law' (1991) *Harvard Journal of Law and Public Policy* 635

—— *Playing by the Rules* (Oxford, Oxford University Press, 1991)

—— 'Fuller's Internal Point of View' (1994) 13 *Law and Philosophy* 285

—— 'A Critical Guide to Vehicles in the Park' (2008) *New York University Law Review* 1109

Schroeder, M, *Slaves of Passions* (Oxford, Oxford University Press, 2007)

Sciaraffa, S, 'On Content-Independent Reasons: It's Not in the Name' (2009) *Law and Philosophy* 233

Sereny, G, *Into that Darkness: An Examination of Conscience* (New York, First Vintage Book Editions, 1983)

Setiya, K, *Reasons Without Rationalism* (Princeton, NJ, Princeton University Press, 2007)

—— 'Practical Knowledge Revisited' (2009) *Ethics* 388

—— 'Knowledge of Intention' in A Ford, J Hornsby and F Stoutland (eds), *Essays on Anscombe's Intention* (Cambridge, MA, Harvard University Press, 2011)

Shapiro, S, 'The Bad Man and the Internal Point of View' in S Burton (ed), *The Path of Law and Its Influence: the Legacy of Oliver Wendell Holmes, Jr* (Cambridge, Cambridge University Press, 2000)

—— 'What is the Internal Point of View?' (2006) 75 *Fordham Law Review* 1157

—— *Legality* (Cambridge, MA, Harvard University Press, 2011)

Sheer, R, 'The "Mental State" Theory of Intentions' (2004) *Philosophy* 121

Shoemaker, S, 'Self-knowledge and Inner-sense' (1994) *Philosophy and Phenomenological Research* 249

—— 'Introspection and the Self' in *The First-Person Perspective and Other Essays* (Cambridge, Cambridge University Press, 1996)

—— 'On Knowing One's Own Mind' in *The First-Person Perspective and Other Essays* (Cambridge, Cambridge University Press, 1996)

—— 'First-Person Access' in *The First-Person Perspective and Other Essays* (Cambridge, Cambridge University Press, 1996)

—— 'Moran on Self-Knowledge' (2003) *European Journal of Philosophy* 391

Simmonds, N, *Law as a Moral Idea* (Oxford, Oxford University Press, 2007)

Smith, M, *The Moral Problem* (Oxford, Blackwell, 1994)

Smith, S, 'Cracks in the Coordination Account?' (2005) *American Journal of Jurisprudence* 249

Soper, P, *The Ethics of Deference* (Cambridge, Cambridge University Press, 2002)

Sorensen, R, 'The All-Seeing Eye: A Blind Spot in the History of Ideas' in M Green and JN Williams (eds), *Moore's Paradox: New Essays on Beliefs, Rationality and the First Person* (Oxford, Oxford University Press, 2007)

Stanley, J and Williamson, T, 'Knowing How' (2001) *Journal of Philosophy* 411

Stewart, I, 'Kelsen and the Exegetical Tradition' in R Tur and W Twinning (eds), *Essays on Kelsen* (Oxford, Clarendon Press, 1986)

Stocker, M, 'Desiring the Bad: an Essay in Moral Psychology' (1979) *Journal of Philosophy* 738

Stone, M, *Positivism as Opposed to What? Law and the Moral Concept of Right*, Cardozo Legal Studies Research Papers No 290, available at http:// ssrn.com/ abstract=1554500

Stout, R, *Action* (Buckingham, Acumen, 2005)

Stump, E, *Aquinas* (London, Routledge, 2003)

Teichman, R, *The Philosophy of Elizabeth Anscombe* (Oxford, Oxford University Press, 2009)

Tenenbaum, S, *Appearances of the Good* (Cambridge, Cambridge University Press, 2007)

Tersman, F, *Moral Disagreement* (Cambridge, Cambridge University Press, 2006)

Thompson, M, *Life and Action* (Cambridge, MA, Harvard University Press, 2008)

Toh, K, 'Hart's Expressivism and his Benthamite Project' (2005) 11 *Legal Theory* 75

—— 'Raz on Detachment, Acceptance and Describability' (2007) 27 *Oxford Journal of Legal Studies* 403

Tur, R, 'The Kelsenian Enterprise' in R Tur and W Twinning (eds), *Essays on Kelsen* (Oxford, Clarendon Press, 1986)

Velleman, JD, *Practical Reflection* (Princeton, NJ, Princeton University Press, 1989)

—— *The Possibility of Practical Reason* (Oxford, Oxford University Press, 2000)

Vinx, L, *Hans Kelsen's Pure Theory of Law* (Oxford, Oxford University Press, 2007)

Vogler, C, 'Anscombe on Practical Inference' in E Millgram (ed), *Varieties of Practical Reasoning* (Cambridge, MA, MIT Press, 2001)

—— *Reasonably Vicious* (Cambridge, MA, Harvard University Press, 2002)

—— 'Modern Moral Philosophy Again: Isolating the Promulgation Problem' (2007) *Proceedings of the Aristotelian Society* 347

Waldron, J, 'Why Law: Efficacy, Freedom or Fidelity' (1994) *Law and Philosophy* 259

—— 'Positivism and Legality: Hart's Equivocal Response to Fuller' (2008) *New York University Law Review* 1135

Wallace, J, 'Practical Reason' in *Stanford Encyclopaedia of Philosophy* (online)

Watson, G, 'Free Agency' (1975) *Journal of Philosophy* 205

Williams, B, 'Ethical Consistency' (1966) *Proceedings of the Aristotelian Society* 103

—— 'Internal and External Reasons' (1966) *Proceedings of the Aristotelian Society* 103, reprinted in *Moral Luck* (Cambridge, Cambridge University Press, 1993)

Wilson, A, 'Is Kelsen Really a Kantian?' in R Tur and W Twinning (eds), *Essays on Kelsen* (Oxford, Clarendon Press, 1986)

Wilson, G, 'Comments on Authority and Estrangement' (2004) *Philosophy and Phenomenological Research* 440

Wittgenstein, L, *Philosophical Investigations* (E Anscombe (trans), Oxford, Blackwell, 1953)

—— *Remarks on the Philosophy of Psychology* (E Anscombe (trans), Oxford, Blackwell, 1980)

Wolff, RP, *In Defense of Anarchism* (New York and London, Harper Torch Books, 1970)

—— *The Autonomy of Reason* (New York, Harper Torchbooks, 1973)

Wood, A, *Kantian Ethics* (Cambridge, Cambridge University Press, 2008)

Zipursky, B, 'Legal Obligations and the Internal Aspect of Rules' (2006) 75 *Fordham Law Review* 1229

Index

acceptance thesis
  detached viewpoint 92–4
  different norms we do not fully endorse
    97–8
  non-cognitivism see under intentional
    action, non-cognitivism
  parasitic thesis see parasitic thesis
  problems with 88–90
  social version (SVAT) 90–2
  third point of view 94–7
active/passive selves 36
actuality
  active/passive selves 36
  actuality/potentiality, distinction 65–9, 73
  authoritative/normative conflict 37–8
  definition of term 3
  deliberative viewpoint 27–8
  good-making characteristics 30, 35–6
  guidance and control 38–40
  guise of the good 30
  intentional action 30–4, 39–40
  internal/external actions 36–7
  law as 25, 213–15
  legal rules 28–9
  naïve explanation 34, 35, 38–9
  non-intentional action 34
  normativity issues 36–8
  and potentiality, distinction 6
  practical reason 3, 19, 26, 35–6, 214–15
  promulgation puzzle 34–6
  reasons and rules, key questions 25
  sanction-based explanations 37
  symmetry illusion 31–4
  two-component model see two-component
    model
  why-question see why-question
    methodology
Akrasia 54
Alexy, R 129–30
analogical argument 149–52
Anscombe, Elisabeth 13, 120
  acceptance thesis 99
  deliberative viewpoint 102–3
  expressions of intentions 124
  groundless knowledge 48, 51
  guise of the good model 41n, 42
  Intention 61–5, 68
  perverse desires 57–8

practical reason 22, 176–7
  Theophrastus principle 50
  theory of action 86–7
  why-question see why-question
    methodology
Aquinas, Thomas 13, 21, 22
  analogical argument 149
  deliberative viewpoint 102–3
  equivalence thesis 163
  expressions of intentions 123–4
  operative principle 196
Aristotle 13, 21, 22, 120
  acceptance thesis 99
  actuality/potentiality, distinction 65–9
  analogical argument 149–50
  central analysis/focal meaning 77
  deliberative viewpoint 102–3
  good desires 52
  operative principle 196
  practical reason 60
  theory of action 86
Austin, John 79, 80, 98
authority
  authoritative commands 70–1, 73–4
  authoritative/normative conflict 37–8
  see also legal authority and autonomy;
    legitimate authority, presumption

beliefs and desires 42–4, 58
Bratman, M 43–4

capacity and change 67–9
claims of legal authorities
  action 127
  capacity 126–7
  character of 125–30
  expressions of intentions 123, 135–8
  failure to perform 137–8
  intentions about actions 131–5
  mistaken beliefs 136–7
  moral correctness 129–30
  practical knowledge 124–5
  propositional content 127–9
  Rule of Law desiderata 125, 131, 135,
    136, 137
  unified manner 125–6
  see also legitimate authority, presumption
Colvyan, M 188–9

complex legal rules 173–4
conceptual and practical capacities 174–9
constructive interpretative theory 210–13

Davidson, Donald
  acceptance thesis 88–9, 99
  beliefs and desires 42–3
  intentional action 116–17
deliberative viewpoint 102–3
  actuality 27–8
  Anscombe/Aquinas 102–3
  deliberative/theoretical viewpoints,
    distinction 86–7
  first-person/deliberative perspective
    59–61
  indispensability 171–2, 187–97, 193–7
desire
  beliefs and desires 42–4, 58
  good desires/pure desires 52–4
  perverse desires 57–8
  as result of valuing 54
Dworkin, Ronald 71, 76
  concept of interpretation 176
  constructive interpretative theory 210–13
  robust value see robust value realism

Energeia see intentional action; legal rules,
  compliance
Enoch, David 181–2, 187–91, 195–7
  legal normativity, unchallenging view of
    201–5
equivalence thesis 162–6
Evans, Gareth 48, 49
exclusionary reasons
  analogical argument 149–52
  and guise of the good 139–40, 146–53
  intention in action paradox 152–60
  key distinctions 143–4
  normal justification thesis 141–2
  phenomenological argument 146–8
  presumption of authoritative force 142–3
  second-order reasons 144–5
  teleological argument 148
  transparent grounding reasons 142
  unified account 140–3
  see also legitimate authority, presumption

failure to seek the good 55–7
Finnis, John 76, 77
first/third person asymmetry 172, 174–5
freedom and submission 20–1

Gibbard, Alan 81–2, 98–9
good desires/pure desires 52–4
good-making characteristics

actuality 30, 35–6
guise of the good 41, 45–58 passim
legal authority and autonomy 22–3
legitimate authority, presumption 163–5
mistaken grasp 206–7
Green, L 127
Grice, Paul 5, 203–4
groundless knowledge 51
guidance and control 38–40
guise of the good
  actuality 30
  beliefs and desires 42–4, 58
  criticisms/defence of model 54–8
  desire as result of valuing 54
  and exclusionary reasons 139–40, 146–53
  failure to seek the good 55–7
  good desires/pure desires 52–4
  good-making characteristics 41, 45–58
    passim
  groundless knowledge 51
  incontinence (Akrasia) 54
  meaning 41
  mental state, memory/reflection 44
  objections see objections
  perverse desires 57–8
  practical knowledge 50–2
  transparency condition 47–50
  unintelligible actions 54–5
  voluntary/involuntary actions 41–2
  why question see why-question
    methodology

Hampshire, S 131–2
Harman, Gilbert 185–7
Hart, HLA 23, 28n, 29, 35, 36
  intentional action 78–80, 80–5 passim,
    131–2
  internal point of view 75–8, 99
heteronomy v autonomy 17–18
Hume, David 43, 207, 208
Hurd, H 163

identifying formula for acts 174, 179–81
incontinence (Akrasia) 54
inseparability thesis 190–2
intentional action 30–4, 39–40, 61–9
  actuality 30–4, 39–40
    potentiality, distinction 65–9, 73
  beliefs and motives 82–4
  capacity and change 67–9
  Davidson 116–17
  exclusionary reasons 152–60
  former stages/later stages 61
  grounding reasons 157–9
  guise of the good 152–3

intentions about actions 131–5
inversion thesis 104–5
key features 61–5
motion 66–7
non-cognitivism
    acceptance thesis 80–5
    beliefs and motives 82–4
    Concept of Law (Hart) 78–80, 80–5
    passim
    internalising/being governed by norms
    81–2
    reflective critical attitude 79–80
    sanction theory 79, 80
    social rules 78–9
    understanding of ends/goals 84–5
non-observational, but might be aided by
    observation 62–3
order conceived/imagined by agent 62
paradox 152–60
parasitic thesis (Hart's) 78–80, 80–5
    passim
practical/theoretical syllogism 63–5
reasons for actions 154–6
sanction theory 79, 80
service conception 159–60
subjective meaning 104–5
two-component view 116–18
see also internal point of view
internal point of view
    conclusions 98–9
    discussion 76n
    Hart's model 75–8, 99
    intentional/voluntary action 76–7
    key issues 78
    legal positivism 75–6
    social normativity 77
    see also intentional action
internal/external actions 36–7
interpretation
    concept 176
    constructive interpretative theory 210–13
inversion thesis 104–5, 110–16
    intentional action 104–5
    Kelsen 104–5
    legitimate authority 110–11
    normative/authoritative characteristics
    111–13
    regulative/guiding function 113–14
    subjective meaning 115–16, 117–18
    transparency condition 114–15
    two-component view 116–18

jurisprudential antinomy 101, 102

Kant, Immanuel

jurisprudential antinomy (Kant/Kelsen)
    101, 102
    practical reason 21–2, 23
    self-legislative thesis 16–21
    will/norm relationship 104
Kelsen, H 23, 78
    inversion thesis 104–5
    jurisprudential antinomy 101–4
    legal normativity 118–21
    Pure Theory of Law 106–10

legal authorities' claims see claims of legal
    authorities
legal authority and autonomy
    anarchistic account 15–16
    empirical account 15
    freedom and submission 20–1
    good-making characteristics 22–3
    heteronomy v autonomy 17–18
    implausible formulations 14–15
    key issues 13–14
    normativity of law 13
    objective standards 18–19
    practical reason 19–20, 21–3
    presupposition 11–12
    received view 11
    strategy of study 12–13
legal normativity
    conclusions 118–21
    intentional action, subjective meaning
    104–5
    inversion thesis see inversion thesis
    jurisprudential antinomy 101
    unchallenging view of 201–5
    see also normativity of law
legal positivism 75–6
legal rules
    actuality 28–9, 71–3
    authoritative commands 70–1, 73–4
    compliance 69–74
    ethical-political account 139–40
      see also exclusionary reasons
    redundancy 200–1
    types 166
    unified account 140–3
legitimate authority, presumption
    acting on presumption 160–1
    equivalence thesis 162–6
    expression of intention 161
    good-making characteristics 163–5
    inversion thesis 110–11
    moral authority/correctness claims 168–9
    responses to authority 161–2
    Rule of Law see under Rule of Law
    desiderata

legitimate authority, presumption *cont.*
spontaneous social practice 162
teleological argument 163–4, 165–6
see also claims of legal authorities;
exclusionary reasons

mathematical realism 188–91
mental state, memory/reflection 44
modestly objective values 178–9
moral authority/correctness claims 168–9
moral puzzle 37–8
Moran, R 48–9
motion 66–7
motivational/normative role of reasons
207–10

naïve explanation 34, 35, 38–9
Neurath, Otto 178, 181
non-cognitivism see under intentional action
normal justification thesis 141–2
normative and value realism 181–2
normative/authoritative characteristics
111–13
normativity of law 13
see also legal normativity

objections
constructive interpretative theory 210–13
good-making characteristics, mistaken
grasp 206–7
legal normativity, unchallenging view of
201–5
legal rules' redundancy 200–1
motivational/normative role of reasons
207–10
sanction fear 199
objective values 171–2
O'Neill, O 22
O'Shaughnessy, B 51–2

parasitic thesis
acceptance thesis see acceptance thesis
deliberative/theoretical viewpoints,
distinction 86–7
Hart's intentional action 78–80, 80–5
passim
Kelsen's inversion thesis see inversion thesis
meaning 75
Parminedes 65
Paulson, Stanley 101, 103
perverse desires 57–8
phenomenological argument 146–8
Plato
good desires 52
normative truths 186

practical capacities 174–9
practical knowledge 50–2
claims of legal authorities 124–5
practical reason
actuality 3, 19, 26, 35–6, 214–15
Anscombe 22, 176–7
first-person/deliberative perspective
59–61
Kant 21–2, 23
legal authority and autonomy 19–20,
21–3
see also intentional action
practical/theoretical syllogism 63–5
presumption of authoritative force 142–3
promulgation puzzle 34–6
Pure Theory of Law (Kelsen) 106–10
Putnam, H 189

Quine, WO 189

Raz, Joeph 13, 23, 76
acceptance thesis, detached viewpoint 85,
92, 94–5, 96
claims of legal authorities 125–30
equivalence thesis 163
normal justification thesis 110–11
reasons for actions
appropriate way condition 204
justificatory/explanatory reasons 202–3,
205
triggering reasons 201–2
reasons and rules, key questions 25
responses to authority 161–2
robust value realism
complex legal rules 173–4
conceptual and practical capacities 174–9
critiques of 182–7
deliberative viewpoint/indispensability
171–2, 187–97, 193–7
Dworkin 182–5
first/third person asymmetry 172, 174–5
grounding reasons for rules 177
identifying formula for acts 174, 179–81
inseparability thesis 190–2
knowing how 177–8
marginal/non-paradigmatic sense 175–6
mathematical realism 188–91
modestly objective values 178–9
normative and value realism 181–2
objective values 171–2
theoretical answer 172–3
Rule of Law desiderata 125, 131, 135, 136,
137
legitimate authority, presumption 166–8,
169

sanction fear 199
sanction theory 79, 80
sanction-based explanations 37
Satan's desires 57–8
self-legislative thesis 16–21
service conception 159–60
Setiya, K 54
social normativity 77
spontaneous social practice 162
Stangl, Franz 95–7
Stocker, M 55–7
subjective meaning see under inversion
    thesis
symmetry illusion 31–4

teleological argument 148
Tenenbaum, S 54
Theophrastus principle 50
transparency condition 47–50
transparent grounding reasons 142

two-component model
    actuality 26–7, 29–30, 35
    inversion thesis 116–18

unintelligible actions 54–5

value realism see robust value realism
Velleman, D 57–8
voluntary/involuntary actions 41–2

Watson, G 53
why-question methodology
    actuality 28, 30, 59
    exclusionary reasons 144–5
    guise of the good (Anscombe) 45–7
    see also intentional action
will/norm relationship 104
Wittgenstein, L 44, 48, 49
Wolff, RP 13, 14, 73
    anarchist conclusion 15, 16, 17, 21, 215